Ethical Issues in International Communication

Also by Alexander G. Nikolaev

INTERNATIONAL NEGOTIATIONS: THEORY, PRACTICE AND THE CONNECTION WITH DOMESTIC POLITICS

LEADING TO THE 2003 IRAQ WAR: THE GLOBAL MEDIA DEBATE (*co-edited with E.A. Hakanen*)

Ethical Issues in International Communication

Edited by
Alexander G. Nikolaev

Introduction, selection and editorial matter © Alexander G. Nikolaev 2011
Individual chapters © Contributors 2011

All rights reserved. No reproduction, copy or transmission of this publication may be made without written permission.

No portion of this publication may be reproduced, copied or transmitted save with written permission or in accordance with the provisions of the Copyright, Designs and Patents Act 1988, or under the terms of any licence permitting limited copying issued by the Copyright Licensing Agency, Saffron House, 6–10 Kirby Street, London EC1N 8TS.

Any person who does any unauthorized act in relation to this publication may be liable to criminal prosecution and civil claims for damages.

The authors have asserted their rights to be identified as the authors of this work in accordance with the Copyright, Designs and Patents Act 1988.

First published 2011 by
PALGRAVE MACMILLAN

Palgrave Macmillan in the UK is an imprint of Macmillan Publishers Limited, registered in England, company number 785998, of Houndmills, Basingstoke, Hampshire RG21 6XS.

Palgrave Macmillan in the US is a division of St Martin's Press LLC, 175 Fifth Avenue, New York, NY 10010.

Palgrave Macmillan is the global academic imprint of the above companies and has companies and representatives throughout the world.

Palgrave® and Macmillan® are registered trademarks in the United States, the United Kingdom, Europe and other countries.

ISBN 978–0–230–27289–7   hardback

This book is printed on paper suitable for recycling and made from fully managed and sustained forest sources. Logging, pulping and manufacturing processes are expected to conform to the environmental regulations of the country of origin.

A catalogue record for this book is available from the British Library.

Library of Congress Cataloging-in-Publication Data
Ethical issues in international communication / edited by Alexander G. Nikolaev.
p. cm.
Summary: "A collection of essays from scholars around the globe examining the ethical issues and problems associated with some of the major areas within contemporary international communication: journalism, PR, marketing communication, and political rhetoric"— Provided by publisher.
Includes bibliographical references and index.
ISBN 978–0–230–27289–7 (alk. paper)
1. Communication, International—Moral and ethical aspects.
I. Nikolaev, Alexander G.
P96.I5.E75 2011
175—dc22   2011004363

10 9 8 7 6 5 4 3 2 1
20 19 18 17 16 15 14 13 12 11

Printed and bound in the United States of America

Contents

List of Contributors	vii
Introduction: The Essence of the Debate *Alexander G. Nikolaev*	1

Part I   From Theory to Practice

1	Cultural Diversity and Moral Relativism in Communication Ethics *Clifford G. Christians*	23
2	What Does It Mean to be Moral? A Cross-Cultural and Cross-Religious Analysis of Morality among Muslims and Christians in Britain and France *Stephen M. Croucher*	35

Part II   The Ethics of International Political Rhetoric

3	The Rhetoric of Democracy *Gerard Elfstrom*	55
4	'America Will Call Evil by its Name': 'Evil' as a Theologically and Morally Loaded Notion in American Foreign Policy Discourse *Anna Kasafi Perkins*	71

Part III   Ethical Issues in International Journalism

5	Saving or Drowning? The Paradox of Attempting Ethics in International News and Communication *Iman Roushdy-Hammady*	87
6	Identities, Ethics and International Communication in the French Context *Élisabeth Le*	103
7	The Dilemmas of War and Peace Reporting *Richard Lance Keeble*	119

Part IV   International PR and Public Communication

8	Ethics, Cultures and Global Social Marketing Health Campaigns *Terry L. Rentner and Lara Lengel*	137

9 An Ethical-Theory-Based Analysis of the Social
  Responsibilities of Three Global Corporations:
  ExxonMobil, Shell and Pfizer   154
  Cornelius B. Pratt and Wole Adamolekun

10 Cultural and Historical Aspects of Media Transparency
   in Russia   172
   Katerina Tsetsura

11 Visual Ethics in Public Relations: An Analysis of Latin
   American Government Websites   183
   Melissa A. Johnson and Eileen M. Searson

Part V Is Education the Answer?

12 The Invisible Dimension of International Communication:
   Is It Possible to Teach Others 'the Right Ethical Standards'? 201
   Svetlana Sablina and Bella Struminskaya

13 Instead of a Conclusion: Is Education the Answer?
   Or What May All This Mean?   220
   Alexander G. Nikolaev

Index   263

List of Contributors

Wole Adamolekun holds a doctorate in media arts from the University of Abuja, Nigeria. He has more than 30 years of practical industry experience in public relations and corporate communications. In addition to having published several scholarly articles worldwide, he is the author of *Public Relations Possibilities: Selected Seminars and Conference Papers* (2005) and a co-author of *Interactive Public Relations* (2007). Currently, he is General Manager of Corporate Services at the Petroleum Products Pricing Regulatory Agency in Nigeria. He is also Secretary General of the African Public Relations Association, based in Abuja, Nigeria.

Clifford G. Christians is the Charles H. Sandage Distinguished Professor and Research Professor of Communications at the University of Illinois, Urbana. He is Director of the Institute of Communications Research and Chair of the PhD programme, with joint appointments as Professor of Media Studies and Professor of Journalism. His received his PhD in communications from the University of Illinois and he has been on its faculty since 1974, where has won five teaching awards. He has been a visiting scholar at the Department of Philosophy at Princeton University, a research fellow in social ethics and later a visiting scholar at the University of Chicago, and a PEW fellow in ethics at the University of Oxford. He is the author or co-author of eight books, including *Media Ethics: Cases and Moral Reasoning*, which is now in its eighth edition. His research and teaching interests are media ethics, communication theory and the philosophy of technology.

Stephen M. Croucher is an associate professor at the School of Communication and the Arts at Marist College in Poughkeepsie, NY. He researches immigrant assimilation, identity formation/negotiation within Europe and conflict management/conceptualization within the Muslim community. He is the winner of numerous top paper awards at regional, national and international conferences, has authored multiple journal articles on assimilation, religiousness and conflict within Islam, and has authored a book, *Looking Beyond the Hijab* (2008), on the Muslim community in France. He has also co-authored with Daniel Cronn-Mills his second book, *Religious Misperceptions: The Case of Muslims and Christians in France and Britain* (2010).

Gerard Elfstrom is Professor of Philosophy at Auburn University and received his doctorate from Emory University. He has authored books, chapters and articles in a number of areas, including the ethics of international relations, political philosophy, ethics, medical ethics, the philosophy of law, business ethics and the philosophy of science. His most recent books are *New Challenges for Political Philosophy* (1997) and *International Ethics: A Dictionary* (1998).

Melissa A. Johnson is an associate professor and Director of Graduate Studies in the Department of Communication at North Carolina State University. She holds a doctorate in mass communication research from the School of Journalism and Mass Communication at the University of North Carolina, Chapel Hill. Her research focuses on international visual communication, digital and traditional ethnic media, and public relations concepts related to Latinos, Latin America, technology and innovation. In addition to teaching at North Carolina State University, she has taught at the University of North Carolina at Chapel Hill, San Diego State University and Elon University, NC. She also has more than a dozen years of communication practitioner experience, including positions as Vice President of Corporate Relations for a California financial institution and Director of Public Relations for a top-ranked US school of public health. In addition, she has worked in a public relations agency and radio broadcasting.

Richard Lance Keeble is Professor of Journalism at the University of Lincoln. He has written and edited 13 books, including *Secret State, Silent Press: New Militarism, the Gulf and the Modern Image of Warfare* (1997), *The Newspapers Handbook* (2005, fourth edition) and *Ethics for Journalists* (2008, second edition). He co-edited *The Journalistic Imagination: Literary Journalists from Defoe to Capote and Carter* (2007) and *Communicating War: Memory, Media and Military* (2007), and is the joint editor of *Ethical Space: The International Journal of Communication Ethics* (www.communicationethics.net). His books have been translated into Chinese, Ukrainian and Romanian. His research interests include the journalism of George Orwell, the reporting of US and UK militarism, and the links between mainstream journalists and the intelligence services.

Élisabeth Le is Associate Professor of Applied Linguistics (French) in the Department of Modern Languages and Cultural Studies at the University of Alberta, Canada. Her research areas are pragmatics and (critical) discourse analysis. In her interdisciplinary work, she uses linguistic methodologies as some of the tools with which to study social phenomena appearing through political, media and intercultural discourse. She has authored articles in the following journals: *Text, Journal of Pragmatics, Journal of Language and Politics, Discourse and Society* and *Études Internationales*. Her monograph *The Spiral of 'Anti-other Rhetoric'* (2006) explored the interconnections between media representations of the other and international relations. She is now working on how editorialists use sociocultural identities to participate in political debates.

Lara Lengel began her transnational and intercultural communication research when she was a Fulbright Scholar in North African Tunisia (1993–4). She is Chair and Professor at the Department of Communication, Bowling Green State University, Ohio, teaching MA and PhD-level coursework in communication and culture and in qualitative and humanistic research methods, undergraduate coursework in international communication, and communication and gender at both graduate and undergraduate levels. She is the author of a number of publications, including *Intercultural Communication and Creative Practice* (2004) and *Casting Gender: Women and Performance in Intercultural Contexts* (with John T. Warren, 2005), and numerous articles appearing in, among others, *Text and Performance Quarterly, Gender & History* and the *Journal of Communication Inquiry*. She has co-directed nearly $500,000 of federal grant programmes funded by Fulbright, the US Department of State Middle East Partnership Initiative and the US Department of State Bureau of Educational and Cultural Affairs.

Alexander G. Nikolaev is Associate Professor of Communication in the Department of Culture and Communication at Drexel University, Philadelphia. He received his doctorate from the Florida State University where he also taught for four years. His areas of research interest and expertise include public relations, political communication, international communication, international negotiations, international news coverage and discourse analysis. He has years of practical work experience in the fields of journalism and public relations in the US and Eastern Europe. He has written a number of articles in these areas in trade and scholarly journals as well as some book chapters in the US and overseas. He is also the author of *International Negotiations: Theory, Practice, and the Connection with Domestic Politics* (2007) and co-editor of *Leading to the 2003 Iraq war: The Global Media Debate* (2006) with E. Hakanen.

Anna Kasafi Perkins is a Jamaican Catholic theologian who is former Dean of Studies and Lecturer at St Michael's Theological College, an affiliated institution of the University of the West Indies, Mona. Currently, she is the Program Officer in the Quality Assurance Unit in the Office of the Board for Undergraduate Studies at the Mona Campus and the adjunct faculty, and is journal editor at St Michael's. She is an eclectic thinker with a keen interest in the varying impact of religious faith on personal, sociopolitical and economic life. Among her more recent publications are: a co-authored article entitled 'Political Leadership and Economic Development: Assessing Jamaica's Post-independence Experience', published in *Social and Economic Studies* (June 2008) and a chapter '"God (Not) Gwine Sin Yuh": The Female Face of HIV-AIDS in the Caribbean and a Theology of Suffering', in *Calling for Justice Throughout the World: Catholic Women Theologians on the HIV/AIDS Pandemic* (2009).

Cornelius B. Pratt is a professor in the Department of Strategic and Organizational Communication at Temple University, Philadelphia. He is also an honorary visiting professor of mass communication at Bingham University, New Karu, Nasarawa State, Nigeria. He served for nearly six years in the US Department of Agriculture, in Washington DC and for 11 years on the faculty at Michigan State University, the last eight as full professor. He has held academic posts at Howard University (2005–6), Virginia Tech (1983–91) and Weber State University (1981–3). He holds doctoral and master's degrees from the University of Minnesota, Twin Cities. His research interests include international and strategic communication, ethics, public relations and health communication.

Terry L. Rentner is Associate Professor and Chair of the Department of Journalism in the School of Communication Studies at Bowling Green State University, Ohio. She teaches public relations and persuasion at undergraduate and graduate levels. She has received 12 state and two federal grants totalling over $700,000 to support her high-risk drinking research and programming efforts, including a $300,000 grant from the US Department of Education awarded in 2005. She also received a number of Bowling Green State University teaching, achievement and leadership awards in 2007, 2008 and 2009.

Iman Roushdy-Hammady is a native of Egypt. She is currently a post-doctoral fellow at Rollins School of Public Health, Religion and Health Collaborative, Emory University, Atlanta. She is also a consultant on the Arabic Program, School District of Philadelphia. She received her PhD in Medical Anthropology and Middle Eastern Studies from Harvard University in 2002. She has a BA in Economics and an MA from the

Department of Anthropology/Sociology/Psychology at the American University in Cairo. She has worked in a number of research and academic institutions including Fox Chase Cancer Center, Philadelphia, Harvard University and Drexel University, Philadelphia. She has written articles in medical and anthropological journals, as well as chapters in edited book volumes and encyclopedias. Her publications focus on two areas: the anthropology of health/disease and of Arabic television and film.

Svetlana Sablina is Associate Professor in the Department of Sociology, Deputy Dean of the Faculty of Economics and Deputy Director of the Centre for European Studies at Novosibirsk State University, Russia. She specializes in the study of social stratification, focusing on such issues as status inconsistency, the middle class and poverty. Her current interests include organizational communication audits, public communication campaigns, international education ethics and barriers to intercultural communication. She teaches a variety of courses at both graduate and undergraduate levels. She has published over 30 articles, book chapters and books. Her book *Communication and Public Relations: Western Theories, Methodologies, Practices* (second edition, 2008) received the Russian Communication Association Award for the best book in communication theory in 2007–8.

Eileen M. Searson is a graduate student at North Carolina State University studying for a masters degree in communication. She holds a bachelor's degree in public health education and promotion from James Madison University. She previously worked as a recruiter for a diabetes prevention study, 'The Healthy Living Partnership to Prevent Diabetes', at Wake Forest University. After completing her studies, she plans a career in public relations.

Bella Struminskaya is a graduate of Novosibirsk State University and the University of Mannheim, Germany. She studied sociology at Novosibirsk State University from which she received her bachelor's degree in sociology under the guidance of Svetlana Sablina in 2008. She also studied Business Administration at the University of Marburg, Germany with a scholarship from the German Academic Exchange Service (2006–7). She received her master's degree in sociology from the University of Mannheim, Germany in 2010. She has professional marketing experience in the areas of IT and telecommunications. Currently she is working as a researcher at GESIS - Leibniz Institute for the Social Sciences in Mannheim.

Katerina Tsetsura is Associate Professor of Public Relations at the Gaylord College of Journalism and Mass Communication, University of Oklahoma, Norman. Her research interests include international and global public relations, global media and public relations ethics, and issues management in countries with transitional economies. Her research appeared in several books (such as *The Global Public Relations Handbook* [2003] and *Global Journalism* [2008]), annuals (*The Global Corruption Report 2005: Transparency International*), journals (*Asian Communication Research, KB Journal* and *Public Relations Journal*), online research centres (the Institute for Public Relations) and has been published in three continents. She is a member of AEJMC, IPRA, PRSA, ICA and NCA, and is a leading researcher of the Global Media Transparency project. She is currently collecting data on media practices in the US and around the world for a forthcoming book, *Truth and Global Media Transparency* (with Dean Kruckeberg).

Introduction: The Essence of the Debate

Alexander G. Nikolaev

The volume you are holding in your hands is devoted to contemporary ethical issues and problems in international communication. This book is written by scholars from across the globe about global ethical issues for a global audience.

Importance of the topic

As some scholars would argue, we live in the time of the *clash of civilizations*. Although it is a very controversial proposition, we can state the fact that, according to many international organizations, the number of wars as well as international and ethnic conflicts since the end of the Cold War has increased dramatically. Simultaneously, we live in a time of globalization and unprecedented international economic integration and cooperation that cross multiple cultural borders. These major aspects of contemporary political, economic and social lives emphasize the importance of the ethical element in international communication.

In a time when even the most extreme leaders find it difficult to use national or racial superiority as their war slogan and when the fight for resources is not considered to be a just or honourable reason to go to war either, politicians as a rule invoke moral justifications for their actions.[1] That is why we live in the era of 'humanitarian' interventions. Whatever the real reasons for a war are, more often than not, politicians claim that they have moral obligations to start killing people on the other side who are usually presented as violators of some universal ethical standards. So, it would be interesting to look at those claims and those standards. What are they? Do they actually exist? When, how, why and to what extent can we consider moral grounds for solving international problems?

Simultaneously, even if we really want to and must cooperate, ethical issues in international communication can create multiple problems for everybody involved. Anybody who has ever worked overseas knows that intercultural misunderstandings involving ethical aspects present a great obstacle to international cooperation. Businesspeople know how ignorance in relation to local ethical standards can ruin a successful business deal. Politicians know how one insensitive comment can destroy a long and sensitive political process. Public relations (PR) people and journalists working overseas constantly get in trouble only because they do not think about the difference between local codes of ethics and their own. In short, it is important to look at those codes and see what we can do so that our people are not considered to be insensitive or 'imperialistic' and, at the same time, we would feel comfortable working with people who use different ethical rules and regulations. Is there a way to solve this problem? This book will claim that yes, probably, there is one.

In general, the topic of the effect of culture on international communication is not a new one. It has been covered in detail and quite comprehensively by many authors. At the same time, the specific effect of *ethics* and *morals* in this area did not attract a lot of attention from scholars. The main idea behind this volume is that in order to really learn other cultures and, consequently, to be able to find truly mutually beneficial solutions for complex international problems, we 'must delve below' superficial cultural knowledge and try 'to find foundational principles that can be used to ground moral decisions' (Ferre and Willihnganz, 1991, p. 13).

Theoretical debate

The main problem that underlies ethical issues in international communication is that culture is a complex and deep-seated psychological structure that runs the lives of millions of people who share a similar history, language, physical environment, religious beliefs, etc. And any type of simplistic approach to cultural variables is dangerous and counter-productive. But the problem is that different communication scholars and practitioners use different types of reasoning dealing with international issues. For example, some of them argue that if you ask people all over the world whether they want freedom, democracy, fairness and a long happy life, everybody would say 'yes'. Consequently, these values are proclaimed to be universal. Those people who apply this type of approach are called *universalists*.

Indeed, it is very difficult to argue that in all likelihood, everybody in the world would really respond to such a question positively. But representatives of every nation would mean different things when answering this question. The main problem is that 'freedom', 'fairness', 'democracy' and 'respect for human life' are not values themselves but simply terms, words or even better *labels* representing different things for different nations. We can always find in a dictionary a linguistic label – a set of symbols and sounds – that is used by the linguists and interpreters to represent in one language something found in another one. But no dictionary in the world could explain to us what this nation actually means when using this term within its culture or how close its understanding of this linguistic label is to ours. Consequently, when the universalists proclaim the universality of values, they proclaim nothing more than some relative universality of labels (Nikolaev, 2007, p. 255). Moreover, each culture has its own interpretation of these labels.

But the universalists respond to this type of reasoning with their own arguments. They believe that 'Indeed, there are constants in most fundamental human values. Also, there are basic concepts of good and evil that transcend cultural boundaries' (Kruckeberg, 1996, p. 89). 'It is easy to assume that if there are any moral truths, they must be timelessly true, perhaps because morality tends to present itself as universalizable' (Lear, 1984, p. 165), that is, 'the radical universalists give absolute priority to demands of the cosmopolitan moral community over other perceived lower moral communities' (Kruckeberg, 1996, p. 85; see also Donnelly, 1989). That is why universalism is mostly a Western type of culture phenomenon.

But people from other (non-Western) cultures may disagree: 'When ... philosophers and social scientists talk so uncritically about the universality of moral beliefs, what they are doing is ignoring the cultural meanings embedded in foreign practices and beliefs and substituting their own, more familiar ones' (McDonald, 1986, pp. 146–7).

At the same time, it is important to note that not everybody in the West is a universalist. There is a strong group of international communication practitioners and scholars who believe that 'it is dangerous to establish one mode of practice as the norm and thereby label all other practices as deviant' (Roth *et al.*, 1996, p. 152). These people are called *internationalists* (Nikolaev, 2007, Chapter 8). For example, Donaldson argues that simply transferring one's values into the international arena is a 'recipe for error and cultural arrogance' (Donaldson, 1989, p. 12). These people conduct a spirited debate with the universalists in an attempt to refute their main arguments. For example, to the universalists' argument that if moral truths exist, they must be timelessly true (see the quote by Lear above), the internationalists respond that 'history strongly suggests that someday we will view some of our present practices as ethically flawed ... [one] should not automatically assume that he or she understands another society's practices well enough to criticize them, let alone attempt to change them' (Jaksa and Pritchard, 1994, p. 19). Indeed, slavery and racial segregation used to be a norm of American society, whereas now we consider them immoral and unethical. Who knows how the future will change our current beliefs. Maybe in two hundred years the ideas we are now ready to die for – those 'timeless truths' – will be also considered immoral and unethical (Nikolaev, 2007, Chapter 8).

It is a little unclear from the literature who is going to be the judge in difficult ethical situations – that is, who is going to interpret what constitutes 'timeless truths'. But from the recent rush of 'humanitarian' interventions and 'democratization' wars, it is quite obvious that representatives of Western cultures mostly assumed this difficult role. For them the answer is obvious – they possess the ultimate and universal knowledge of what those truths are. They just know from the depth of their hearts that what they believe in is universally true and the only moral way to live.

In response, internationalists argue that what the universalists are doing is substituting the whole psychological structure of another culture with their own cultural projections and continuing to comfortably operate in this environment whilst at the same time truly believing that they understand what the other side is supposed to think. In other words, they establish their world as the model for everybody else. And they not always do it subconsciously. In fact, there is a whole body of literature that tries to justify such an approach theoretically. It tries to demonstrate Western moral superiority and, consequently, establish Western notions of *right* or *wrong* as universal. This is what internationalist communication scholars write about such literature:

> The views expressed in this literature establish United States customs as the 'norm' and those of practitioners in other countries as 'other.' This approach leads to development of ethics codes that attempt to impose U.S. standards on practitioners from other countries and on U.S. nationals working elsewhere. Such an approach is problematic because U.S. standards are highly specific and legalistic and leave little room for cultural variation. It also establishes the U.S. method of conducting business as the most ethical without calling into question

U.S. practices. For example, this literature might be viewed as suggesting not only that U.S. and Japanese practitioners might handle an airplane crash differently, but also that the U.S. tendency to protect the company name and wealth from lawsuits is more ethical than the Japanese desire to apologize and make restitution to affected families. (Roth *et al.*, 1996, p. 154)

The universalists object, saying that 'if we have to respect the rationality and autonomy of every culture, then it turns out that there is one culture whose rationality and autonomy we cannot respect – our own' (Kruckeberg, 1996, p. 86). The internationalists respond that it is rather unclear how respect for other cultures leads to disrespect of one's own. It would logically seem to be the other way round – if you respect other cultures, you can count on reciprocal respect of your own culture by these others. If every culture is special, you can be proud of your own culture as being special and unique. Once an undergraduate student wrote in his final paper on international communication that: 'Successful [cultural] immersion does not come at the expense of one's own background, but rather functions as an important compliment to it.' It is quite amazing how an 18-year-old easily understands something that many professors and diplomats manage to miss.

However, the universalists continue:

Our moral beliefs present themselves as basic truths about how human beings should act, but we are now supposed to respect incompatible moral beliefs just so long as they are actually embodied in a culture. By the standards of rationality available in our tribe these two stances are incompatible: being forced to accept that alternative incompatible moral outlooks ... cannot help but undermine the confidence of reflective moral agents. (Lear, 1984, p. 147)

From the internationalist point of view, there are some misconceptions here. First of all, nobody was ever talking about giving up one's own culture for another one. Secondly, nobody has ever talked about 'forcing to accept' somebody's 'moral outlooks' either. Usually, we talk about respect and non-interference but not full acceptance. Finally, we do not have to change our own culture – we just have to understand, respect and learn how to deal with some elements of another one. And nobody forces us to do it. If we don't want to do it, we don't have to. But a philosophical position similar to the one expressed in the quote above can easily explain why many international communicative actions fail.

Quite often, so-called universal human rights are used by the universalists as an argument in support of the universality of what is right and what is wrong. Donnelly (1989), for example, argues that prohibition against degrading or inhumane treatment or the arbitrary deprivation of life, and an equitable share of the means of subsistence are the universal values accepted worldwide. Donaldson (1989) identified ten minimal human rights applied and honoured internationally. They include such rights as the right to physical security, the right to minimal education and the right to political participation. Donnelly writes that: 'It may be necessary to allow limited cultural variations in the form and interpretation of particular human rights, but we must insist on their fundamental moral universality' (1989, p. 124). For the universalists 'such rights would seem universal by definition' (Kruckeberg, 1996, p. 88).

From their point of view, internationalists find in this type of reasoning the same problem as with some previous universalists' arguments – they never say who is going to interpret these human rights labels; that is, who is going to define what is a violation of a certain human right and what is not – what, for example, constitutes 'degrading or inhuman treatment, [or] arbitrary deprivation of life'. They also point out the fact that not everything is that simple when it comes to the very notion of 'the universal human rights'. For example, 'in 1982 and 1983 the US was alone in voting against a declaration that education, work, healthcare, proper nourishment, and national development are human rights ... The United States insisted that it does not recognize a "right to food"' (Sardar and Davies, 2002, p. 70; see also Blum, 2001). Since universalism is a predominantly Western phenomenon, the question is: which set of human rights will the universalists be using as their frame of reference – the one recognized by their own country or a more comprehensive one proposed by representatives of other cultures and suggested by the United Nations (UN)? But it seems that the 'right to food' is at risk of not being an important part of the universalists' own interpretation of the 'universal human nature'.

On behalf of the internationalists, Sardar and Davies (2002) write that the ideology of ethical universalism 'defines what is democracy, justice, freedom; what are human rights and what is multiculturalism ... In short, what it means to be human. The rest of the world ... must simply accept these definitions'. This ideology 'defines human rights as it wishes, then uses [the] emotive language of human rights as a stick to beat any country that does not fall in line' (pp. 201–2).

On behalf of the universalists, Spaemann (1989) has replied that 'common features' of the universal human nature are 'self-evident' (p. 5). But Sardar and Davies respond as follows:

> That all are created equal is both a 'self-evident' truth and meaningless if it remains 'self-evident' rather than explored, questioned and permitted to express differences and diversity. All people are indeed created equal, but live with the actual inheritance of human inequalities, the legacy of real history. Equality of opportunity, equal right to exercise the liberty to be themselves, equal freedom to define and live out their beliefs as they understand them, requires more than just treating everyone the same. The libertarian rhetoric of equal rights and self evident equal creation can be as doctrinaire, illiberal, intolerant and inequitable as any ideological system. (2002, pp. 205–6)

Internationalists believe that generating universal interpretations for human rights may be problematic. For example, the absence of a universal free healthcare system in the US (and especially its system of HMOs) is considered to be a gross violation of human rights (in particular, the right for physical security) by the rest of the world. The American two-party system and the role of money in this political system are also considered to be gross violations (in particular, the right to political participation) by many other countries. The same can be said about such labels as 'minimal education' (secular versus religious, free versus paid), 'capitalism' (American model versus Rhine model),[2] etc.

Some internationalists argue that universalism is philosophically impossible. They argue that no person in the world can possibly see and comprehend human values of all the human beings living all over the world. But this is a mandatory requirement for finding and proclaiming universal human values – theoretically and scientifically, one has to know and understand all (or at least most of) the moral standards and values in the world in order to detect and select common ones. So, internationalists ask: how can one person know and profoundly understand all the deep-seated cultural interpretations of all the moral values of the Chinese, Australians, South Africans, Brazilians and Russians at the same time? They say that it is simply impossible. The internationalists state that the universalists simply do not understand their own psychological and social limitations as human beings. What human beings usually do is to take their own values – the ones they know and understand because they were brought up in a certain culture – and merely project their interpretation of these values onto other people without realizing it (Nikolaev, 2007, p. 261).

Norms and values are adopted 'out of awareness' and are accepted 'as common sense, even as human nature' (Fisher, 1997, p. 10). This is from where the illusion of the commonalities of the moral values as well as the infamous concept of the so-called 'universal human nature' emanate. But actually 'There are fewer universal commonalities in human thought process than most people think' (Fisher, 1997, p. 28). There is:

> [a] need to be wary of those who claim universality for certain beliefs ... The supposed commonalities of human nature prove evanescent where mindsets and perception habits are concerned ... Even someone who might be judged as needing psychiatric help in one society may be considered quite sane in another. Culture and personality studies conducted by anthropologists have documented stark contrasts in the most fundamental aspects of human experience: cosmology, ethics, meaning of death, family roles, governance ... The importance of this kind of radical variation in values and behavior can hardly be overestimated ... The counsel of the psychological anthropologist applies: while people may be alike in basic human qualities, they do not necessarily think alike. (Fisher, 1980, pp. 28–9, 38)

The value system of each society formulates 'an ethic which, when shared by the society and internalized by individuals, functions to control behaviors' (Fisher, 1997, p. 105). This system defines such concepts as shame, sin, guilt, honour and dignity. This system also establishes the limits of morality: 'These limits differ markedly, of course, from one society to another' (p. 67). Consequently, 'The common sense or obvious consideration domestically becomes not so common or obvious internationally ... What is right and wrong or reasonable and unreasonable takes on different coloration' (p. 18). That is, 'culture is variable; there is no one universally preferred or natural way of life, and standards for evaluating cultures must, to a large extent, be comparative and relative. What is appropriate in the desert might not work in New York' (p. 44).

Internationalists argue that what universalists are doing is simply proclaiming their interpretation of everything as universal: 'the normal and unconscious assumption is that the habitual ways of thinking of one's own society are a matter of *human nature* and therefore have universal application' (Fisher, 1997, p. 30). Indeed, these people merely project what is called their own 'mindset' onto the rest of the world. 'Mindset' is a 'fixed mental attitude formed by experience, education, prejudice, etc.' (p. 2). 'We too comfortably find ourselves relying on our domestic experience and normal ethnocentric common sense rather than focusing directly on new dimensions of problem solving that are demanded by international realities' (p. 2).

Internationalists say that universalists do not understand that 'an ethos or way of customary thinking is aligned with some degree of cultural uniqueness' (Fisher, 1997, p. 168), that is, moral standards are quite unique for each culture. And even most of what they call basic human perceptions – such as human rights – can be strongly skewed: '[as to] the perception of threat, human rights, or appeals to world opinion, it frequently turns out that assumptions held in one country regarding these matters are not matched in another' (pp. 1–2). For instance, the American ethos is considered only 'superficially egalitarian' (Hodge, 2000, p. 50) and, consequently, is not considered to be applicable to international human rights issues by many nations.

For example, 'projecting much more of an American frame of reference' onto foreign events led to such disastrous miscalculations as the Vietnam War (Fisher, 1997, p. 30). Robert McNamara admitted that: 'We ... acted according to what we thought were the principles and traditions of this nation. We made our decisions in light of those values. Yet we were wrong, terribly wrong' (quoted in Fisher, 1997, p. 7).

The universalists argue that there is a 'consensus' on the moral positions that underlie the notion of 'virtue' (Kruckeberg, 1996, p. 89; see also Donnelly, 1989, pp. 121–2). But the internationalists reply that this is a white-man Anglo-Saxon Protestant-Christian ideology consensus – a far cry from a universal ideology. For instance, Margaret Wertheim maintains that universalists:

> seem not to be able to imagine life itself in any guise other than the one they themselves are enmeshed in ... It is quite unrealistic to expect that someone brought up on a diet of exclusively American media should comprehend the dynamics of Arab culture or appreciate the struggle needed to survive in an African village ... In the land of the free, the underlying ethic of too much discourse is that one is free only to do things 'our way'. As Henry Ford said of his motor car: 'You can have it in any colour you like as long as it's black.' In this case, of course, the singular option is white. (Quoted in Sardar and Davies, 2002, p. 135)

Sometimes, the universalists claim that a certain 'moral consensus' is seen in the results of some research programmes that were conducted overseas. The internationalists have several objections in this area. First of all, they argue that the actual result of such research is simply a set of labels that are interpreted in a rather arbitrary way. Secondly, the results of a research programme conducted in a Third World country and funded by a rich country will always be suspect to all reasonable people.[3] Thirdly, in some countries (especially in Eastern civilizations) people may tend to agree with researchers simply out of politeness. Finally, people may not simply be able to explain how their value system differs from another one. Here is just one example:

> Unfortunately, if one asks foreign colleagues to explain the underlying philosophy and fundamental assumptions that apply to the way their government functions, the chances are that the answer, even if the question is taken seriously, will be a confusion of schoolbook pronouncements and unstudied rationalizations. Most people do not routinely dwell on the way that they are programmed to think about government and its operations. It is not necessary, the logic of government is taken for granted. (Fisher, 1997, p. 90)

The same can be said about values and ethics in general. People of a certain culture are usually not capable of clearly explaining their cultural value base. They just subconsciously know it. But formulating, categorizing, explaining and clearly thinking about it – this is something they simply may not be capable of. That is, 'I know what it is but I can't explain it to you'. Therefore, superficial surveys, according to the internationalists, simply cannot produce any valuable data when it comes to such deep and complex issues as morals.

Another argument put forward by the universalists is globalization – that the world is becoming more homogeneous. But the internationalists respond by stating that what their opponents do not realize is that only 10 per cent of culture is visible, while 90 per cent is invisible to an outsider (Hodge, 2000, p. 32). So, to concentrate on the 10 per cent of visible similarities and ignore the 90 per cent of culturally deep-seated reasons for differences is not appropriate. Certainly, many people in the world now wear Nike trainers and Levi's denim jackets. But the main idea is that 'Deep cultural values ... are more resistant to change than superficial cultural expressions are' (Hodge, 2000, p. 33). That is why people more easily accept superficial things – such as blue jeans, baseball caps or even elections – but inside still remain who they are (e.g., Russians, Arabs, Africans, Chinese or Brazilians). Thus, according to the internationalists, the world seems to be getting more homogeneous, but in fact it is just a dangerous and deceptive illusion. That is probably why we are actually seeing more political fragmentation (secessions) and ethnic conflicts than ever before.

The internationalists also continue by saying that the self-confidence of the universalists can be explained by the fact that they do not fear any repercussions. In their usual guise as representatives of the so-called super powers, they are absolutely sure that nobody will ever dare to come to their countries and try to impose another set of cultural values on them. They are very sure of this one-way flow of force, that is, their 'confident self image [is] based on a sense of moral, economic, or military *superiority* (or all three)' (Fisher, 1997, p. 106). But if something like that had ever happened, they would have immediately remembered that their cultures and countries are unique and that nobody has a right to interfere with their cultural, economic and political judgments.

The universalists often say that: 'The best possible life for everyone is achievable only when everyone follows the rules of morality, rules that quite frequently may require individuals to make genuine sacrifices' (Kruckeberg, 1989, p. 11). But the internationalists argue that it is precisely the universalists who in this case violate their own moral rules because it is they who are not willing to sacrifice anything and who continue to live comfortably while everybody else in the world is supposed to behave in the manner defined for them by the universalists.

The universalists also argue that there is a set of values that are universally undisputed: among these, they usually mention such values as respect for human life, freedom and democracy, and some others, but the value of human life is always number one. They consider it the *ultimate* universal value. But some internationalists respond by stating that in some cultures, life is measured not from the moment of birth but from the moment of conception. Consequently, under such a supposition, a human foetus is already a complete human being and killing this embryo is as serious a crime as killing an adult. Many religions of the world consider abortion an immoral act and a mortal sin. Therefore, at an international level, the question 'what is a human life?' is not an idle issue but a matter of practical significance.

Another problem here is the notion of what is considered a 'valued' human life. Some extremists proclaim the lives of 'infidels' worthless. But we should not be quick to condemn them. How are they different from some Western leaders who call the death of thousands of innocent civilians 'collateral damage' and the death of one of their own citizens a 'senseless and brutal act of terrorism'? Many countries in the world still use capital punishment and consider it a valuable crime-fighting tool.

And every nation in the world glorifies its own soldiers who kill many enemy fighters (somebody's children and parents). When our allies get killed, we call it 'mass murder', but when our allies kill, we call it 'isolated cases of arbitrary deprivation of life'. As was mentioned above, while many people die of hunger, the right to food is still a problematic issue. In general, we know that every society would authorize killings if it deemed it necessary. And the universality of values is precisely the tool that is used to justify such killings of so-called 'evil' people because an 'evil person' is usually defined as somebody who does not adhere to the 'universal' (for this read personally and culturally preferred by somebody else) moral standards or set of values. 'When we encounter different cultural symbols, people merely seem different, perhaps, even colorful. But when they express different values, they seem unnatural, dangerous, or evil' (Hodge, 2000, p. 33). In other words:

> When ... philosophers and social scientists talk so uncritically about the universality of moral beliefs, what they are doing is ignoring the cultural meanings embedded in foreign practices and beliefs and substituting their own, more familiar ones. What allows them to do this without apparently meeting contradictions by the facts is their confused view of the meaning of a 'prohibition against murder' as [a] quasi-empirical, quasi-conceptual entity. (McDonald, 1986, pp. 146–7)

But the bottom line of the very idea of human life boils down to the notion of the meaning of life – its main purpose – and the question 'what do people live (and die) for on this planet?' would be answered quite differently by people of different nations. Some would say success, some God, some pleasure, some family, some their country and society, some spiritual development, etc. What is the correct universal answer? Nikolaev (2007, Chapter 8) suggests that unless we can find such an answer, we cannot even think about the universal meaning of human life.

One of the most difficult concepts is the notion of freedom and, in particular, the freedom of speech. The dominant Western idea is that the freedom of speech is when every member of a society can express his or her point of view freely (that is, to say whatever he or she wants). But the internationalists believe that the freedom and, in particular, 'the freedom of speech is not only the right to say what you think but, more importantly, it is the right to be heard' (Nikolaev, 2007, p. 268). In their opinion, 'the Western-civilization notion of the freedom of speech is the principle of "a voice crying in the wilderness" – you can say whatever you want but nobody cares' (p. 268).

In general, applying the Western notion of freedom to other cultures may be quite destructive: 'This notion of "freedom" – or more appropriately, libertarian individualism which promotes every individual's potential for fulfillment ... the withdrawal of all collective, communal and social responsibility – undermines everything that indigenous cultures, traditions and history stand for' (Sardar and Davies, 2002, p. 125).

The same can be said about the notion of democracy. Actually, it is a very complex idea and requires quite an extensive explanation. And such detailed explanations can be found in a book written by Nikolaev in 2007 (pp. 268–73). Therefore, just a few words will be devoted to this topic here.

It may sound amazing for some but the word 'democracy' means different things to different nations. For example, for most mainstream Muslims, the notion of democracy can be expressed and explained in one word – Islam. That is why we have to understand that for Iranians, for example, the structure of their state – where the final say belongs to a council of holy men – is the ultimate model of democracy.

Another example may be Russia, where the notion of democracy is different from the Muslim and American perspectives. In order to understand the Russian idea of democracy, it is necessary to understand the concept of *sobornost*, which can be loosely translated as 'togetherness' or 'cathedralness' – the image of a huge house of worship where the whole nation is gathered in spiritual unity as one big parish. This tradition goes all the way back, over 1,000 years ago, to the Novgorod Republic political tradition and to the form of political decision making called *veche*. This tradition emphasized consensus over the idea of majority rule. The rights of minorities had to be strictly observed and guaranteed. It is still impossible to conduct a successful communication campaign in Russia without taking into account this part of the Russian mentality.

Russians completely reject the American interpretation of the value of *fairness* which in the American version reads 'let the best [for this read the strongest] guy win'. In the Russian culture, the loser (not the winner) is the national hero. All losers are supposed to be taken care of and their rights and safety must be guaranteed. Most Western civilizations have trouble understanding this. Reading Dostoyevsky may help here.

Russians prefer a different system for choosing their leaders. For them, a really democratic leader is not necessarily the one voted into office but the one who, first of all, cares about ordinary people (mostly those who would be called 'losers' in American society) and, secondly, who climbed all the way up from simple origins into the elite due to his or her hard work and talent.

For the Chinese, a really democratic society is one organized as a big family with its own patriarchs and obedient and respectful children (but here we have to note that the notion of family is different for different nations as well). And even the Japanese state, which is on the surface structured as a Western-type parliamentary democracy, in its essence has little to do with democracy as it is understood in the West.[4] This is where some people may get confused and substitute the outward superficial structure of the state government for the actual meaning that different nations have for the idea of the 'democratic state'.

To avoid erroneous interpretations of the whole issue of democracy, we have to consider what is called the *implicit social role* that the government plays in a certain society (Fisher, 1997, pp. 85–96). For example, in the US the main implicit social role of the government is to provide safeguards for individual freedoms and self-fulfilment for each American citizen, while in Russia – and to a large extent in Japan (pp. 151–2, 154, 157–8, 161–2) and China – the implicit social role of the government is 'to restrain people, to curb the impulses which undermined group well-being ... to attend to the citizens' needs and in turn to provide guidance, check performance, and demand obedience' (p. 91). Therefore, it is exactly the opposite of what an American means by democracy.

So, when we talk about democracy, we have to anticipate that we are going to see culture-specific deviations in every country and that there is nothing wrong with that. But what seems to be wrong is to criticize other nations for those differences because they make at least some forms of democracy sustainable in those other types of cultures.

Family values have already been mentioned above. Some universalists say that 'in all cultures, parents have duties toward their children, children have duties to their parents' (Spaemann, 1989, p. 5). The problem is that we cannot even compare such duties in American society (where children are supposed to leave home at 18, become completely independent and see their parents twice a year – on Christmas and Thanksgiving) and many South European, African, Middle Eastern or Chinese societies (where many generations may live their whole lives under one roof and rely heavily on each others' support in all matters – independence in such societies is not a core value). In the latter type of societies, a person who would want to become completely independent from the family would be considered a pariah, an immoral individual who wants to relinquish his or her societal duties. In such cultures the whole society is based on the family network support. Children are taught to be dependent on their families and to take care of others. It is exactly the opposite of the American way, where children are taught to be independent from a very early age. The family values in the American and more traditionalistic[5] types of societies are not similar – they are actually poles apart. This is not to say that one is better than the other – they are simply different. That is why in *traditionalistic* societies an extreme desire for ultimate independence and individual freedom is not a symbol of democracy and freedom but rather a sign of a sick and immoral mind. However, respect, help and discipline are considered to be ingredients of a 'democratic' and 'free' society.

Therefore, internationalists believe that every international communicator has to understand that such labels as 'freedom', 'democracy', 'human life' and 'family' have completely different – and very often opposite – meanings for the representatives of different nations. Without this simple understanding, we are not only dangerously close to chauvinism and the idea of national superiority, we are also dangerously close to business and political failure. That is, extreme universalism can be called *ethical labelism* and, actually, has little to do with honouring all human values but indeed simply argues in favour of imposing certain *interpretations* of those values on the rest of the world.

It may be possible to create what can be called a general protocol of moral understanding or simply primitive ethical guidelines for separate culture groups – such as the Protestant Anglo-Saxon culture group, the North-Mediterranean or Catholic South-European culture group, or the Orthodox Christian East European culture group – but even in this case, it is quite clear that they will be extremely difficult to implement, especially when politics or other national interests come into play.

In general, the internationalists argue that every international communicator 'must accept that all civilizations have the same right to exist, the same freedom to express themselves, and the same liberty to order their society guided by their own moral vision. Moreover, all the people of the world have the right and freedom to disagree' (Sardar and Davies, 2002, p. 169).

Some people would say that it is unfair to criticize the West all the time and forget about the other side of the coin. This is a very fair statement. Often the Americans and the British suffer as a result of cultural stereotypes and misconceptions too. Representatives of other nations also often lack cultural awareness and understanding when they are talking to the representatives of these two countries. Indeed, this entire volume is written not specifically for Western communicators but for representatives of every nation with a simple idea – that other cultures must be thoroughly studied and understood before any communicative action can succeed, whatever culture it may be.

It is imperative to make an important point here. Certainly, there are some practices that, in all likelihood, most people on earth would find appalling and repulsive – such as violence against women or child labour. But we have to remember two things. First of all, nearly all of these practices are rooted in economic circumstances (not in cultural characteristics) and as those circumstances change, they change as well. That is, the best way to fight them is not by force, threats or condescending and patronizing moral lectures, but by economic aid and development. Secondly, as history shows, countries tend to develop on their own towards an improved humanitarian situation over time. Certainly, they may be moving much more slowly than we would want them to, but it is important to be patient here. Any excessive pressure usually creates a boomerang effect – accusations of cultural imperialism and support for more extreme traditional ways of doing things. As such, the best way to promote change is education and personal example. However, in order for this to work, we ourselves have to be flawless and serve as models for the future (that is, not only should soldiers be representatives of our nations in other countries but so should teachers, nurses and doctors). But how can we provide such models if we ourselves often disrespect other cultures, choose ignorance and arrogance over education and understanding, and frequently use threats and violence to solve problems? We have to learn how to understand others better and only then will international communication be much easier. This is good advice for people who are not lazy and not arrogant.

All the above provides merely a brief overview of a broad and spirited debate that is ongoing between universalists and internationalists. It highlights the main differences between people who want to protect and respect every culture in the world and those who want to claim the high moral ground exclusively for themselves. And those who claim that moral high ground always use ethical appeals in their international communication.

Content and structure of the book

The use (or rather misuse) of ethical appeals, themes and arguments in contemporary international communication became so common all over the world that it actually developed into a major communication problem and requires detailed consideration and exploration. The important questions that repeatedly emerge in this area and, consequently, will be addressed in this volume can be formulated as follows:

- Can we apply the same ethical standards while discussing political and social issues worldwide?
- If we cannot, why?; if we can, which standards and how?
- How will differences in ethical standards affect such professional fields as international PR or public communication?
- Can we use ethical appeals in international political rhetoric and international journalism?
- Is branding somebody 'evil' (in cross-national political discourse or journalism) moral honesty or a propaganda trick?

These are just some of the issues and problems that will be addressed in this book. Moreover, the structure of the book will reflect our collective attempt at finding answers to even the most challenging questions. It is written by scholars from all over the globe (Canada, Egypt, Germany, Jamaica, Nigeria, Russia, the UK and the US) covering a big portion of our planet (Africa, Europe, Latin America, the Middle East, North America and Russia) and discussing many areas of international communication (philosophy, journalism, international PR and public communication, political rhetoric and education).

We will start with a theoretical discussion. So far, two groups – the universalists and the internationalists – kept arguing and accusing each other of either being imperialistic or of being completely devoid of any moral principles at all. Is there a way to make peace between the two? Probably not entirely, but it is at least possible to reject the extreme forms of these two approaches and modify them in such a way that they become more user-friendly and useful in practice.

In such an attempt, Clifford G. Christians will try to develop universalist theories that are not imperialistic. Such theories, with internal coherence, would arguably benefit the area of international communication ethics and move the whole field forward. Part I of the book will be continued by Stephen M. Croucher and his investigation of ethical problems emerging in conflict situations between Christians and Muslims in Europe.

Part II – the international political rhetoric unit – will discuss the rhetoric of democracy (Gerard Elfstrom) as well as main theological underpinnings of the rhetoric of 'good' and 'evil' (Anna Kasafi Perkins).

Part III will cover ethical issues in international journalism. We will take a look at how Arabs are covered in the Western media and at related ethical dilemmas (Iman Roushdy-Hammady) as well as at how the French daily newspaper *Le Monde* deals with problems of journalism ethics and national identity (Élisabeth Le). In addition, the chapter written by Richard Lance Keeble will focus on the media (both mainstream and alternative) in the UK and will explore a number of central ethical issues in war and peace reporting.

Part IV, which covers international public relations and public communication, will consider some ethical dilemmas in international social marketing health campaigns (Terry L. Rentner and Lara Lengel), major ethical issues encountered by three global corporations conducting their operations in Africa (Cornelius B. Pratt and Wole Adamolekun), the problem of media non-transparency in international media relations (Katerina Tsetsura) and the issue of visual ethics in relation to Latin American government websites (Melissa A. Johnson and Eileen M. Searson).

In the last part of the volume, Part V, two international education practitioners (Svetlana Sablina and Bella Struminskaya) will demonstrate a system of actively creating communication ethical codes. They will show that students can be taught to find mutually acceptable ethical premises and work based on them, instead of trying to teach each other 'the right ethical standards' for communication practices. Finally, the book will conclude with an attempt to summarize and make sense out of the wealth of information and viewpoints covered in this volume (Alexander G. Nikolaev), which will try to find a path towards solutions for some major ethics-related international communication problems.

Please, enjoy the book and we all hope that you will find it enlightening as well as useful in your scholarly and professional lives.

References

Albert, M. (1993). *Capitalism Against Capitalism*. London: Whurr Publishers.
Blum, W. (2001). *Rogue State*. London: Zed Books.
Donaldson. T. (1989). *The Ethics of Business*. New York: Oxford University Press.
Donnelly, J. (1989). *Universal Human Rights in Theory and Practice*. Ithaca, NY: Cornell University Press.
Ferre, J.P. and Willihnganz, S.C. (1991). *Public Relations and Ethics: A Bibliography*. Boston: G.K. Hall & Co.
Fisher, G. (1980). *International Negotiations: A Cross-cultural Perspective*. Yarmouth, Maine: Intercultural Press.
——. (1997). *Mindsets: The Role of Culture and Perception in International Relations*. Yarmouth, Maine: Intercultural Press.
Hodge, Sh. (2000). *Global Smarts: The Art of Communication and Deal Making Anywhere in the World*. New York: John Wiley & Sons.

Jaksa, J.A. and Pritchard, M.S. (1994). *Communication Ethics: Methods of Analysis*, 2nd edn. Belmont, MA: Wadsworth.
Kruckeberg, D. (1989). 'The Need for an International Code of Ethics', *Public Relations Review*, 15 (Summer), 6–17.
——. (1996). 'Transnational Corporate Ethical Responsibilities', in H.M. Culbertson and N. Chen (eds), *International Public Relations: A Comparative Analysis*. Mahwah, NJ: Lawrence Erlbaum Associates, pp. 81–92.
Lear, J. (1984). 'Moral Objectivity', in S.C. Brown (ed.), *Objectivity and Cultural Divergence*. Cambridge University Press, pp. 135–70.
Marshal, R. and Tucker, M. (1992). *Thinking for a Living: Education and the Wealth of Nations*. New York: HarperCollins.
McDonald, H. (1986). *The Normative Basis of Culture: A Philosophical Inquiry*. Baton Rouge: Louisiana State University Press.
Nikolaev, A.G. (2007). *International Negotiations: Theory, Practice and the Connection with Domestic Politics*. Lanham, MD: Rowman & Littlefield.
Roth, N.L., Hunt, T., Stavropoulos, M. and Babik, K. (1996). 'Can't We All Just Get Along?: Cultural Variables in Codes of Ethics', *Public Relations Review*, 22 (Summer), 151–61.
Sardar, Z. and Davies, M.W. (2002). *Why Do People Hate America?* New York: Disinformation.
Sennett, R. (1998). *The Corrosion of Character: The Personal Consequences of Work in the New Capitalism*. New York: W.W. Norton & Company.
Spaemann, R. (1989). *Basic Moral Concepts*, T.J. Armstrong (trans.). London: Routledge.

Notes

1. It seems like realism is winning only among international relations scholars. Real politicians prefer the *idealism* type of rhetorical strategies. Simply saying that we are fighting for our interests or resources is considered unethical by most people nowadays.
2. On the differences between the Rhine and American models of capitalism, see Albert, 1993; Marshal and Tucker, 1992; and Sennett, 1998.
3. It is important to note that it is always possible to find an extremely small group of Westernized (or pseudo-Westernized) people in every society who find it profitable to live in a symbiotic relationship with the incoming outsiders. But they do not represent their entire society by any means. Unfortunately, it is this group of people that is usually chosen by Western researchers as their research subjects (mostly because they are easier to gain access to and because of their language skills). Consequently, the research results always come out severely skewed and, as such, these tiny groups of people – so-called dissidents – serve as the 'living proof' for all the universalists' ideas.
4. For more information, see Okabe Kazuaki's article, available at www.tabunka.org/newsletter/true_democracy.html (date accessed 22 November 2010).
5. *Traditionalistic*: adhering to tradition especially in cultural or religious practices (Hyperdictionary.com: www.hyperdictionary.com/dictionary/traditionalistic, date accessed 22 November 2010).

Part I
From Theory to Practice

1
Cultural Diversity and Moral Relativism in Communication Ethics

Clifford G. Christians

Media ethics is at a crossroads. Our premier challenge is moral relativism and unless we resolve it intellectually, the future of media ethics is limited. Ethical relativism is a long-standing issue since Nietzsche made it inescapable. But in this first decade of the twenty-first century, relativism has taken on a comprehensiveness that threatens our conceptual progress in communication ethics.

For cultural relativism, morality is a social product. What is considered good is approved by the majority in a given culture. As all cultures are equal in principle, all value systems are equally valid. Cultural relativity now typically means moral relativism. As communication is a cultural phenomenon and social institution, this field abets the conflation of cultural relativism with moral relativism, rendering cross-cultural and transnational principles incoherent.

The challenge for media ethics in a global age is whether cultural diversity can be honoured while moral relativism is simultaneously rejected. In other words, can a different kind of universal principle be constructed from the ground up, one that is not imperialistic in character? Is there a pathway out of relativity that is intellectually credible but also facilitates diversity instead of ignoring it? The proposal here is to decouple cultural diversity from ethical relativism and then deal philosophically with moral relativism in terms of normative theory and realism. This is my argument in raw form. My focus is metaethics.

Cultural relativism[1]

We prize diversity in communication theory and practice. Indigenous languages and people groups have come into their own. Ethnic self-consciousness these days is considered to be essential to cultural vitality.

The world's cultures each have a distinctive beauty. We celebrate tolerance across genders and of religions and countries different from our own.

Alongside the rapid globalization of communications has been the reassertion of local identities. Media technologies are globalizing rapidly, but local identities are reasserting themselves at the same time. Cultural relativism is attractive and ordinarily presumed within this splendid variety of human life. We can understand and evaluate human beliefs and behaviour only by knowing the cultural context.

The term 'cultural relativism' first appeared in 1948 in the *American Anthropologist* journal after Franz Boas introduced the idea in 1887: 'Civilization is not something absolute, but ... is relative, and ... our ideas and conceptions are true only so far as our civilization goes' (Boas, 1887, p. 589). The concept became axiomatic for international studies generally and anthropology in particular.

While serving as a methodological tool for research, cultural relativism has carried a romantic appeal at the same time. Contrary to an ethnocentrism of judging other groups against a dominant Western model, other cultures were not considered inferior, only different. Boaz recognized that scientific methods required an escape from cultural imperialism and immersion in native languages and local cultures in order to understand them in their own terms from the inside out. As Alfred Kroeber describes the field:

> Anthropologists became aware of the diversity of culture and the tremendous range of its variations ... They became aware of culture as a universe or vast field in which we of today and our own civilization occupy only one place of many. The result was a widening of a fundamental point of view, a departure from unconscious ethnocentricity toward relativity. (1933, p. 11)

What is more, the benefits have been enormous. When seeing cultures that differ from our own, we recognize that our beliefs and behaviours are culture-bound rather than the natural state of affairs. Cultural relativism also makes it obvious that our definitions of humanity must include features from as varied a sample of individual cultures as possible. Certainly it is complicated to implement. As Alfred Kroeber puts it: 'Relativism poses certain problems when from trying merely to understand the world we pass on to taking action in the world, and right decisions are not always easy to find' (1949, p. 318). But with this warning in place, cultural relativism fosters tolerance.

Cultural diversity enriches human life. The vast variety in educating children broadly suggests new possibilities. Meeting basic human needs – food, clothing housing and medical care – demonstrates the ingenuity of this species in adapting to geography and resources. The verbal symbol *death* suggests a wide variety of understanding: medical cessation of brain waves or heartbeat, a disembodied soul meeting God, and separation from a human community requiring a seven-day wake for passage to the life beyond.

Cross-cultural communication requires the equality motif of cultural relativism in order to preserve cultural diversity. International negotiations, for example, depend on it totally and unequivocally:

> It is important to realize that the two sides at the negotiating table are absolutely equal, that their demands are as important to them as ours to us, that their positions are as reasonable as ours. In order to realize that, we have to understand how their positions were formed and where they are coming from – not in our misperception but in their reality. But for that we have to admit the reality, value, and independence of their culture ... The deeper they comprehend and respect the other side's culture the better negotiating results they will achieve and the better they will be able to protect the interest of their own country. (Nikolaev, 2008, p. 252)

Rather than superficial attention to courtesies, quirks in language and obvious habits, a deep understanding of culture is necessary in transnational communications. Cultures are complex, multilayered, express our worldviews and make life meaningful. Nikolaev demonstrates that our use of basic concepts across cultures belie their fundamental differences in meaning. Freedom, fairness, democracy and respect for life 'represent different things for different nations' and cannot be given a patina as universal values (2008, p. 289).

However, it should be noted that throughout this overview, I have interpreted cultural relativism in *epistemological* terms. I have given it continuity with its origins in anthropology as cognitive, aesthetic and conceptual in character. For its first half-century, the epistemological definition prevailed. But, as George Marcus and Michael Fisher (1999) argue, after the Second World War, cultural relativism was popularized to mean that since cultures are separate and equal, value systems are equally valued no matter how different they are. Cultural relativism became redefined as moral relativism.

Those of us in communications tend to follow this redefinition and in doing so we exacerbate the problem of relativism rather than resolve it. Our emphasis on particulars is one reason. We work at the juncture of globalization and local identities. Both of them are happening simultaneously, but in communications (and in news especially) we emphasize specifics. This age is caught in the contradictory trends of cultural homogeneity and resistance. Unique to our complicated era is communication technology on a worldwide scale, but tribalism is fierce at the same time and identity politics have become dominant in world affairs. Open information is a working formula for sustaining the planet, but ethnic self-consciousness these days is considered to be essential to cultural vitality. The integration of globalization and multiculturalism is the extraordinary challenge, but the media's penchant for immediacy in everyday affairs makes integration difficult. In our passion for ethnography, for diversity, for the local, we typically allow cultural relativity to slide into philosophical relativism.

Moreover, our preoccupation with narrative in communication studies usually leaves cultural relativism unattended. Stories are symbolic frameworks that organize human experience. Through narratives we constitute ways of living in common. Stories become public discourse when they are driven by good reasons. Narratives of good reasons make sense collectively and form the warrant for communal decision making (Fisher, 1987). Narratives are linguistic forms through which we argue, persuade, display convictions and establish identity. In a nutshell, they contain the meaning of our theories and beliefs. The moral domain is considered to be intrinsic to human life. We are not constituted as ethical selves antecedently, but moral values unfold dialectically in human interaction. Ethical understanding is a cultural product. Moral commitments are embedded in the practices of particular social groups and they are communicated through a community's stories. Moral values are situated in the cultural context rather than being anchored by philosophical abstractions. Contextual values replace ethical absolutes. The domain of ethics shifts from principle to story, from formal logic to community formation.

In some cases, narrative points us in the right direction. It anchors the moral domain in culture instead of rationalist individualism. But *narrative ethics* is conflicted in its own terms, about which value-driven stories ought to be valued. How does one determine the status of context-dependent, everyday discourse within context dependency? What in narrative itself distinguishes good stories from destructive ones? On what grounds precisely does narrative require fundamental changes in existing cultural and political practices? Narrative leaves the critical dimension under-determined.

Communication ethics grounded in narrative stakes out its territory in radically different terms than the ethics of rationalism, but it is co-opted by the status quo. After providing a thick reading of how societies work in a natural setting, narrative ethics is mute in its own terms on which valuing to value. Whatever is identified experimentally cannot in itself yield normative guidelines. If phenomena situated in immediate space and present time are presumed to contain everything of consequence, the search outside the immediate and particular is meaningless.

On behalf of anthropological research and its tradition of cultural relativism in epistemological terms, Clyde Kluckhohn (1949) insisted that all humans have moral standards and no society takes a laissez-faire approach to morality. Just because some customs are relative does not mean that all are relative. Polygamy is practised in some societies, with various types of monogamy in most. However, in no society do men have free play with women. While there are disagreements over details, policies and interpretations, these differences do not themselves mean that no moral judgments can be made about major historical events – the Holocaust, Stalinism, genocide, genital mutilation, Nazism, apartheid in South Africa, etc. Some societies practise euthanasia or capital punishment, but no known society has hunting seasons for people – your licence permits you to shoot three in October.

Cultural relativism outside its epistemological territory is overwrought. It is indispensable for curbing ethnocentrism, and its promotion of cultural diversity is critical in social scientific research. However, in the moral domain it is both misused and erroneous. The first step in dealing with today's crisis in media ethics is to restrict cultural relativism to epistemology and then deal with ethical relativism philosophically.

Ethical relativism

The heavy demands on media ethics today do not come first of all from cultural relativism, but from the long-standing philosophical struggle over ethical relativism.[2] In its modern version, it was Friedrich Nietzsche (1844–1900) who in the nineteenth century developed a totalizing assault on moral values. Since there is no transcendent answer to the 'why' of human existence, we face the demise of moral interpretation altogether. For Nietzsche, morality had reached the end of the line. In its contemporary version, defending a suprasensory good is not beneficent but is in fact imperialism over the moral judgments of diverse communities.

With ethical relativism in the Nietzschean tradition, the right and valid are only known in local space and native languages. A context that is intelligible, a proposition that is true, an argument that is legitimate, and judgments of right and wrong are accepted by the internal criteria of their adherents. Therefore, these concepts and propositions are considered to have no validity whatsoever outside their indigenous home.

In his first book, *The Birth of Tragedy*, Nietzsche insisted that 'only as aesthetic phenomena are life and the world justified' (1967 [1872], pp. 5, 24). He announced a philosophy beyond good and evil that 'places morality itself not only in the world of appearances but even among deceptions, as semblance, delusion, error and interpretation' (1967 [1872], Preface; see also Nietzsche, 1967 [1887]). In a world where God has died and everything lacks meaning, morality is appearance, even a fool's paradise.

In contrast to the traditional belief that ethics was essential for social order, Nietzsche argued that moral values had become worthless. In *Will to Power* he insisted that there is no longer an answer to the human 'why' and this nihilism means the 'end of the moral interpretation of the world' (1967 [1880], pp. 1–2). Because he was questioning God's existence, and with it the viability of moral commands, Nietzsche turned to aesthetic values that need no supernatural sanction. 'One can speak of beauty without implying that anything ought to be beautiful or that anybody ought to create the beautiful' (Kaufmann, 1968, p. 130).

These oppositional voices in the eighteenth and nineteenth centuries have burgeoned into a wholesale attack, so that in our own time, immutable and universal imperatives have been generally invalidated. Defending an abstract good is no longer seen as beneficent, but rather as imperialism over the moral judgments of diverse communities.

In fact, the modernist project to establish universal and unchanging normative claims has failed. The concept of norms themselves has eroded. Metaphysical certitude has been replaced by philosophical relativism. Moral principles are presumed to have no objective application independent of the societies within which they are constituted.

As we work on ethical principles for communication, believing them to be more urgent than ever, the social fashion is to be emancipated from moral standards and to disavow moral responsibility. We are witnessing the demise of the ethical, living in what Nietzsche (1966 [1886]) called the era beyond good and evil. In summarizing the postmodern argument against ethics, Zygmunt Bauman uses Nietzsche's perspective: ethics in postmodern times has been replaced by aesthetics (1993, pp. 178–9). Popular culture gets caught up in the technological imperative, creating programmes at times of artistic wholeness, but driven by the conditions of aesthetic space rather than ethics.

Ethical relativism is deep, wide and largely unattended – in fact, abetted by our concern in communications for diversity and narrative. Which agenda is therefore imperative for us? It is a pathway of two steps – protonorms and realism. If these can be established with credibility, media ethics has a framework within which it can move forward constructively.

Protonorms

Ethical rationalism has discredited itself over history by breeding totalitarianism. Those who claim knowledge of universal truth typically use it to control or convert dissenters. Transcendental metaphysical universals are now understood as imperialistic. Ethical theories in the twenty-first century ought to be grounded first in beliefs, not in objectivist absolutes. For communication ethics to be meaningful over the long term, we have to transform the idea of moral universals itself. And this must be done without presuming rationalist foundations, without the luxury of an objective morality from which to begin.

Scholars today doing credible work on universals understand norms to be historically embedded rather than abstract and absolutist. The primary issue is identifying a different kind of universal, one that honours the splendid variety of human life while articulating cross-cultural norms. There are several universal frameworks that step outside professional ethics and media institutions to work from the point of view of the general morality. These normative models are rooted in philosophical reflection, while having an explicit orientation to communications.

Kwasi Wiredu (1996), for example, writes from an African philosophical perspective. The human species lives by language. Languages everywhere are communal, giving their speakers particularity, while the shared lingual character of our existence makes intercultural communication possible. Wiredu calls the relationships among humans that of sympathetic impartiality, reflecting the commonness of our biologic-cultural identity as *homines sapientes*. Thomas Cooper's (1998) strategy for asking whether universals are possible involves learning from indigenous groups, those who experience their moral perspective and practice modes of communication first-hand without an industrial overlay. Their integration of heart and mind demonstrates a fundamental commitment to authentic communication. Lee Wilkins (2008) develops a universal model through neuroscience. Neuropsychology documents that through evolutionary naturalism, the human species has a sense of right and wrong. This biological inheritance is the ground for universalizing moral development and an ethics of care throughout the species. These kinds of theories rest on presuppositions to which we are committed inescapably; they reflect core beliefs about human existence.

For the sake of clarification, let me elaborate on another of these credible approaches to universals. In a study of ethical principles in 13 countries on four continents, the sacredness of human life is consistently affirmed as a universal value in *Communication Ethics and Universal Values* (Christians and Traber, 1977). The rationale for human action is reverence for life on earth. The scientific view of the natural world cannot account for the purposiveness of life itself. Living nature reproduces itself in terms of its very character. Therefore, within the natural order is a moral claim on us for its own sake and in its own right. Our duty to preserve life is taken for granted and is outside subjective preference. Reverence for life on earth is a pretheoretical given that makes the moral order possible.

The veneration of human life is a protonorm similar in kind to the proto-Germanic language – *proto* meaning beneath – a lingual predecessor underlying the Germanic languages as we know them in history. Reverence for life on earth establishes a level playing field for cross-cultural collaboration on the ethical foundations of responsible communication. It represents a universalism from the ground up. Various societies articulate this protonorm in different terms and illustrate it locally, but every culture can bring to the table this fundamental norm for ordering political relationships and such social institutions as the media. In fact, our human livelihood is rooted in the principle that 'We have inescapable claims on one another which cannot be renounced except at the costs of our humanity ... Universal solidarity is the basic principle of ethics and the normative core of all human communication' (Peukert, 1981, pp. 10–11). The primal sacredness of life is a protonorm that binds humans into a common oneness. This theoretical model appealing to universals is not based on metaphysical givens, but indicates that one cannot proceed intellectually without taking something as given.

Unconditional *a priori*s or a fixed human nature or philosophical foundationalism carry no resonance at present. Ethical relativism rightly combats such appeals. But in both the East and West we can successfully embed norms within culture and history. As an indicator of our distinctiveness, the human species generates symbolic patterns along the boundaries between moral norms and actual behaviour, the deepest self and our collective roles, the intentional and the inevitable (Wuthnow, 1987). Through the intrinsic self-reflexivity of natural language, we arbitrate our values and establish the differences and similarities of our worldviews. Thomas Nagel's *The View From Nowhere* (1986) documents those epiphanal moments coming with dynamic force from outside us, though not grounded *a priori*. In an ironic twist on conventional scepticism, normative claims are not a medieval remnant but are the catalyst for innovation.

Realism

Our creative ability works within the limits of an established natural order, creativity within a structured cosmos. People shape their own view of reality and we are under an obligation to take each other's cultural worlds seriously. But this fact does not presume that reality as a whole is inherently unstructured until it is shaped by human language. A world that exists as a given totality forms the presupposition of historical existence. Reality is not merely raw material, but is ordered vertically and through an internal ordering among its parts. Vegetables are ordered to people as food, for example. Some kinds are hierarchical – subspecies within species, and species within genus – but relations among humans are horizontal. There is no slave race to serve a master race, and the human species will not mutate into something else. This coherent whole is history's source, its beginning, an intelligible order that makes history itself intelligible. From a realist perspective, we discover truths about the world that exist within it.

This is ontological realism. It does not appeal to an objective sphere outside our subjectivity. Realism of this kind is inscribed in our human beingness. All human languages are translatable into another and as such can be understood. Every normal human being can learn another language and some people in every language are purely bilingual. All languages enable abstraction, inference, deduction and induction. All human languages serve cultural formation, not merely social functions. All humans understand the distinction between raw food and cooked food. Among human beings are common universals entailed by their creatureliness as lingual beings. Step two in our philosophical work is a legitimate realism on this side of Einstein, Freud and Darwin.

On a broader and deeper level, social constructionism is the dominant pattern in today's social sciences. In the liberal arts and sciences, relativism means a constructivist methodology. Both problems and their solutions are considered made, constructed, fabricated. For the interpretive turn in social scientific approaches to communication, the notion of humans as constructors and deconstructors is presumed.

But the ubiquity of constructionist methodologies does not threaten universalist theories rooted in realism. We do possess an irrevocable creative imagination, the unusual capacity to interpret experience, evaluate action and transmit these to public discussion. Symbols open up reality by making the invisible perceptible. Human beings implant intelligent systems on their world for themselves, but do so within the broad constraints of their natural existence. From a realist perspective, we discover truths about the universe that exist within it. Discovering values is incommensurable with constructionism. These two perspectives are antinomies – an antinomy in the sense that both sides can be justified independently as self-evident. The credibility of one paradigm does not in itself destroy that of the other. Those who believe that values are constructed do so authentically, and the opposite view of realism presented here is likewise intellectually legitimate.

Conclusion

As communication ethics faces the monumental challenge of relativism, this chapter has outlined a constructive intellectual pathway through which media ethics can proceed with integrity.

Cultural relativism ought to remain in the epistemological realm. In so doing, it serves as a deterrent to ethnocentrism and promotes cultural diversity, that is, a comprehensive and inclusive understanding of our humanness.

When cultural relativism is misconstrued in popular terms as moral realism, the fallacy of confused categories should be made apparent. Moral relativism justified by cultural diversity yields arbitrary definitions of goodness, as if to say: 'This is good because most people in a social group identify it as good.' But the communities we describe ethnographically are not necessarily good. From David Hume to G.E. Moore, we have recognized the fallacy of deriving 'ought' statements from 'is' statements. To assert prescriptive claims from an experiential base entails the illogic of confused categories.

Moreover, when popular moral relativism is unquestioned, we usually have not faced up to the pernicious politics that insists on the prerogatives of a nation, caste, religion or tribe. Cultural relativism turned into a moral claim is stultifying. If moral action is thought to depend on a society's norms, then 'one must obey the norms of one's society and to diverge from those norms is to act immorally ... Such a view promotes conformity and leaves no room for moral reform or improvement ... What constitutes right action when social consensus' does not indicate the wrongness of a society's practices and beliefs (Velasquez et al., 2009).

Since Nietzsche, ethical relativism has been arguing against absolutes. The universal sacredness of life and other normative models that are presuppositional start over intellectually. They reject ethical rationalism. The argument from relativism is directed against ethical objectivism. Protonorms accept that critique and construct a universal paradigm on totally different grounds. Therefore, protonorms conditioned by realism are acceptable, not imperialistic. They arise from the ground up and do not emasculate local difference.

In order to make philosophical work on ethical relativism fruitful, media ethics needs to nurture the philosophical imagination across the board. All the ethical issues we face should be rooted in philosophical beliefs about the character of human beings and the meaning of life. Debates over issues such as ethical relativism are not only an intellectual exercise but a venue for learning how to live.

References

Bauman, Z. (1993). *Postmodern Ethics*. Oxford: Blackwell.
Boas, F. (1887). 'Museums of Ethnology and their Classification', *Science*, 9, 589.
Christians, C. (2005). Ethical Theory in Communication Research', *Journalism Studies*, 6(1), 3–14.
——. (2009). 'Theoretical Frontiers in International Media Ethics', *Australian Journalism Review*, 31(2), 5–18.
Christians, C. and Traber, M. (eds) (1997). *Communication Ethics and Universal Values*. Thousand Oaks, CA: Sage.
Cooper, T.W. (1998). *A Time Before Deception: Truth in Communication, Culture, and Ethics*. Santa Fe, NM: Clear Light.
Fisher, W. (1987). *Human Communication as Narration: Toward a Philosophy of Reason, Value, and Action*. Columbia, SC: University of South Carolina Press.
Kaufmann, W. (1968). *Nietzsche: Philosopher, Psychologist, Anti-Christ*. Princeton University Press.
Kluckhohn, C. (1949). *Mirror for Man: The Relation of Anthropology to Modern Life*. New York: McGraw-Hill.
Kroeber, A. (1933). *Anthropology*. New York: Harcourt, Brace and Company.
——. (1949). 'An Authoritarian Panacea', *American Anthropologist*, 51(2), 318–20.
Marcus, G. and Fisher, M. (1999). *Anthropology as Cultural Critique: An Experimental Moment in the Human Sciences*, 2nd edn. University of Chicago Press.
Nagel, T. (1986). *The View From Nowhere*. New York: Oxford University Press.
Nietzsche, F. (1966 [1886]). *Beyond Good and Evil*, W. Kaufmann (trans.). New York: Routledge.
Nikolaev, A.G. (2008). *International Negotiations: Theory, Practice and the Connection with Domestic Politics*. Lanham, MD: Lexington Books.

——. (1967 [1872]). *The Birth of Tragedy*, W. Kaufmann (trans.). New York: Random House.
——. (1967 [1880]). *Will to Power: Attempt at a Revolution of All Values*, W. Kaufmann (trans.). New York: Random House.
——. (1967 [1887]). *On the Genealogy of Morals*, W. Kaufmann and R.J. Hollingdale (trans.). New York: Random House.
Peukert, H. (1981). 'Universal Solidarity as the Goal of Communication', *Media Development*, 28(4), 10–11.
Velasquez, M., Andre, Claire, Shanks, Thomas and Meyer, Michael J. (2009). 'Ethical Relativism'. Markkula Center for Applied Ethics, www.scu.edu/ethics/practicing/decision/ethicalrelativism.html, date accessed 23 November 2010.
Wilkins, L. (2008). 'Connecting Care and Duty: How Neuroscience and Feminist Ethics Contribute to Understanding Professional Moral Development', in S.J.A. Ward and H. Wasserman (eds), *Media Ethics Beyond Borders*. Cape Town: Heinemann Publishers.
Wiredu, K. (1996). *Cultural Universals and Particulars: An African Perspective*. Bloomington, IN: Indiana University Press.
Wuthnow, R. (1987). *Meaning and Moral Order: Explorations in Cultural Analysis*. Berkeley and Los Angeles, CA: University of California Press.

Notes

1. Relativism is elaborated and given a different orientation in Christians (2009).
2. For an expanded version of this argument, though with a different orientation, see Christians (2005).

2
What Does It Mean to be Moral? A Cross-Cultural and Cross-Religious Analysis of Morality among Muslims and Christians in Britain and France

Stephen M. Croucher

What does it mean to be a moral person? Are there universal traits that make someone a good person as opposed to an evil person? There really are no easy answers to these questions. What it means to be a moral person is a matter for individual interpretation by each of us. Each of us thinks there are specific traits, values or behaviours that make someone good or bad. Such beliefs are culturally based (Pojman, 2005), subjective in nature, not based on scientific fact and often not based on logical reasoning either. Furthermore, from a sociocultural perspective, the evaluation of *what is moral* is often based on an individual's religious beliefs and thoughts. The religious teaching of one faith can dictate the actions and beliefs deemed to be morally just and acceptable (Mitchell, 1980), while actions and beliefs of non-believers may in some cases be deemed unjust, unacceptable and immoral. The following examples are illustrations of this point.

In the summer of 2007, two years after the July 2005 London bombings, I sat in a hotel lobby conducting an interview with Lawrence, a bank representative from London. He described how he sees Muslims as lacking ethical principles:

> I don't really think Muslims are that good of a people honestly. I mean if you look at them, uh they do all sorts of bad and morally wrong things. I just saw on the news how a Muslim man killed his daughter because she uh wouldn't marry the man he wanted her to, now how right is that huh?

During the same summer, I met with Ali, an Algerian-born Muslim immigrant in France who works as a store clerk in Paris. He discussed how he sees Christians as severely lacking and in need of a 'moral compass' to guide them to God:

> I look around me and I see many uh many Christians who have lost their way. They uh they have no moral compass. They don't know what they want in life. All they want is more money, and uh more control over people and over other countries. How is that morally correct and good? I don't think it is. I think they need to know God.

While these two men come from different countries and religions, they both share a belief that the other individual's religion is lacking in morality and ethics. Religious beliefs and morality are intrinsically linked to one another (Pojman, 2005). As individuals from religious faiths make and interpret morality and ethics in similar and different ways, the intersection of these creations and interpretations is a prime location for potential disagreement and conflict (Croucher, 2008). As organized religion has a profound effect on the interpretation and practice of morality, an examination among different religious groups as to their interpretation and practice of morality could offer an insight into the cultural nuisances of this construct. Therefore, this analysis explores what it means to be a moral and or ethical person among two religious groups, Christians and Muslims. Specifically, Christians and Muslims in Britain and France are examined.

Geertz (1973) asserted that religion is an integral part of culture, yet few communication studies operationalize religion, even though religious differences influence communication (Cohen and Hill, 2007; Fuller, 2006). Communication studies also tend to neglect non-Christians. Oetzel *et al.* (2006) and Kandath (2006) argued that the Muslim world has been understudied in communication research. While political science and Islamic studies have conducted comparative analyses of these two nations, few communication studies have compared them (Croucher, 2006; Favell, 1998; Fetzer and Soper, 2005; Keaton, 2006; Laurence and Vaisse, 2006; Weller, 2006). Thus, a comparison of these nations within communication studies is warranted.

Ethics and morality

How should one lead one's life? Are there specific ways of living and thinking that are universally understood to be right or wrong? What is in fact the nature of right and wrong? These are just some of the questions addressed by scholars who study ethics and morality. Thomas Hobbes answered many of these questions in his 1651 work *Leviathan,* paid particular attention to the nature and purpose of morality, arguing that humans act to protect their own interests in a state of nature that is made up of relatively equal individuals. While individuals are relatively equal, we strive to make ourselves stand out from others in a state of competition, to reach our own goals and to outachieve others. This state of nature leads to a life devoid of enforced laws, rules and/or justice, as such concepts are non-existent. Yet, for Hobbes, such a state does not benefit anyone; thus, we work together in a social contract and obey a ruler, a Leviathan. Therefore, for him, morality is following a social contract among our peers for social order so as to avoid a *natural hell* (Pojman, 2005).

Morality as a branch of philosophy examines how we ought to lead our lives. Within this field of study, the analysis of the influence of culture and its impact on the development of ethical standards has increasingly become of interest to those studying in this area (Casmir, 1997; Hall, 1997; Johannesen, 1990). Different cultures conceptualize morality and ethics in different ways. There is an abundance of literature examining the differences in morality and ethics across cultures. In Judeo-Christian culture, and equally in Western culture, ideals such as autonomy, freedom of choice and justice prevail in shaping the Christian view on morality and ethics (Johannesen, 1990; May and Sharratt, 1994). In Islamic culture, morality and ethics are based on religious concepts and are rooted in the Qur'an (Ali, 1990; Haneef, 1996).

Conflict

An individual's ethics impact values, beliefs and how one approaches others in a conflict (Rahim, 2001). Hocker and Wilmot (1991) define conflict as 'an expressed struggle between at least two interdependent parties who perceive incompatible goals, scarce resources, and interference from the other party in achieving their goals' (p. 12). Individuals manage conflicts in varying ways. If individuals are taught that it is ethical to value the individual over the other as opposed to the group, or the other over the individual, the individual's conflict style will be affected (French and Albright, 1998).

Cultural influences cannot and should not be dismissed or ignored when analysing conflict (see, for example, Brew and Cairnes, 2004; Cai and Fink, 2002; Kim and Leung, 2000; Oetzel, 1998; Oetzel *et al.,* 2006). Specifically, cross-cultural differences like nationality, religion and language, as well as values and beliefs (such as ethics), are important variables for analysis. Little is known about the interaction of conflict with moral and ethical standards in other parts of the world. Therefore, this chapter examines the relationship between conflict and such norms in two relatively understudied religious cultures in communication studies – Britain and France.

Context

Britain

Britain has an officially sponsored church, the Church of England, which for centuries facilitated religious discrimination. However, a series of actions diminished the power of the Church and brought forth more equal protection for religious groups in Britain: the 1828 recognition of the rights of Protestant Nonconformists, the Roman Catholic Relief Act of 1829 and the Jewish Relief Act of 1859 each granted more rights to religious groups and allowed more political participation (Weller, Feldman and Purdman, 2001). As new religions entered Britain, the government slowly adapted to allow groups to have more legal rights (Fetzer and Soper, 2005).

Britain's greatest exposure to the Muslim world in the modern era was its colonial rule of the Indian subcontinent from 1600 to 1947 (Chamberlain, 1974; Croucher and Cronn-Mills, 2010). It was during this rule that the perceptions and misperceptions of what it meant to be a *proper* British man and a *proper* Indian emerged (Vertovec, 2002). Britain experienced one of its largest waves of Muslim (and Hindu) immigration after the 1947 partition of India. Due to the British Nationality Act, Commonwealth immigrants had full access to British citizenship. While this law was intended to allow white colonial subjects to gain automatic citizenship, it also permitted millions of non-white Indians to gain citizenship (Adolino, 1998). As a result of British colonialism, the British had a paternalistic attitude towards early Indian immigrants. Fetzer and Soper (2005) assert that because of this paternalistic attitude, these Indian immigrants were treated unequally. Even with calls to limit immigration mounting over the past 40 years, the immigrant population in Britain increased from one to three million in 1991 (Hoge, 2002) to around five million in 2001.

Currently, there is no legal protection on the books in Britain to defend religious minority groups. The Race Relations Act of 1976 prohibits discrimination on racial or ethnic grounds but does nothing to protect religious groups from similar discrimination (Croucher and

Cronn-Mills, 2010). Religious discrimination remains a critical problem in Britain (Rex, 2002).

In the wake of the 7 July 2005 terrorist attacks, in which 52 people died and more than 700 were injured (Greater London Authority, 2006), some in Britain called for heightened surveillance and control of the Muslim community. An article in the 8 July 2005 issue of *The Independent* discussed how the bombings were an attempt to divide British Muslims from British non-Muslims (Fisk, 2005). Calls were made in the media to stop immigration from Muslim lands in order to protect Britain's Christian people. Croucher and Cronn-Mills (2010) found that numerous Christians and Muslims in Britain blamed the *other* for the growing racism and hate in Britain. A primary cause for the growing racism and hate was that both groups accused the other of not having strong enough morals. But what is right? It is clear that overt and covert discrimination has increased in Britain, and religious coexistence has become strained.

France

France is also experiencing religious tension. However, unlike Britain, which has an official church and makes attempts to adapt in 'some ways' to its religious minorities (Fetzer and Soper, 2005), France is sterner in its resolve for secularism. Secularism, or *laïcité*, dating back to the French Revolution, is a matter of French law. In 1905, the French government officially declared France a secular state (Jones, 1994). As France increasingly comes into contact with Islam, this secularism is challenged (Croucher, 2009).

France's primary contact with Islam has been through its former colonies in North Africa, particularly Algeria. France fought a bloody civil war over Algerian independence (1954–62), in which thousands of French troops and more than a million Algerians died (Silverstein, 2004). This war left lasting scars on social, cultural and political relations between Christians and Muslims in France.

As in many other European nations, vast numbers of Muslim immigrants have migrated to France as either workers or as retired soldiers after the First and Second World Wars. France recruited approximately 150,000 workers from North Africa between 1915 and 1918 to help rebuild France. Many of these workers returned to North Africa between the two World Wars. However, during the *Trente Glorieuses* (the 30 glorious years of 1945–75), as France experienced a labour shortage, many Muslims from North Africa returned to France and took up employment in much-needed sectors. Most of the labour was from Italy, Morocco, Algeria, Tunisia, Spain and Portugal (Togman, 2002). 'Many of the

North African men, since only men were typically recruited for labor, who immigrated to France during this period, established their own lives and then many called upon their families to join them in France' (Croucher, 2009, p. 3).

Today, Islam is the second largest and fastest growing religion in France (Croucher, 2009). This growth has led to growing tensions over whether or not the secular French government should recognize Muslim holy days, the Muslim wish to wear religious symbols in public schools and the Muslim assertion that French employers can arbitrarily fire Muslims without legal recourse (Derderian, 2004). The response from the government and many Christians on the street has been that it is ethically unjust to recognize any religion's holy days or symbols and that limiting the rights of an employer puts restraints on a free-market society (Croucher and Cronn-Mills, 2010). The debate over the moral and ethical standing of religion's place in French society is vital, especially as France grapples with conflicts over the hijab.

Like Britain, France is responding to various sociocultural, political and economic issues. However, one issue that is uniquely French and that has encompassed a moral debate is the wearing of hijabs and other religious symbols in French public schools (Croucher, 2008, 2009). Dating back to the first veil affair in 1989, whether a school has the moral right to forbid someone to wear a religious symbol in a school or not has been a hot topic in French politics (Kidd, 2000). Political and religious groups have weighed in on the matter and in 2004 the government responded with a ban on the wearing of all religious symbols in public schools. This 2004 Act was labelled as morally repugnant by the overwhelming majority of the Muslim community and by a few in Jewish and Catholic communities as well, while being hailed as a defence of secularism by many secular citizens and many in the Catholic community (Ganley, 2004; Graff, 2005).

In Britain and France, how Muslims and Christians perceive events differs culturally. Moreover, the moral and ethical importance and rationale placed on events appear to differ *greatly*. Just as many Muslims in France deem the 2004 ban on the wearing of religious symbols in schools to be morally repugnant, many Christians perceive it to be ethically just to place such a restriction on individuals in order to protect secularism. In Britain, many Muslims argue that Christians lack strong moral values because they allow and support government efforts in 'spying' on mosques and Islamic prayer groups. As Pojman (2005) states, what is deemed morally and ethically *right* or *just* often differs based on an individual's religious beliefs. Therefore, the remainder of this analysis answers the following research question: in what ways do Muslims and Christians in Britain and France have similar or differing views on morality and ethics?

Method

In Britain, 29 Muslims (15 men and 14 women) and 38 Christians (20 men and 18 women) were interviewed. British participants ranged in age from 18 to 69. Of the British-Muslim participants, 17 were born in Pakistan, 2 in Bangladesh and 10 in Britain. All 38 of the British-Christians were born in Britain. In France, 45 Muslims (24 men and 21 women) and 44 Christians (20 men and 24 women) were interviewed. French participants ranged in age from 19 to 72. Of the French-Muslim participants, 14 were born in Algeria, 8 in Tunisia and 23 in France. Each of the 44 French-Christian participants was born in France. Participants were contacted through previously established social networks (Croucher, 2006, 2008, 2009).

This project used standard open-ended interviews, which can provide rich descriptions of communities (Patton, 1990; Philipsen, 1992). Interviews were conducted between 2005 and 2007. All interviews were conducted in English, French (by the principal investigator) and Arabic (through a translator). These interviews included a wide array of topics, including ethical behaviour, how morals and ethics guide interactions with others and how they approach conflicts with others. Interviews were analysed using a grounded theory approach, which looked to see what patterns emerged within the transcripts (Glaser and Strauss, 1967). Based on the grounded theory analysis, two significant themes emerged. The following section describes these two themes.

Findings and discussion

Definition of morality

Christians and Muslims described similar as well as differing ideas as to what *morality* is. For many Christians in Britain and France, morality was defined as individual, societal and governmental actions that help to maintain social order. This social order is reminiscent of the social contract discussed in *Leviathan*, one that encourages freedom of will and thought, but preferably not at the expense of societal order or tradition, and it is generally a social order that carefully weighs religion against secularism.

Alain, a shopkeeper in Paris, offered a simple definition of morality. He said morality is being able to 'know what is right and what is wrong for you and your family. It is uh knowing what is best for your country'. Janet, a student in London, similarly said that morality was 'a willingness and belief that what you are doing is good and uh a just thing to do'.

Suzanne, a florist from Lille, said that morality is not going against what is best for the community: 'Morality is doing what is good for the community, what is good for the people close to you. When you not do what good for them, you not have morality.' Michael, a military officer in Liverpool, expressed a similar sentiment. He described how morality is simply 'standing up for your community, family and government'. Ultimately, these individuals expressed how the idea of morality is doing good things and not going against what is best for an individual's family, community or government. Other Christians in both nations took this sentiment a step further and said that in order to be truly moral, one must not disrupt the social order of society. Alfred, a groundskeeper in Exeter, asserted that moral people:

> do not ruffle feathers of those around them [pause] because doing something like that is just impolite. Why would you want to do such a thing. Being rude is tantamount to be unethical and only thinking about yourself.

Similarly, Jacqueline, a stylist in Bordeaux, stated that morality means knowing when to speak and when not to speak in any given situation:

> People speak when they should not speak. People often cause trouble and make others angry or uncomfortable and really I ask, is this the right thing to do? Is this the moral or ethical thing to do? I uh I personally think it better to leave many things unsaid.

Connor and Xavier disagreed with Jacqueline. Connor, a store clerk in London, stated that it was virtually impossible for him to see morality as ignoring:

> saying what is on my mind and protecting what is right in the world. I must protect what is good for my family and government and Christ, but there needs to be a careful balance. Really uh, the balance between what is good for the government and religion needs to be balanced in a moral choice so one does not control the other.

The feelings of Xavier, a restaurant manager in Paris, on morality were almost identical:

> I think morality means speaking your mind and being sure of who you are and what kind of government and life you want here and after you are dead with God. But uh, talk of religion and government must be balanced.

The Muslim participants did not share the talk of balancing religion and God in morality. While Muslim conceptualizations of morality differed only slightly from those of Christians, the significance of God to morality was a major difference. Fatima, an Algerian immigrant to Paris who works as a clerk in Paris, stated that morality is 'the belief that your actions are ones that are good and just, and actions or deeds that help your family and community'. Khalid, a Pakistani immigrant to London who works as a civil servant, defined morality as a way of living that 'attempts to help those around you better themselves and uh, focuses more on good actions and less on things like greed and ego'.

As for the relationship between morality and social order, Muslims asserted that morality is important to maintaining social order. However, they often referred to Islamic scripture when referring to social order. The following are just two examples of such incidents. Ahmed, a Pakistani immigrant to Manchester who works in a factory, discussed how social order is important:

> moral actions help us keep things together. It uh, all come from the Qur'an. The holy book teaches us how to be moral, it teaches us morality and ethics and because of it we Muslims know right from wrong and can be holy men and women.

Rana, a Moroccan immigrant to Marseille, made a similar assertion:

> Morality and what is ethical in society, this is something we Muslims learn from Qur'an. We learn from [the] book how to keep society together. It is something very sacred to us. It is something very important to us. We want society, family and community to be together and safe.

While both religious groups refer to the relationship between morality and social order, the key difference is that Muslims refer to the Qur'an as guiding them in how to maintain social order. While the Christian

Bible does offer teachings on similar issues, the Christians in this project did not refer to it as a guiding beacon in their everyday moral lives. Similarly, for the Muslim population, the Qur'an weighed heavily in how they looked at the formation of their morals. While the Christians interviewed for this project talked about a careful balance between God and government, the Muslims did not call for this balance. For example, Nura, a Pakistani immigrant to Liverpool working as a schoolteacher, stated that it was impossible for her to separate God from government:

> It is morally impossible for me to say God should not have a say in what the government does or says. I think Allah, he must have influence over government. All people of faith must inform governments when they do things that are morally corrupt and unjust. Only then can we truly be a just and good society.

Clearly, this is a case of an individual blending religion and secularism into their interpretation of morality. For Nura, God's word is imperative in order to judge what is right and wrong with official governmental decisions and actions. However, for the Christians interviewed, it is best for governmental decisions to be devoid of religious influence. Zayd, an Algerian immigrant to Paris working as an athletic trainer, made a similar claim to Nura. He declared that a business or government without God at the helm is inherently unethical and doomed to failure:

> I do not understand why, why do people not want God a part of their lives. When God is not part of a business or government, the government, the government does not have the faith of the people. It is seen as unjust, as immoral. The two, justice or morals and governance, cannot be separate for me.

While the Christian and Muslim participants in this project were similar in many ways, the importance they placed upon religion differs significantly. What also emerged from interviews concerning morality was how morality relates to an individual's conceptualization of conflict. Specifically, differences emerged in how Christians and Muslims in Britain and France looked to their moral upbringings during conflict situations.

Morality and conflict

Conflict is inevitable. How individuals conceptualize conflict is greatly affected by their culture, values and morals (Croucher and Cronn-Mills,

2010; Rahim, 2001). Participants discussed how their approaches to conflict situations between members of their own religious group and members of differing religious groups were often moulded by differing views on what was considered moral or ethical. Muslims interviewed for this project pointed to the Qur'an and Islam as reasons for their tendency to avoid or want to compromise in conflict situations, regardless of the other individual's religion. Christians did not refer to their religion or religious texts as reasons for their general conflict preferences, describing themselves as having general tendencies towards the dominating and compromising conflict styles.

Hessa, a French-born Muslim woman working as a bartender, described how she was not a fan of conflict situations. She said that according to the Qur'an, conflict between individuals should be avoided if at all possible:

> From reading the Qur'an and growing up in the Islamic faith, I know that conflict is something that should be used only, only when very necessary. I know many other people here, I have uh many Catholic friends who think it is good to argue with others, to have conflict. I don't think this is right.

Mihran, a British-born Muslim working as a psychologist, talked about how conflict to him is something that is to be used as a last resort. His approach to conflict is greatly related to his Islamic identity:

> I have many clients, many Muslim and many Christian clients who all have problems with anger and have many conflicts in their lives. Conflict is a major issue for people. I must say though that for my Muslim clients, how they look at conflict and how I look at conflict relates very closely to the Qur'an. The Qur'an teaches us what is right and what is wrong in life. It guides us to do things that are just and to only have conflict when absolutely necessary, something to do only if we must do it. Most Christians I work with do not have this kind of background or gift in their lives.

Waahid, an Algerian immigrant to France working as a taxi driver, also said that because of the Muslim belief in using conflict as a last resort, he found involvement in conflict to be immoral:

> I think conflict is a bad thing. When people are part of a conflict, they show they are weak and that they let evil control their

decisions. This not a good thing to let happen I think. As a good Muslim I don't let conflict control my life and I don't let conflict happen, I avoid conflict if possible.

Nishan, a Pakistani-born Muslim in London, said that when confronted with potential conflict with someone who is not Muslim, the conflict is worse because, in his opinion, non-Muslims:

do not have the same values as we Muslims do. They uh, they do not think the same way we do about life and about people or the community. I think when there is a problem Christians want to make it worse by having argument and having to talk about all things. It much easier to avoid the problem. This is hard to do when you have conflict with Christians.

Jalal, an Algerian-born Muslim working as a nurse in Lille, suggested that Christians do not take Muslims seriously during conflicts:

[They] do not think Muslims are equal to them in a given situation. I think this is why uh when we have a conflict, they uh treat us differently. They look at us and treat us like children. We are not children. We are not different from them. We uh are taught in Islam and by Qur'an to treat all people equally, but I uh do not think they uh taught that in Christianity.

Cantara, a Pakistani immigrant to Britain, also suggested that how Muslims and Christians interact during conflict situations is greatly influenced by religious background. Specifically, she stated that as long as all involved in a conflict remember the good things their families taught them, conflict could be minimized:

Not all conflict between people has to be bad, I mean I uh do not like it but it can be alright I suppose. I think it can be better if all people in a conflict remember what they learned as children from their parents or uh from their religion like Islam or Christianity. Values, morals and beliefs are all important to helping reach a good compromise.

Bibi, a British-born Muslim woman working as a martial arts instructor, also believed consensus could be reached during a conflict situation.

She said that as long as people remember their values and what is just or moral, people could create a more peaceful society:

> I think it very possible for all people in conflict to come to agreement on what is best if people uh, if people remember where they come from and remember their past. If people remember we are not very different. It doesn't matter if we are Muslim, Christian or Hindu or Jewish or anything. We all have beliefs and other ideas, but we need to only be good to each other I think.

The Christians interviewed in this project, unlike the Muslims, expressed a general tendency towards wanting to dominate conflict situations. Moreover, these individuals did not reference the Bible when it came to describing the reason for their approaches to conflict situations. Christina, a massage therapist in London, discussed how she was really not a fan of conflict, but would prefer to be in control of it when it occurs:

> I think when a conflict happens, it is best to be in control of it. In fact, if I think something may be going to a conflict, I think I just go for it and get it over with. It is just easier in the long term I think.

Spencer, a musician in Paris, made a similar remark. He asserted that he prefers to end conflicts as soon as they begin, at almost any cost:

> When I see an argument, it really does not bother me. It is something that I think just needs to happen but I like to end it and uh end it anyway I can. I do not care what I have to do to end it really. I just need to end it and when I end it I like to win too.

Barry, a store manager in London, suggested that winning arguments and conflicts was a part of what he was taught as a child:

> When I was a kid, goodness, all I remember learning was that we needed to win. I heard it from my folks, my teachers, and even at church. If you look at the Bible we read about battles and overcoming diversity, it's about battling and winning in the end. It really is a Christian way.

Diana, a French tour guide, also suggested a relationship between Christian philosophy and a desire to control and win in arguments or conflicts:

> I am not trying to say the Bible or Christ is an angry book or man. But, if you think about it, Christianity and many of the Christian nations are known for being controlling and bossy. It is horrible but I think that may be why I have no problem wanting to control a conflict.

Francois, a restaurant owner in Paris, described how he was just brought up not thinking about others in a conflict: 'I never remember hearing people tell me to think about how a conflict can affect others. Really conflicts were about how they affect you and that was it.'

When it comes to reasons why the Christians in this sample said they were not taught to think of others when it came to conflict situations, they attributed this to a focus on individuality. Oliver, a British schoolteacher in Manchester, said:

> As a young child I remember learning that a goal in life was a pursuit of autonomy, you know freedom of choice and in life. This was very important for us all. So I think that uh in life this is something I look for even today.

Patricia, a French advertising representative, also discussed how as a child she was taught to be independent:

> Independence and things that lead us to be independent are considered to be the most important things in life really. So uh when I have a problem, like a conflict at work, I look at what is the best thing to do that will help me remain independent because that is the right thing to do.

What is apparent from these examples, as opposed to the answers given by the Muslim participants, is that not one of the Christian participants referred to the teachings in the Bible or Christianity as a reference point for dealing with conflict. The importance of religious beliefs is a key difference in how these two groups approach conflict.

While these two groups share a large number of similarities in how they conceive morality and ethics, there are many subtle differences in how morality influences their lives. Moreover, how religious teaching and morality affect conflict preferences also differs significantly between the two groups. The individual and collective nature of these two religious groups is a clear reason why these subtle differences exist. Christianity is generally a more individualistic religion and Islam is a more collectivistic one. Therefore, it makes sense that the choices of these individuals would reflect these historic cultural traditions.

Croucher (2008) asserts that further research is needed to examine the influence of cultural socialization on children's moral development within diverse religious groups. Such cross-cultural examinations could provide a valuable insight into how cultural groups like religious and ethnic communities can better work together to bring about productive problem-solving endeavours. Furthermore, future work should endeavour to explore further ways to bring together the different conceptualizations of ethics between various religious communities. As different groups increasingly come into contact with one another, it would be beneficial to comprehend how individuals approach right and wrong and how these approaches influence conflict. Such an endeavour would enhance overall intercultural communication and specifically could improve overall Christian-Muslim relations.

References

Adolino, J.R. (1998). *Ethnic Minorities, Electoral Politics and Political Integration in Britain*. London: Printer.
Ali, M.M. (1990). *The Religion of Islam*. Dublin, OH: Ahmadiyya Anjuman Isha'at Islam Lahore USA.
Brew, F.P. and Cairnes, D.R. (2004). 'Styles of Managing Interpersonal Workplace Conflict in Relation to Status and Face Concern: A Study with Anglos and Chinese', *International Journal of Conflict Management*, 15(1), 27–56.
Cai, D. and Fink, E. (2002). 'Conflict Style Differences between Individualists and Collectivists', *Communication Monographs*, 69, 67–87.
Casmir, F.L. (1997). 'Some Introductory Thoughts', in F.L. Casmir (ed.), *Ethics in Intercultural and International Communication*. Mahwah, NJ: Lawrence Erlbaum, pp. 1–5.
Chamberlain, M.E. (1974). *Britain and India: The Interaction of Two Peoples*. Hamden, CT: Archon Books.
Cohen, A.B. and Hill, P.C. (2007). 'Religion as Culture: Religious Individualism and Collectivism among American Catholics, Jews, and Protestants', *Journal of Personality*, 75(4), 709–40.
Croucher, S.M. (2006). 'Looking Beyond the Hijab: An Analysis of French Muslim Cultural Adaptation', unpublished Doctoral dissertation, University of Oklahoma.
——. (2008). *Looking Beyond the Hijab*. Creskill, NJ: Hampton Press.
——. (2009). 'A Mixed Method Analysis of French-Muslims Perceptions of La Loi 2004-228', *Journal of International and Intercultural Communication*, 2, 1–15.
Croucher, S.M. and Cronn-Mills, D. (2010). *Religious Misperceptions: The Case of Muslims and Christians in France and Britain*. Cresskill, NJ: Hampton Press.

Derderian, R.L. (2004). *North Africans in Contemporary France: Becoming Visible*. New York: Palgrave Macmillan.
Favell, A. (1998). *Philosophies of Integration: Immigration and the Idea of Citizenship in France and Britain*. New York: St Martin's Press.
Fetzer, J.S. and Soper, J.C. (2005). *Muslims and the State in Britain, France, and Germany*. Cambridge University Press.
Fisk, R. (2005). 'The Reality of this Barbaric Bombing', *The Independent*, 8 July, www.independent.co.uk/opinion/commentators/fisk/robert-fisk-the-reality-of-this-barbaric-bombing-497971.html, date accessed 23 November 2010.
French, W. and Albright, D. (1998). 'Resolving a Moral Conflict through Discourse', *Journal of Business Ethics*, 17, 177–94.
Fuller, R. (2006). 'Wonder and the Religious Sensibility: A Study in Religion and Emotion', *Journal of Religion*, 86, 364–84.
Ganley, E. (2004). 'Islamic Group Says Officials Abusing Law on Religious Symbols', *Associated Press Worldstream*, 21 October, http://web.lexis-nexis.com/universe.
Geertz, C. (1973). *The Interpretation of Cultures*. New York: Basic Books.
Glaser, B.G. and Strauss, A.L. (1967). *Discovery of Grounded Theory: Strategies for Qualitative Research*. Chicago: Aldine.
Graff, J. (2005). 'Streets of Fire', *Time Online*, 6 November, www.time.com/time/europe/html/051114/story.html, date accessed 23 November 2010.
Greater London Authority (2006). *Report of the 7 July Review Committee*. London: City of London.
Hall, B.J. (1997). 'Culture, Ethics, and Communication', in F.L. Casmir (ed.), *Ethics in Intercultural and International Communication*. Mahwah, NJ: Lawrence Erlbaum, pp. 11–42.
Haneef, S. (1996). *What Everyone Should Know about Islam and Muslims*, 14th edn. Chicago: Library of Islam.
Hocker, J. and Wilmot, W. (1991). *Interpersonal Conflict*, 3rd edn. Dubuque, IA: Wm. C. Brown.
Hofstede, G.H. (2001). *Culture's Consequences*, 2nd edn. Thousand Oaks, CA: Sage.
Hoge, W. (2002). 'New Immigration Plan in Britain Would Restrict Asylum Seekers', *New York Times*, 31 May, A4.
Johannesen, R.L. (1990). *Ethics in Human Communication*, 3rd edn. Prospect Heights, IL: Waveland Press.
Jones, C. (1994). *Cambridge Illustrated History: France*. Cambridge University Press.
Kandath, K. (2006). 'Critical Approaches to Community Conflict in Developing Countries: A Case Study of India', in J. Oetzel and S. Ting-Toomey (eds), *The SAGE Handbook of Conflict Communication*. Thousand Oaks, CA: Sage, pp. 501–15.
Karapin, R. (2000). 'Major Anti-minority Riots and National Legislation in Britain and Germany', in R. Koopmans and P. Statham (eds), *Challenging Immigration and Ethnic Relations Politics*. Oxford University Press, pp. 312–47.
Keaton, T.D. (2006). *Muslim Girls and the Other France: Race, Identity Politics, & Social Exclusion*. Bloomington, IN: Indiana University Press.
Kidd, W. (2000). 'Frenchness: Constructed and Reconstructed', in W. Kidd and S. Reynolds (eds), *Contemporary French Cultural Studies*. New York: Arnold Publishers, pp. 154–62.

Kim, M. and Leung, T. (2000). 'A Multicultural View of Conflict Management Styles: Review and Critical Synthesis', in M. Roloff and G. Paulson (eds), *Communication Yearbook 23*. Thousand Oaks, CA: Sage, pp. 227–69.

Laurence, J. and Vaisse, J. (2006). *Integrating Islam: Political and Religious Challenges in Contemporary France*. Washington DC: Brookings Institution Press.

May, L. and Sharratt, S.C. (1994). *Applied Ethics: A Multicultural Approach*. Englewood Cliffs, NJ: Prentice Hall.

Mitchell, B. (1980). *Morality: Religious and Secular*. Oxford University Press.

Miyahara, A., Kim, M.S., Shin, H.C. and Yoon, K. (1998). 'Conflict Resolution Styles among "Collectivist" Cultures: A Comparison between Japanese and Koreans', *International Journal of Intercultural Relations*, 22, 505–25.

Money, J. (1999). *Fences and Neighbors: The Political Geography of Immigration Control*. Ithaca, NY: Cornell University Press.

Oetzel, J. (1998). 'The Effects of Self-construals and Ethnicity on Self-reported Conflict Styles', *Communication Reports*, 11, 133–44.

Oetzel, J., Arcos, B., Mabizela, P., Weinman, A.M. and Zhang, Q. (2006). 'Historical, Political, and Spiritual Factors of Conflict: Understanding Conflict Perspectives and Communication in the Muslim World, China, Colombia, and South Africa', in J.G. Oetzel and S. Ting-Toomey (eds), *The SAGE Handbook of Conflict Communication*. Thousand Oaks, CA: Sage, pp. 549–74.

Patton, M.Q. (1990). *Qualitative Evaluation and Research Methods*. London: Sage.

Philipsen, G. (1992). *Speaking Culturally: Explorations in Social Communication*. Albany, NY: State University of New York Press.

Pojman, L.P. (2005). *How Should We Live? An Introduction to Ethics*. Belmont, CA: Wadsworth.

Rahim, M.A. (2001). *Managing Conflict in Organizations*, 3rd edn. Westport, CT: Quorum Books.

Rex, J. (2002). 'Islam in the United Kingdom', in S.T. Hunter (ed.), *Islam, Europe's Second Religion*. Westport, CT: Praeger, pp. 51–76.

Silverstein, P.A. (2004). *Algeria in France: Transpolitics, Race, and Nation*. Bloomington, IN: Indiana University Press.

Togman, J.M. (2002). *The Ramparts of Nations. Institutions and Immigration Policies in France and the United States*. Westport, CT: Praeger.

Vertovec, S. (2002). 'Islamophobia and Muslim Recognition in Britain', in Y.Y. Haddad (ed.), *Muslims in the West: From Sojourners to Citizens*. Oxford University Press, pp. 19–35.

Weller, P. (2006). 'Addressing Religious Discrimination and Islamophobia: Muslims and Liberal Democracies: The Case of the United Kingdom', *Journal of Islamic Studies*, 17(3), 295–325.

Weller, P., Feldman, A. and Purdman, K. (2001). *Religious Discrimination in England and Wales*. London: Home Office Research.

Part II
The Ethics of International Political Rhetoric

3
The Rhetoric of Democracy

Gerard Elfstrom

Democracy has become a brand (Nathan *et al.*, 2008). In the twenty-first century, it is difficult to find anyone who does not claim to favour democratic government. Though the word 'democracy' does not appear in the United Nations Universal Declaration of Human Rights, Article 21 declares: 'The will of the people shall be the basis of the authority of government; this will shall be expressed in periodic and genuine elections which shall be by universal and equal suffrage and shall be held by secret vote or by equivalent free voting procedures' (United Nations, 1948). The student demonstrators in Tiananmen Square in Beijing, China in 1989 issued calls for democracy even though none had first-hand experience of democratic government (Kristof, 1989). Even China's communist government has cautiously experimented with democratic government by allowing open elections in some villages (Liu, 2009). Though many observers believe Russia has become disturbingly authoritarian, its government nonetheless insists that it is a *sovereign democracy* (Figes, 2009). Alas, the desire to spread democratic institutions was also prominent among the justifications offered by the Bush Administration in support of its invasion of Iraq (Bush, 2003). Rhetorically at least, democracy is likely as near a universal value as any to be found in the present age.

Nonetheless, democratic government is not universally praised. Following Iran's revolution in 1979, Ayatollah Khomeini announced that Iran would not have democratic government, since democracy is a product of the non-Islamic West. In its place, Iran would have an Islamic republic (Bakhash, 1984, p. 73). In Russia, the euphoric embrace of democracy that followed the collapse of the Soviet Union has given way to distrust of democratic government and the endorsement of order and stability by ordinary Russians. Many are convinced that only an authoritarian government is able to provide these things for them. Stalin, though responsible for the deaths of tens of millions of Russians, has re-emerged as one of their heroes (Figes, 2009). Recent public opinion polls in Asia reveal that many ordinary people agree with Putin-era Russians, that is, they claim to value order and stability and to be largely indifferent to the lure of democratic government (Nathan *et al.*, 2008). Lee Kuan Yew, once Prime Minister of Singapore, has argued forcefully and articulately that Western-style democracy is unsuited to Asian societies (Zakaria, 1994). Lee asserted that Asian culture requires that the community has greater value than the individual. Since democracy gives greatest weight to the individual, he believed that it is incompatible with Asian culture. Even in the US, frequently cited as a bastion of democratic government, only slightly over half the eligible electorate votes in presidential elections and considerably less than half turns out for non-presidential elections (McDonald, 2009; Tomasky, 2008). Though ordinary Americans are prone to voice wholehearted enthusiasm for democratic government and to casually denigrate other forms of government, their professed devotion is belied by their tepid record of voting.

Given the general enthusiasm for democratic government professed by august institutions and ordinary people, it should be simple to find compelling arguments to support it. Surprisingly, such overwhelmingly convincing arguments are difficult to uncover. In addition, the global enthusiasm for democracy does not make clear whether democratic government is a fundamental moral right of human beings or whether it is simply the governing mode that happens to work better than others. In addition, we wish to know whether democratic government is most suitable for all peoples and all societies under any and all circumstances whatsoever, or whether it is only most suitable sometimes and in some places.

The value of the individual

This chapter's analysis is grounded on the assumption that the life and welfare of the individual human being are of greatest importance. Any worth possessed by a democratic or alternative form of government must be sought in its relation to this fundamental value. However, if this assumption is accepted, it is possible that people's lives and well-being can be best served by authoritarian government and also that their lives and welfare may conflict with democracy. Moreover, it is not a trivial assumption, as a number of articulate and influential people deny it. Denunciation of the contemporary world's individualism has become a common theme of contemporary rhetoric. Communitarians, religious figures and spokespersons for traditional societies all sound this note. This chapter lacks space to give these critics the attention they deserve. However, its basic rhetorical response is that no government can possess value apart from the benefit it bestows on individual human beings. Any human construction that fails in this way is not defensible.

It is certainly true that some individuals deny that their own lives have intrinsic value and others are eager to sacrifice themselves for the sake of a cause or institution. In addition, it is not uncommon for people to assert that their lives have value and/or meaning only insofar as they contribute to the value of something beyond themselves. But it is not difficult to address these concerns. In the 1970s, two philosophers with divergent political ideologies, John Rawls and Robert Nozick, distinguished between the requirements of a political order and the values individuals should be allowed to pursue in their personal lives (Rawls, 1971, pp. 264–5, 520–9; Nozick, 1974, pp. 307–9). They argued that defensible governing structures must place ultimate value on individual human lives. Nonetheless, within this overarching concern, individuals, while leading their private lives, should be allowed to pursue such values as they see fit. Of course, this view has the unsettling implication that some people may gain the most value from their lives by devoting them to some other cause or movement. However, if that is what gives their lives greatest fulfilment, the jarring note disappears, since their devotion to a cause is what gives their lives value.

The reasoning of Rawls and Nozick can be reconstructed as follows. Many individuals may indeed find fulfilment only by submerging their lives in a communal whole. They may also wish to find meaning by devoting themselves to some larger cause in which their personal interests will be secondary to the value of the whole. This is common enough. The difficulty Rawls and Nozick find is that different individuals will devote themselves to quite distinct and frequently conflicting causes or communities. Other individuals, in turn, may be completely repulsed by communal activity and find little value in submerging their lives in a larger cause. The only governmental order that will allow each of these diverse individuals with distinctive values and personalities to achieve maximal gratification is for government to remain aloof from these private matters and allow each individual to pursue them as he or she desires. For example, a common difficulty that many societies now face is that some members of their community may devote themselves to Islam while others are equally committed to Christianity. The only way for each of those individuals to pursue the type of life they find most rewarding is for the government to allow all, even conflicting, religious groups to follow their beliefs.

Ayatollah Khomeini's endorsement of an Islamic republic (that is, a Shahless theocracy) can be addressed with many of the same resources (Bakhash, 1984, p. 73). However, to begin with, it is worth noting that Khomeini's views are not entirely alien to those of Christian Europe. For much of the Middle Ages, all European governments were, at least in theory, subject to the authority of the Catholic Church. On the face of it, this is an entirely reasonable position. From the perspective of believers, the supreme deity is the fundamental authority of the universe. As such, the authority of the supreme deity should override all else. Because many religious groups are intently focused on the supreme deity and much concerned with its mandates, it is reasonable to suppose that these groups share the ultimate authority of the deity. But if this is correct and plausible, why have the great majority of the world's nations separated religious from secular authority? A significant portion of the answer to this is found in the religious and personal diversity of the world's people in the present day. If each individual nation were populated entirely by individuals with a single set of religious beliefs, a theocracy might prove both workable and desirable. The difficulty is that almost no nations of the world (including Iran) now find themselves in this circumstance. Furthermore, a fair portion of the world's current population is without religious belief. When a number of groups with varying religious beliefs find themselves within a common set of national boundaries, they have two choices: either they can try to eliminate the other groups and rule supreme or they can adopt a policy of tolerating all religious beliefs. However, the latter option precludes theocratic government.

Of course, Lee Kuan Yew has the most direct challenge to the premise that individual life and well-being are of utmost importance. He believes that this assumption directly conflicts with traditional Asian values. He is quoted as saying: 'Eastern societies believe that the individual exists in the context of his family. He is not pristine and separate. The family is part of the extended family, and friends and the wider society ... There is grave disquiet when we break away from tested norms, and the tested norm is the family unit. It is the building block of society' (Zakaria, 1994, p. 113). Notice that Lee does not purport to make a claim about universal principle. He is making a factual claim about Asian culture and values. However, his argument has several facets. In addition to a claim about values, he ties his position to a view of the requirements of social order. Another prominent theme of his interview is: 'The expansion of the right of the individual to behave or misbehave as he pleases has come at the expense of orderly society. In the East the main object is to have a well-ordered society so that everybody can have maximum enjoyment of his freedoms' (Zakaria, 1994, p. 111). Recently, this latter theme received an echo in the comments of an Asian movie celebrity, Jackie Chan. Chan is quoted as saying: 'I'm gradually beginning to feel that we Chinese need to be controlled. If we're not being controlled, we'll just do what we want' (Lee, 2009). It is likely to be unsurprising that the leadership of mainland China has similar views. The head of the Chinese parliament is quoted as saying: 'Without a single Communist Party in control, Mr. Wu argued, a nation as large as China "would be torn by strife and incapable of accomplishing anything"' (Wines, 2009).

Though Lee entwines his claim about Asian values with the requirement of an orderly society, the two differ, at least in theory. Hence, each will receive a separate response. As might be supposed, Lee's comments prompted a firestorm of controversy. However, one distinguished Asian, Kim Dae Jung, issued a thoughtful response. Kim was a prominent South Korean political leader who was a courageous dissident during the period of military dictatorships and served a term as President from 1998 to 2003. His response had two strands. Firstly, he asserted that a precedent for individualism could be found in past Asian writing and practice. Secondly, he denied that culture is immutable. He asserted: 'As an inevitable consequence of industrialization, the family-oriented East Asian societies are also rapidly moving toward self-centered individualism. Nothing in human history is permanent' (Kim, 1994, p. 190). Kim's remarks tacitly acknowledge the truth of Lee's claim about traditional values. The East Asian nations of China, Korea, Japan and Vietnam have all been heavily influenced by Confucianism. Confucianism places greatest emphasis on human relations and puts family relations at the centre of the nexus of human ties. Kim Dae Jung was well aware that South Korea remains the most Confucian of the East Asian societies, but he was also aware of the speed with which it is moving away from its Confucian past. However, if Kim is correct, cultural values may change. If so, Lee's beliefs about Asian values may soon prove obsolete. But are there grounds to support Kim's claims? As it happens, careful students of the matter have found a close, causal relationship between the level of economic development and the emergence of democratic institutions (Foweraker and Landman, 2004, pp. 14–15).

The second theme of Lee's argument focuses on the disorder which he believes Western individualism allows. To bolster his case, he made specific mention of drug use and violent crime in the US (Zakaria, 1994, p. 111). Of course, the concern to maintain order is deeply entrenched in the thinking of the leadership of mainland China. This anxiety long predates the rise of the Communist Party. The claim is that only a strong authoritarian government has the resources to maintain order (Wines, 2009). Part of the difficulty of this issue is that 'order' and 'disorder' are ill-defined. It is not obvious that the US is less orderly than China. Nor is it obvious that India, a large sprawling democracy with a population nearly as large as that of China, is less orderly than China. Politics are far more turbulent in India's fractious democracy than in China's one-party rule, but it has yet to be demonstrated that China's autocratic government brings more social order than India's democracy. Both nations suffer from explosions of violence and ethnic conflict. Further, though India suffers from more visible governmental turmoil, it has yet to be proven that China's authoritarian government is genuinely more orderly or whether state control is able to maintain a façade of calm. Thus, the most that can be said of Lee's authoritarian position is that it is unproven.

A requirement for living a fully human life

Several lines of argument support the idea that democratic government is a necessary requirement for leading human life to its fullest. Prominent among these is the claim that democratic government is a fundamental right of all human beings because it alone is consistent with the requirements of human autonomy. The general approach is Kantian, though Kant himself, being Prussian, favoured autocratic government (Kant, 1983, pp. 113–14). For Kant, the salient features of human beings are their freedom and rationality. Taken together, these qualities make them autonomous, that is, laws unto themselves. This same autonomy also makes them responsible for their actions and hence accountable for them. If that is correct, it is but a short step to the view that the only mode of government consistent with human autonomy is democratic government, that is, government by the people. The difficulty with authoritarian modes of government is that they subject autonomous human beings to laws which they have not made. In consequence, such governments are inconsistent with human autonomy.

However, there are several well-known difficulties with this position. A brief analysis will make clear that democratic government cannot satisfy the requirements of autonomous life as they are described above. Moreover, it is not obvious that a government of any type could meet them. As a matter of fact, appeals to human autonomy are commonly employed to ground anarchism (Wolff, 1970; Nozick, 1974, pp. 51–3). Nonetheless, the type of government apparently most consistent with individual autonomy is direct democracy, that is, government in which all citizens directly participate. However, even with this mode of government, decisions will be made by vote. Individual citizens will commonly find themselves on the losing side of votes, but their community will oblige them to abide by the result even though they not only did not choose it but instead opposed it. There are other difficulties. It may be the case that the assembled citizens will not agree to discuss an issue which a particular citizen believes to be critically important, or the community may consider matters which particular individuals may believe to be unworthy of consideration. If autonomy requires that individuals be subject only to decisions which they accept, even direct democracy must fail to meet the requirements of autonomous human existence.

In addition, in a world with a human population of well over six billion people and nations populated by tens or hundreds of millions of people, direct democracy must be a rare commodity. Democracies these days will be representative democracies, meaning that ordinary individuals will not directly participate in government. Instead, citizens will collectively select individuals to govern on their behalf. But, once again, such decisions will be made by vote, and rarely unanimously. Hence, in the usual course of events, one side will lose. Furthermore, the candidates for office will seldom be the individuals each particular voter, or even most individual voters, would most prefer. To make matters worse, once in office, elected officials will commonly support laws or policies that many individual citizens reject. In addition, nations are so complex that important legislation will commonly be enacted concerning matters about which individual voters are ignorant or unable to understand. Of course, the most basic difficulty of all is that each individual vote counts for almost nothing in an election in which tens of millions of voters participate. So, as is commonly recognized, democratic governments in the twenty-first century have very little connection to the decisions, desires or interests of any given individual citizen. In consequence, it is highly unlikely that democratic government can be justified on the grounds that it is a requirement of individual citizen's autonomy. If there is a universal human right to democratic government, then it must be sought elsewhere.

Aristotle formulated a kindred argument in Classical Greece well over 2,000 years ago. He was convinced that the most excellent human life could be lived only by individuals who take an active part in government. This was because the most excellent life for human beings is a life that makes full use of the most valuable human qualities and, for Aristotle, this required participation in governing activity (Aristotle, 1984, pp. 2027–9).

Though Aristotle's view is attractive in several respects, it falls prey to the objections listed above. He believed that only city states are sufficiently small to allow the type of governing arrangements he advocated (Aristotle, 1984, pp. 2104–5). However, the world currently holds well over six billion people and is likely to have billions more by the middle of the twenty-first century. A world dotted with compact city states is hardly feasible in such circumstances. But nations with millions, tens of millions or hundreds of millions of people are simply unsuited to direct democracy, even if the citizens allowed to participate are restricted to the elite few, as Aristotle wished. There are other pertinent difficulties. In the current era, participating in government is typically a full-time occupation. Being a politician is at present an engrossing career which leaves time for few other activities. It is doubtful that many contemporary politicians are convinced that they are leading the best possible life for human beings. Also, the activity of governing is currently so complex and specialized that each office of government employs only a subset of the range of abilities any human being possesses. Thus, present-day governing careers scarcely meet the standard of excellent existence established by Aristotle.

Another difficulty is that many people are able to employ their abilities in non-governing roles and perform many of the same activities Aristotle associated with the activity of governing. More directly, if we were to construct a roster of the most valuable human abilities and seek out the people who employed these qualities to the highest degree, it is unlikely that most or any of them would be politicians.

Lastly, and most disconcertingly, Aristotle himself believed that the best possible government would be government by a single wise individual (Aristotle, 1984, pp. 2045–6). The difficulty, as he understood it, was in finding a suitable wise individual and keeping such a person in office and uncorrupted. Given this difficulty, Aristotle believed that democracy would function as a serviceable alternative, the best that could be expected given the circumstances of human life. However, Aristotle does have an important link with contemporary theorists of democratic progress. It is currently something of a commonplace that democracy will develop once a middle class of sufficient size and self-confidence emerges. This topic will be examined in more detail later on. For now, it will suffice to point out that Aristotle also believed that the middle class is best suited to democratic governing. He reasoned that the very poor and the exceptionally wealthy share an important quality that would prevent them from governing effectively – both groups are too interested in money, the poor because they have too little and the wealthy because they have too much (1984, pp. 2056–8).

Another argument emerges from the idea that democracy is closely associated with human freedom. Rhetorically at least, human freedom and democratic government are tightly linked in human consciousness. This connection is likely a significant factor behind the current enthusiasm for democracy. One commentator put it this way: 'It is by virtue of the close connection of democracy with contemporary values of liberty, equality, and solidarity that it has acquired such a good name in modern times' (Christiano, 2001, p. 385). Aristotle also found a strong connection: 'The basis of the democratic state is liberty' (Aristotle, 1984, p. 2091). Though both attractive and plausible, there are difficulties with this view. For one thing, there is clearly no necessary connection between democratic government and the values of liberty, equality and solidarity. India, for example, is clearly a democracy. However, it retains a rigid caste system which is founded on radical inequality. All Indian citizens are able to vote, but it is obvious that some individuals and some groups have far more influence on affairs of government than others (Drèze and Sen, 2002, pp. 352–8). The US is commonly viewed (not least by itself) as a bastion of both freedom and democratic government, yet there was scarcely a whimper from US citizens when the Patriot Act removed some of their most basic liberties, such as the right of habeas corpus (Cole, 2004). And, of course, no one should forget that Hitler was placed in office by a democratic vote. *Solidarity* is not an easy notion to pin down. However, it is not obvious that citizens of democracies, such as India or South Korea, feel greater solidarity with one another than citizens of authoritarian states, such as China or Singapore. In fact, citizens of raucous democracies seem to enjoy few things more than tormenting one another. Solidarity, as Hegel believed, is more likely to result from war or shared hardship than from a particular mode of government (Hegel 1949, pp. 210–11). Hence, the citizens of the UK appear to have been far closer to one another in the bleak years following the Second World War than in the recent years of peace and prosperity.

However, James Madison, one of the founding fathers of the US, found a more direct and troubling conflict between democracy and freedom, equality or solidarity: that of the tyranny of the majority. In democracies, one side of any given issue will prevail and may perhaps always prevail. In that circumstance, the majority may use its power to trample over the rights and prerogatives of the minority. Hence, Madison concluded, the majority must be constrained if all are to enjoy the values of freedom and equality (Sunstein, 2009). In the US, this is accomplished by the separation of the powers of government and the Bill of Rights of the US Constitution, as Madison urged. In sum, democratic government may well be closely associated with the values of freedom, equality or solidarity, but there is certainly no necessary or consistent connection. In fact, James Madison found a direct conflict and concluded that the difficulty could be addressed only by constraining democratic processes.

The above arguments purporting to demonstrate that democracy is a fundamental requirement for an excellent human life are unpersuasive. However, another difficulty stands in the way of concluding that democracy is a fundamental right of all human beings. As the world's experience of the past two centuries demonstrates, the establishment of genuinely democratic government requires a demanding set of conditions to function as it should. Democracy is not a matter of simply holding elections. Elections that are not free and open do not satisfy the demands of democracy. Neither do elections in which voters are subjected to intimidation or coercion, or in which they simply vote as their religious, clan or tribal leaders dictate. Even if the above pitfalls are avoided, elections will prove a poor shadow of democracy if citizens are unable to comprehend relevant issues and are indisposed to make their interests and concerns known. But there is also another requirement of genuinely democratic government: citizens must be prepared to demand that governmental leaders be responsive to their interests and concerns. As the American philosopher John Dewey (1937) recognized early in the last century, democratic government requires both certain types of institutions and certain kinds of people. It is far simpler to establish and maintain an authoritarian government: armies can simply sweep into a nation, take over and commence governing. However, democracy cannot exist in the absence of citizens who are confident of themselves, well informed, willing to participate in the machinery of elections and who expect governments to be responsive to their concerns.

In light of the above, it is unsurprising that many accept Aristotle's conclusion that democratic government is a matter for the middle classes. Hence, it is unlikely to be an accident that observers find a strong connection between the emergence of viable middle classes and the creation of democratic government. Those in the middle classes tend to be well educated, prosperous and self-confident. They are less likely than other social groups to be cowed by authority and more likely to presume that governments should bow to their concerns. The wealthy are prone to believe that they alone should hold power, while the impoverished are commonly too downtrodden and desperate to have much interest in the affairs of government or to believe that anyone should be responsive to their needs. Nonetheless, these are claims of matters of fact. It is entirely possible that viable democracies may exist in nations without a significant middle class. However, it is likely that democratic institutions are more fragile in nations without a significant middle class. The wealthy are likely to have a preponderance of political power, both because of their wealth and because they are likely to be highly educated. The poor and uneducated will have little significant source of power other than through their numbers. Sometimes, their massed numbers can overthrow an abusive or unpopular government, but such upheavals are unusual. Further, after the upheavals, it is likely that once again they will be more vulnerable to those with greater resources of wealth and education to draw upon.

Democracy's instrumental value

If democratic government is not a fundamental human right, is not required to lead the most excellent human life and may conflict with human freedom, what other justification or justifications might it possess? Recall that many ordinary people are convinced that stability, prosperity or a decent life are more important than democratic government. Of course, it is possible that their views on this matter are mistaken. However, if their views are justified, then democratic government cannot be a fundamental human right since, when push comes to shove, these people find other things to be more important. But if it is not of fundamental importance, then how important is it? In particular, is democratic government sufficiently important to justify the lofty rhetoric issued on its behalf?

To help focus thinking, consider the example of present-day Iraq. It has a democratic government. Elections are reasonably fair and open. There is free debate at legislative sessions. Nonetheless, ordinary Iraqis are absolutely miserable. Iraq currently suffers from an unemployment rate of over 30 per cent. Salaries for those who have jobs have plummeted. Electricity, water and fuel are available only sporadically. People who head off to work or to markets cannot be sure they will return whole or alive. Glad though they are to be rid of Saddam Hussein, they may certainly be excused for believing that their lives were better under his draconian rule. Hussein was a brutal dictator, but the vast majority of Iraqis were able to live their lives without his interference and conduct their affairs in peace. They are presently optimistic about their futures, but only because present conditions have improved compared to the misery of a few years ago. It is a safe bet that many would be content to return to the stability and orderliness of the Hussein era. Further, it is difficult to argue that they are unjustified in making that choice. Most certainly, the introduction of democratic government has done little to improve their lives (Hammer, 2008).

The example of Iraq clearly shows that stable and decent lives do not inevitably result from the institution of democratic government. If ordinary people are faced with a choice between the two, they are clearly justified in opting for decent and secure lives. That is a brutal and unfortunate choice, of course, but the world sometimes forces such choices on people. However, if democratic government and decent human lives do not inevitably accompany one another, is it possible that they can actually conflict? Bangladesh may be a pertinent example of this. It is among the poorest and most miserable nations on the face of the earth, yet it has an indisputably democratic government (United States Department of State, 2008). It enjoys free elections in which the two major political parties compete ferociously, but it is what may be termed a pathological democracy. The two major political parties devote their talents and energies to fighting one another. When one becomes dominant in government, the other will work tirelessly to undermine its work. Hence, government is a cockpit of unmitigated political haggling and little attention is given to the needs or welfare of the populace. Though there is reason to believe the Bangladeshis are proud of their democratic institutions, it is not unlikely that many ordinary Bangladeshis would be pleased to substitute their current governing system for Lee Kuan Yew's authoritarian government. Though many would believe such a choice to be shortsighted, there is no obvious reason to believe their choice in such a matter would be unjustified or irrational.

The examples of Iraq and Bangladesh show that democracy does not inevitably improve the lives of its citizens and also that democratic institutions may in fact deepen their misery. It is nonetheless possible that democratic government should be valued because it is *more likely than* authoritarian governments to nurture values that are critically important to individual human beings, such as freedom of expression or freedom from tyrannical government.

Unfortunately, one distinguished economist has found no connection between the existence of democratic government and national prosperity (Sen, 1997). It might seem otherwise, for the wealthiest nations of the world are commonly democratic, and the tie between a substantial middle class and democratic government has been noted above. And, as it happens, researchers have found a close link between economic development and democracy, but they conclude that economic development is a causal agent of democratic government rather than the reverse (Foweraker and Landman, 2004). At present, China, with its authoritarian government, is prospering mightily, as is Singapore. The nations well endowed with petroleum reserves are not, by and large, particularly democratic. Nonetheless, if Foweraker and Landman are correct in their analyses, sufficient prosperity will eventually bring democratic government to these nations as well.

Another reasonable and attractive view is that democratic nations may be less likely to go to war than authoritarian governments. The idea is that ordinary citizens are less prone to military adventures than autocrats. This notion was formulated first by Kant, but was revived several years ago and remains the focus of intense discussion (Kant, 1983; Doyle, 1983). Nonetheless, in the latter half of the twentieth century, the democratic US spent many more years at war than authoritarian China or Russia. European nations, which are uniformly democratic, are indeed reluctant to engage in warfare, but this reluctance may owe far more to the years of misery warfare brought to them earlier in the twentieth century than to democratic government. Though the idea that democracies are unwarlike appears plausible, empirical analyses reveal a more complex picture. Emerging, unstable democracies, for example, seem more likely to initiate war than other nations. Well-established democracies in stable domains of the world are less likely to involve themselves in war than others (Rasler and Thompson, 2005). Democratic government is one factor among others in the equation. In certain circumstances, it increases the chance of war, but in others, it decreases the likelihood of warlike activities.

Does anything else remain? One further view is that politicians are more likely to concern themselves with the welfare of their citizens when they face the discipline of the ballot box from time to time. Also, those seeking office are under pressure to make a case for their claim to office. An effective way to gain support from the voting public is to pledge devotion to projects aimed at public welfare. It is also likely that authoritarian governments are less likely to concern themselves with the welfare of their citizens than democracies. However, these are all claims of matters of fact. In consequence, they must be supported by factual information. One positive sign is, as Amartya Sen (1997) notes. that 'No substantial famine has ever occurred in any independent and democratic country with a relatively free press'. Another researcher has found a strong correlation between democratic government and respect for human rights (Davenport, 1999). In addition, Transparency International, the corruption monitoring group, presents a complex picture of the relation between democracy and corruption. It finds corruption to be greatest in emerging democracies, where institutional monitoring of behaviour is at its weakest. Nonetheless, it does conclude that corruption is less likely in democracies, though even strong democracies will not be entirely free of corrupt practice (Transparency International, 2007).

So, the picture that emerges from empirical analysis does not support the soaring rhetoric frequently employed on behalf of democracy. Democratic government seems a result rather than a cause of economic development. This is closely linked to the tie commonly found between the emergence of a middle class and democracy. Nonetheless, democracies are more likely to respect human rights than authoritarian governments and are less likely to be corrupt. Thus, for a variety of reasons, human beings can anticipate their lives will be better with democratic government than authoritarian.

Yet, it may be fitting to reserve the last word on this matter to a nation that recently entered, with some trepidation, the league of democratic nations. The tiny state of Bhutan was among the world's few remaining monarchies. Its inhabitants were somewhat bemused several years ago when their king announced that it was time to establish democratic government. They believed their lives were going well and they were entirely content with their monarchy. Further, they were anxious about the prospect of exchanging a system that was serving them well with a new and untried mode of government. A prominent journalist put the matter this way: 'We've always been stable under the kings but people worry about life without the monarchy in charge' (Agence France-Presse, 2008). Though their king was otherwise convinced, his subject's views were not obviously unjustified or irrational. Nonetheless, being accustomed to obey their king, they obediently followed his directions to initiate democratic government. The king's reason for urging the change was simple: 'Today you have a good king, but what if you have a bad king tomorrow?' (Agence France-Presse, 2008).

References

Agence France-Presse (2008). 'Tiny Bhutan Will Vote Today to Trade Absolute Rule for Democracy', *New York Times*, 24 March, www.nytimes.com/2008/03/24/world/asia/24bhutan.html, date accessed 23 November 2010.

Aristotle (1984). *The Complete Works of Aristotle*, vol. 2, J. Barnes (ed.). Princeton University Press.
Bakhash, S. (1984). *The Reign of the Ayatollahs*. New York: Basic Books.
Bush, G. (2003). 'President Bush Discusses Iraq in Veterans Day Address', 11 November, http://merln.ndu.edu/MERLN/PFIraq/archive/wh/2003111110.pdf, date accessed 23 November 2010.
Christiano, T. (2001). *Democracy. Encyclopedia of Ethics*, 2nd edn. New York: Routledge, pp. 385–9.
Cole, D. (2004). 'Uncle Sam is Watching You', *New York Review of Books*, 51(18), 18 November, www.nybooks.com/articles/17568, date accessed 23 November 2010.
Davenport, C. (1999). 'Human Rights and the Democratic Proposition', *Journal of Conflict Resolution*, 43(1), 92–116.
Dewey, J. (1937) 'Democracy and Educational Administration', *School and Society*, 45, 457–67.
Doyle, M.W. (1983). 'Kant, Liberal Legacies and Foreign Affairs', *Philosophy & Public Affairs*, 12(3), 205–35.
Drèze, J. and Sen, A. (2002). *India: Development and Participation*. Oxford University Press.
Figes, O. (2009). 'Putin vs. the Truth', *New York Review of Books*, 56(7), 30 April, www.nybooks.com/articles/22642, date accessed 23 November 2010.
Foweraker, J. and Landman, T. (2004) 'Economic Development and Democracy Revisited: Why Dependency Theory is Not Yet Dead', *Democratization*, 11(1), 1–20.
Hammer, J. (2008). 'Iraq: Before & After, and Now', *New York Review of Books*, 55(19), 4 December, www.nybooks.com/articles/22111, date accessed 23 November 2010.
Hegel, G.W.F. (1949) *Philosophy of Right*, T.M. Knox (trans.). Oxford University Press.
Kant, I. (1983). *Perpetual Peace and Other Essays*, T. Humphrey (trans.). Indianapolis, IN: Hackett Publishing Company.
Kim, D.J. (1994). 'Is Culture Destiny? The Myth of Asia's Anti-democratic Values', *Foreign Affairs*, 73(6), 189–94.
Kristof, N. (1989). 'Thousands Chant for Democracy within Earshot of China's Leaders', *New York Times*, 19 April.
Lee, M. (2009). 'Spokesman: Jackie Chan Comments Out of Context', *Yahoo News*, 21 April.
Liu, Y. (2009). 'Are Village Elections Leading to Democracy?', *China Elections and Governance Review*, 1, 1–4.
McDonald, M. (2009). 'Voter Turnout', *United States Election Project*, http://elections.gmu.edu/voter_turnout.htm, date accessed 23 November 2010.
Nathan, A.J., Chu, Y-H. and Meyers, J.J. (2008, November 10). 'How East Asians View Democracy', Carnegie Council, www.cceia.org/resources/transcripts/0085.html, date accessed 23 November 2010.
Nozick, R. (1974). *Anarchy, State, and Utopia*. New York: Basic Books.
Rasler, K. and Thompson, W.R. (2005). *Puzzles of the Democratic Peace*. New York: Palgrave Macmillan.
Rawls, J. (1971). *A Theory of Justice*. Cambridge, MA: Harvard University Press.
Sen, A. (1997). 'Human Rights and Asian Values: What Lee Kuan Yew and Le Peng Don't Understand about Asia', *New Republic*, 217, 2–3.

Sunstein, C.R. (2009). 'The Enlarged Republic – Then and Now', *New York Review of Books*, 56(5), 26 March, www.nybooks.com/articles/22453, date accessed 23 November 2010.

Tomasky, M. (2008). 'How Historic a Victory?', *New York Review of Books*, 55(20), 18 December, www.nybooks.com/articles/22156, date accessed 23 November 2010.

Transparency International (2009). 'Frequently Asked Questions about Corruption', www.transparency.org/news_room/faq/corruption_faq, date accessed 23 November 2010.

United Nations (1948). 'Universal Declaration of Human Rights', www.un.org/en/documents/udhr/index.shtml, date accessed 23 November 2010.

United States Department of State (2008). 'Background Note: Bangladesh', www.state.gov/r/pa/ei/bgn/3452.htm, date accessed 23 November 2010.

Wines, M. (2009). 'In China, No Plans to Emulate West's Way', *New York Times*, 10 March, www.nytimes.com/2009/03/10/world/asia/10beijing.html?_r_1&pagewanted-print, date accessed 23 November 2010.

Wolff, R.P. (1970). *In Defense of Anarchism*. New York: Harper & Row Publishers.

Zakaria, F. (1994). 'Culture is Destiny: A Conversation with Lee Kwan Yew', *Foreign Affairs*, 73(2), 109–26.

4
'America Will Call Evil by its Name': 'Evil' as a Theologically and Morally Loaded Notion in American Foreign Policy Discourse

Anna Kasafi Perkins

One of the epithets for which former US President George W. Bush became infamous was used in his State of the Union Address just four short months after 9/11. In that address he described three nations – Iran, North Korea and Iraq – as members of an 'Axis of Evil' constituting a clear and present danger to global peace. In this soundbite, the then leader of the free world expressed the belief that 'evil', a deeply religious concept, existed in geopolitical and geostrategic entities, often embodied in individual leaders like Saddam Hussein ('the evil one') or Osama bin Laden ('an evil man'). Evil, with its visceral connections to notions of sin and rebellion against God, speaks to extreme wrongdoing and is instinctively opposed by its absolute opposite – good.

Implicit in Bush's argument was the recognition of a conflict between the forces of good and evil. Coming face to face with evil demands a taken-for-granted response and fuels an impulse to eradicate evil. Indeed, later that same year, Bush told West Point graduates: 'We are in a conflict between good and evil, and America will call evil by its name' (Rossing, 2004, p. 44). America under George W. Bush did more than name calling or finger pointing. America's major response to the perceived conflict between good and evil is what Stephen Chan (2005) calls a 'War on Evil', a conflation of the terms 'War on Terror' and 'Axis of Evil' (p. viii) – an attempt to eradicate evil from the geopolitical sphere.

This chapter critiques the notion of evil in American foreign policy discourse as exemplified in the epithet 'Axis of Evil'. It draws out the theological roots of the term from the American cultural context, one that has been shaped by Protestant forms of Christianity, which Howard Davis (2002) has described as '[Bush's] gun-slinging Christian heritage' (p. 191). In recent times, America has felt the growing impact of Christian fundamentalist groups like the so-called Religious Right, while conservative religious groups, such as the Moral Majority and the Religious Roundtable, have also directly sought to influence politics, including foreign policy.

Yet the impact of US cultural and religious traditions on its foreign policy pronouncements has passed largely unnoticed. Exploring the impact of such traditions on US foreign policy becomes even more crucial with the deployment of such morally and theologically loaded terms as 'Axis of Evil'.[1] This takes on a particular moral flavour when seen in the light of America's self-understanding as a 'saviour nation' (Ryn, 2003, p. 387), having a divine mission to rid the world of evil and establish democracy and civilization. Viewed theologically, such action may amount to a usurping of the divine role – only God can eradicate evil ultimately. At the same time, the myth of redemptive violence needs to be challenged as it provides a basis for the belief that violence saves; sadly, violence is never redemptive but simply fuels more violence.

Evil in international discourse

While evil has been a potent term in recent international discourse, it is equally a highly problematic one. Renée Jeffery, whose recent work traces the meanings and uses of the notion of 'evil' in modern international relations, argues that, while evil has always had a particular currency in international relations:

> [W]hat has regained a particular level of prominence in recent years is the idea that evil is a dark and malevolent force to be reckoned with and, following from this, that a good/evil dualism is at play in the world. However, unlike the early apocalyptic writers and, indeed, the Manichaeans who conceived of the cosmic war between good and evil in response, at least in part, to the problem of meaningless suffering, this battle is now being presented in predominantly moral terms. (2007, p. 129)

This moral vision of evil is two-pronged – it shines light on both the culpable actions of those who perpetrate evil and the necessary response of those who combat it. Yet if the theological and morally loaded nature of the term is taken seriously, it calls into question the claims of innocence and goodness being made by either side, as will be explored below.

Calling international enemies 'evil' is not new – Ronald Reagan, in 1980, described the Soviet Union as the 'evil empire', which he pledged to fight. The US in turn was described by Ayatollah Khomeini of Iran as the 'Great Satan', the main source of corruption in the modern world. Even within the borders of the US, in the post-9/11 world, some internal critics of US foreign policy call America 'the main source of evil in the world' while other critics see it as a major agent in combating evil (Hunt, 2003, p. 11). Similarly, as some Islamic groups view the West, and the US in particular, as *the* source of evil and corruption in the world, inevitably they see attacking America and its allies as a religious duty. There is a congruence in the position of opposing sides that is striking. Kittredge (2008), citing Lincoln (2006), shows that the apocalyptic features of Bush's speeches are mirrored in those of bin Laden: both constructed their conflict as a Manichean struggle of the Sons of Light against the Sons of Darkness or the camp of the faithful versus the camp of the infidels, both divided history into different epochs under different reigns, both used the image of suffering children and both chastised anyone who would seek to find a middle ground between their radically opposed positions.

As Chan (2005) points out, such dualism also informed the rhetoric of the clerical party after the Iranian Revolution and infused the North Korean response to US accusations about its nuclear intentions. Similar points of contact can be demonstrated between the approaches in both American fundamentalist communities and some Islamic groups. As Jürgen Moltmann demonstrates, such groups understand time in apocalyptic terms and see themselves as a factor in the ending of the world and bringing about a new reality:

> [I]n the apocalyptic Armageddon politics of amassing nuclear armaments for the 'last battle,' as under President Ronald Reagan in the USA, or in Saddam Hussein's rhetoric of the final battle, when he attempted to talk into existence 'the mother of all battles' in Kuwait. The heightening of the friend-foe relationship in the horrific modern world to a final apocalyptic battle between Christ and the Antichrist or between the true Islam and the 'Satan' USA, the West, apostasy and blasphemy, are part of the modern phenomenon of fundamentalism. (1992, p. 113)

Undoubtedly, the description of the world in terms of such a deadly opposition serves to construct and exacerbate that division, making any chance for negotiation impossible. War on evil is therefore the only response.

Religion in foreign policy and international relations

This has to be viewed against the backdrop of a global resurgence of religion in a fashion that is transforming our understanding of international relations (Thomas, 2005). This resurgence is often unremarked upon or dismissed as an aberration, yet it can be cogently demonstrated that religious factors are at work in many circumstances across the globe. At the same time, even within the tradition of international relations, it is possible to identify deep religious roots for accepted notions such as just war and humanitarian intervention. Martin Wight, for example, highlights the existence of a theological perspective behind the diplomatic principle 'he who is not for us is against us' (cited in Thomas, 2005, p. 114).

Wight identifies the root of this not-for-us-is-against-us principle in the impulse for salvation, the desire to eradicate sin and suffering in the world. Perhaps the same impulse lies behind the drive to eradicate evil in order to create a civilization that mirrors the heavenly realm. Such a religious impulse swings between yearning to convert the world and the impulse to condemn it. It then divides the world into the saved and the damned, the orthodox and the heretic, the virtuous and the corrupt – us and those that hate us. Looked at in another way, it can be argued that the theological principle is captured in the following question: 'Who is on the Lord's side?' The 'natural' response is 'I am on the Lord's side', as was implicit in President Bush's call to arms post-9/11 or embodied in the 1998 charge by bin Laden that America had declared war on God. Clearly, to be inattentive to or dismissive of the role of religion in foreign policy has consequences.

The importance of this is not lost on the community of nations. Jamaican self-styled 'word terrorist'[2] Mel Cooke, for example, captures the ambiguity of this not-for-us-is-against-us principle in his aptly titled poem 'Why Do They Hate Us?', while at the same time giving voice to the concerns about the 'War on Terror' of many Jamaicans:

> If you are not with us
> Then you are against
> But every son of A. Smith
> Who serves the rich
> Is capitalism's saint.
> When the scourges of people's lives
> Musarraf of Pakistan
> Pinochet of Chile

The Shah of Iran
Mobutu of Congo
Hussein of Iraq
Are your allies
It should be no surprise
At the appointed hour
Who coulden ketch Quaku³
Ketch him twin ... towa (2008, p. 12)

Cooke's last two lines in the first stanza, written in Jamaican, refers to a Jamaican proverb meaning that if you cannot hurt an enemy, you go after someone close to him or something he holds dear. In this case, the Twin Towers (twin towa) of the World Trade Center were targeted by the hijackers since they were viewed as symbols of the materialistic core of the US. For much of the world, Wall Street and the Pentagon, both targets of 9/11, stand for the economic and military domination of the world by America. Cooke, like many Caribbean people, recognizes the complexity of the issues coalescing around 9/11 and its aftermath, and protests – using the power of 'words of mass destruction' (WMD) – against the intersection of violence and religious fervour, as well as against the way in which the US approach the rest of the world in the wake of this tragedy. He protests against the hypocrisy of the world's only superpower that beds down with dictators and tyrants, among whom he lists friend-turned-enemy and 'evil personified' Saddam Hussein, and then claims that it is hated for its freedom and democracy – or, worse, disingenuously asks 'Why do they hate us?'. Ironically, for a 'terrorist' such as Cooke, the violence with which to strike the evil that he sees in the American Right are the clustered bombs of his words, with poetry being the 'final vehicle'; in so doing, he may 'accidentally hit its banal people' (2008, p. 10). His words echo Hannah Arendt's concerns about the banality of evil while challenging its personification in a person or a state. Davis (2002) was also critical of the use of the simplistic categories of 'good' versus 'evil' by George W. Bush, who dismissed 'the myriad complexities, ambiguities and resentments of a world created out of his nation's own imperial *realpolitik*' (p. 189).

America's mission to confront evil

Beginning in the middle of the 1990s, the concept of evil returned to popular rhetoric to describe the worst humanitarian atrocities, such as the Rwandan genocide and the massacre in Bosnia. Now, in the early decades of the twenty-first century, evil has been indelibly associated with mass-casualty terrorism (Jeffery, 2007) and 9/11 is the epitome of such evil. Sean Hannity (2004) represents one voice that defends the American approach to evil, which it perceived as acting against US interests; such anti-American evil is at play inside US borders and in other parts of the world. In a work pointedly titled *Deliver Us from Evil: Defeating Terrorism, Despotism, and Liberalism*, he paints a picture of evil in the world and America's special mission to confront it. The defeat that he perceives for evil is not simply in the hands of God. America, as divine agent with a special mission, is responsible for 'delivering' the world from evil and establishing a civilization of freedom and democracy. There is much decisive certainty in Hannity's position that builds on a long tradition of America's self-understanding as having a religious mission, which began with John Winthrop in 1630 (Bellah, 2003).

Hannity is sure that evil can be easily recognized in many dimensions of life, but it is recognizable in its purest form in the events of 9/11. He rejects what he calls the liberal 'explanation' of evil as originating in unjust structures and systems, and locates it squarely in the realm of the human heart, which in some individuals is morally warped – evil. He identifies evil with certain ideological positions, liberalism being the main one, which – ironically in his estimation – allows other dangerous forms of evil, like terrorism and despotism, to flourish.

As he calls for a morally trenchant response to evil, Hannity identifies Ronald Reagan as the twentieth century's greatest President, who intimately understood the importance of confronting evil. Reagan is the President to whom George W. Bush is most often compared, particularly in his approach to dealing with evil. Interestingly, Jeffery (2007), while identifying George W. Bush as the foremost proponent of evil discourse in American presidential history, illustrates that he is not as unusual as he first appears. In fact, while George W. Bush leads the way in this respect followed by Reagan, surprisingly, Bill Clinton comes next. According to Jeffery, while George W. Bush is often compared to Reagan, in many ways Bush's understanding of evil more closely approximates that of his predecessor.

It was during the Clinton presidency that evil became associated with acts of terrorism. So, although Bush is usually the one credited with having brought the idea that evil forces exist in the world back into contemporary American politics, it was actually Clinton who did so in explicit terms. Jeffery concludes that Bush's 'understanding of evil is profoundly religious if, at times, theologically confused' (2007, p. 132). She argues convincingly that the former President did not always use the word in black and white terms; in fact, he used evil in several, but often incommensurable, ways: to describe the nature of evil, to demonize the adversary and to depict its absolute opposition to good. The West Point speech, which gives this chapter its title, is an example of Bush's conception of evil as the absolute opposite of good. For Bush, the word 'evil' is manifold: evil describes the acts carried out by individuals as well as an independent force that exists in the world. He draws on multiple understandings of 'evil', such as evil agents, as well as apocalyptic notions of a cosmic battle between good and evil. Given the confused and confusing nature of Bush's use of the term and the importance of its role in contemporary international political discourse, it is clearly necessary to reflect briefly on this very notion, which fascinates as well as confuses us (Häring, 1998).

In Jeffery's estimation, what Bush did was simply to raise the public profile of evil. She sees the fact that Clinton's and Bush's uses of this term so closely approximate each other as possibly symptomatic of 'wider [radical religious] trends taking hold in America in the late twentieth and twenty-first centuries' (2007, p. 148). Those who are shaped by and are shaping these religious trends have come to view Islam as the primary source of evil and Saddam Hussein as a prime candidate for the role of the Antichrist or, since his death, the forerunner of the Antchrist. Hence, political discourse about evil finds fertile ground in the general rise of radical religion among a large section of the American population. Clearly, the long reliance of US presidents on the term 'evil', with its usage sharply increasing from the middle of the twentieth century, has deep roots in these radical American religious traditions.

Theological reflection on nations defeating evil

The former UK Prime Minister Tony Blair was quick to endorse the Bush declarations. Eight days after 9/11, he told the Labour Party that out of the tragedy and evil of 9/11 would come a force for 'lasting good' – terrorism would be destroyed, hope would be given to the nations, greater understandings would arise between countries and faiths, and justice and prosperity would arise for the poor and dispossessed (Scranton, 2002, p. 6). In this telling, the tragedy of 9/11 elicited a response that was all-encompassing and panacea-like, solving all the problems of the world which hitherto had been unsolvable. The moral high ground was claimed forthwith. At the same time, it conveniently ignored the existence of the victims of injustice within the American, British, Muslim and other populations.

Such claims – that a lasting good will originate from the defeat of evil – taps into the deeply theological roots of the term. Defeating evil is a soteriological act, that is, it brings about salvation, in this case in the form of civilization, freedom and democracy. In the poetry of the aggressive lyricist again:

> Bush says it is freedom of choice.
> Freedom of voice
> Freedom of worship
> Freedom to rejoice in
> Just being different
> It is not that we hate your freedoms as such
> Just
> Those are the very freedoms denied us. (Cooke, 2008, p. 12)

The US believes that out of evil will come a promised legacy of good, but only if it, acting as the divine agent, defeats evil and delivers the good(s) of freedom and democracy. No other nation could provide the moral framework to lead the fight against evil (William Kristol, cited in Wallis, 2003). Cooke gives the lie to these claims. He questions the actions of the powerful saviour nation and shows them to be less moral than at first blush.

Viewed theologically, therefore, attempts by nations like the US to finally eradicate evil are actually futile, as Wallis (2003) argues. According to Wallis, in Christian theology it is not nations that rid the world of evil, but rather God *and* the people of God when they exercise moral conscience. He charges in the best Niebuhrian fashion that nations 'are too often caught up in complicated webs of political power, economic interests, cultural clashes and nationalistic dreams' (2003). He is unequivocal that God has not given the responsibility of overcoming evil to a particular nation, much less to a superpower with enormous wealth and particular national interests.

People are indeed called to fight against evil, but the *final* eradication of evil lies in the hands of God. Therefore, in a certain way, the discourse of some US leaders and media celebrities about evil demonstrates a kind of theological confusion or even deep theological error (or bad theology, as Wallis terms it). If it is God's role to rid the world of evil and God has not yet done so, then perhaps theirs is an unwitting attempt to usurp the divine role or perhaps an attempt to outshine God, who has not been able to rid the world of evil. Human beings are attempting to do what God has not managed to do up to this point. There is sinfulness (idolatry or blasphemy) at play. At the same time, the eschatological dimension of the problem of evil has been overlooked or ignored. This final eradication of evil at the hands of God is part of the *last things*, events at the end of the world.

The Book of Revelation is the text that provides the final answer to earthly suffering. After God rids creation of all evil and evildoers, He will personally heal and minister to His holy ones and free them from suffering (Kurz, 2004, p. 177). The earthly struggle against evil is viewed as a reflection of the battle between God and Satan which, having been lost by Satan in heaven, has continued on earth (Rev. 1:7–9). It is a futile battle, however, as God has already won. Our role is simply to carry out the divine will in the earthly realm knowing that the battle has already been won in the cosmic realm. This is captured in the symbolism of Revelation 20, where the Devil, the Beast and the False Prophet are thrown in the pool of fire and sulphur. This symbolizes the expectation that all rebellion against God – earthly and heavenly – is finally crushed at the Last Judgment. When that happens:

> The problem of evil will finally meet a thoroughly just solution: People who do unrepented evil deeds will be punished; the good will be rewarded. The injustices that the good suffer from in this life will be rectified in the next life. Total justice will finally, and actually for the first time, be publicly established. The bad news for evildoers is good news for the upright, who have been victimised and oppressed and persecuted by them in this life. (Kurz, 2004, p. 175)

Human participation in eradicating evil

Häring (1998) asks rhetorically if evil can be overcome by human beings and replies that the answer is not simple. Even so, he comes down on the side of declaring that evil can be overcome, a deeply problematic position, as we have demonstrated. Nonetheless, he cautions that there are two great dangers along the way: 1) the confusion between perception and projection, which can lead to the worst perversions; 2) human beings, societies and institutions being declared representatives and embodiments of evil. These dangers have played themselves out in the 'War on Terror'.

Häring's (1998) concerns are echoed over and over again: 'The locating of evil in the person of single men, nations or organizations has certainly not quarantined evil. Rather, it has legitimized any action which claims to be intended to bring the light of democracy and freedom to a world under threat' (Chan, 2005, pp. 90–1). Nor has it served to destroy evil for good (that after all is the work of God).

Identifying evil on the international stage led America to one response – war – a problematic practice. The 'War on Terror' was declared with the moral purpose of defending civilization and defeating evil. Any state that was not on board for this project was considered to be against it – there was no neutrality and no position from which a justified and justifiable critique could be launched. Scranton charges, as would Walzer (2004), that from its conception, the 'War on Terror' was flawed (Scranton, 2002, p. 8). Matusik states that: 'Any naïve externalization of evil proves to be dangerous in that it is attached to its own ignorance of the sources of evil' (2008, p. 129). Matusik therefore questions the very notion of war on evil, whether it is defined in political (evil empire, axis of evil, evil ruler) or sacral terms (jihad on Great Satan, infidels targeted by a suicide bomber).

When Häring's (1998) second danger plays itself out, each terrorist is seen as an instance of the transcendent evil force. What are unconnected centres of inhuman violence become connected as part of a larger global and cosmic strategy:

> That is why the conflict readily bleeds from one locus to another – Afghanistan then, Iraq now, Iran or some other land of evil soon – and why, for that matter, the targeted enemies are entirely interchangeable – here Osama bin Laden, there Saddam Hussein, here the leader of Iran, there of North Korea. They are all essentially one enemy – one 'axis' – despite their differences from one another, or even hatred of one another. (Carroll, 2004, p. 18)

In exploring President Bush's spontaneous description of the 'War on Terror' as a crusade, Carroll (2004) compares the meaning and impact of both the 'War on Terror' and the medieval crusades. (The negative resonance of crusades for the Muslim community cannot be ignored.) He contends that taboos tend to fall in all-out war, 'whether crusade or jihad' – that is, actions considered unacceptable in routine circumstances are often the norm during war. One thousand years ago, for example, Christian crusaders used the severed heads of Muslim fighters as missiles; today Iraqi insurgents decapitate hostages (Carroll, 2004, p. 14). No side is wholly innocent. The disingenuousness of the self-professed 'good' side in this equation is also captured by the word terrorist Cooke:

> Why do they hate us? ...
> ... They will never know,
> Watching Geraldo

And star reporters
Deify mercenaries
As civilian contractors
Show four-fold mutilation,
Cut 15 murdered civilians
Panties over head in Abu Grahib
Beheading made at high-speed (2008, pp. 11–12)

Christian crusade was the mirror image of jihad, as both 'threatened nothing less than apocalyptic conflict between irreconcilable cultures' (Carroll, 2004, p. 16). Violence becomes established as the appropriate response to all that is wrong with the world. But such sacred violence has a momentum of its own, often turning against an internal enemy as well as the enemy outside. This was amply demonstrated in the routine demonization of Muslims within the US and Europe after 9/11. Carroll laments that, as in the time of the crusades, such sacred violence was used to enforce doctrinal uniformity. Similarly, the US Attorney General defined criticism of the Bush Administration during the 'War on Terror' as treason and Congress enacted legislation justifying the erosion of civil liberties in an appeal to patriotism.

The myth of redemptive violence

Contemporary theologian Walter Wink sheds light on the futility of such attempts at ridding the world of evil through violent national action. Wink (1999) locates the futility of such action in the 'myth of redemptive violence', the belief that violence saves, that war brings peace and that might makes right. The myth that violence saves may seem not to be mythical because it seems to work. Wink makes the startling claim that we tend to overlook the religious character of violence. Violence is deeply religious, as it demands of its devotees absolute obedience-unto-death. He describes this myth as 'the simplest, laziest, most exciting, uncomplicated, irrational, and primitive depiction of evil the world has ever known' (1999, p. 53). Children, especially boys, may be socialized into this orientation towards evil and never outgrow the need to locate evil outside of themselves.

This myth contributes significantly to international conflict, as survival of the nation becomes 'the highest earthly and heavenly good' (Wink, 1999, p. 56). In such a situation the nation assumes god-like proportions ('No other god but the state'). Such an imperialist state can demand the ultimate sacrifice of its citizens and can by divine decree use violence to rid the world of its enemies. God – any god, Christian, Muslim, Hindu – is seen to have blessed and favoured the supremacy of the chosen nation and ordained the defeat of its evil enemy. In circumstances where the myth of redemptive violence underlies such imperialist or nationalist states, talk of defending democracy and Christianity are vain echoes as they cannot accept the existence of any higher power other than the myth itself. Even those oppressed by the manifestations of the myth of redemptive violence buy into its righteousness. This is so because the myth offers salvation through identification with the leader and nation that confront and defeat the enemy powers. Salvation comes by identifying with military might, not repentance and truth. 'The myth of redemptive violence is, in short, nationalism become absolute ... Its salvation is not a new heart but a successful foreign policy' (Wink, 1999, pp. 61–2). Sadly, in resorting to violence in order to solve conflict, neither party ever learns from the encounters.

Deliverance from evil is a central promise of scripture and the daily prayer of every Christian (Matthew 6:7–15). '[Yet] the summons to collaborate in history to overcome evil is a call to be responsible for a world which is endangered by evil and an invitation to praise its creator, so that God can be all in all' (Suess, 1998, p. 46). The exercise of moral conscience therefore requires a kind of humility and spirit of repentance which should accompany any attempt at changing the world for good, eradicating evil. Acknowledging evil in oneself and one's nation *and* the presence of the divine in the enemy may be difficult, but it is an important way of exercising moral conscience in the defeat of evil.

In conclusion, discourse on evil in international political dialogue, and particularly in US foreign policy, is deeply moral in its character. Apart from calling into question the nature and meaning of evil, it questions the role of individuals and nations in the 'fight against evil'. In dividing the world into 'us' versus 'them', 'good' versus 'evil', politicians hark back to a Manichean notion of the world that ignores the ambiguity of the motives, actions and justice of the self-proclaimed 'good side'. However, in the final analysis, only God has *the* absolute and definitive role in eradicating evil. To believe otherwise is to attempt to usurp God's role in salvation and to ignore the theologically and morally loaded nature of the concept of evil.

References

Bellah, R.N. (2003). 'Can We Be Citizens of a World Empire?', talk delivered at Iliff School of Theology, Denver, Colorado, 28 January 2003, and at Pepperdine University, Malibu, California, 6 March 2003, www.robertbellah.com/lectures_8.htm, date accessed 24 November 2010.

Carroll, J. (2004). 'The Bush Crusade', *The Nation*, 20 September, pp. 14, 16–18, 20, 22.
Chan, S. (2005). *Out of Evil: International Politics and Old Doctrines of War*. London: I.B. Tauris & Co.
Cooke, M. (2008). *11/9*. Kingston, Jamaica: Blouse and Skirt Books.
Davis, H. (2002). 'The Lion, the Witch and the Warmonger: "Good", "Evil" and the Shattering of the Imperial Myth', in P. Scranton (ed.), *Beyond September 11: An Anthology of Dissent*. London: Pluto Press, pp. 188–94.
Hannity, S. (2004). *Deliver Us from Evil: Defeating Terrorism, Despotism, and Liberalism*. New York: Regan Books.
Häring, H. (1998). 'Beyond Theory, Practice and Imagination', *Concilium: International Journal of Theology*, 1, 25–42.
Hunt, M. (2003). 'In the Wake of September 11: The Clash of What?', in Joanne Meyerowitz (ed.), *History and September 11th: Critical Perspectives on the Past*. Philadelphia: Temple University Press, pp. 8–21.
Jeffery, R. (2007). *Evil and International Relations: Human Suffering in an Age of Terror*. New York: Palgrave Macmillan.
Kittredge, C.B. (2008). 'Echoes of Paul in the Speeches of George W. Bush', in C.B. Kittredge, E.B. Bradshaw and J.A. Draper (eds), *The Bible in the Public Square: Reading the Signs of the Times*. Minneapolis: Fortress Press, pp. 55–66.
Kurz, W. (2004). *What Does the Bible Say about the End Times?* Cincinnati, OH: St Anthony's Messenger Press.
Lawrence, B.B. (2003). 'Conjuring with Islam, II', in J. Meyerowitz (ed.), *History and September 11: Critical Perspectives on the Past*. Philadelphia: Temple University Press, pp. 175–89.
Lincoln, B. (2006). *Holy Terrors: Thinking about Religion after September 11*. University of Chicago Press.
Matustik, M.B. (2008). *Radical Evil and the Scarcity of Hope: Postsecular Meditations*. Bloomington and Indianapolis, IN: Indiana University Press.
Moltmann, J. (1992). 'Fundamentalism and Modernity', *Concilium: International Journal of Theology*, 3, 115–21.
Rossing, B. (2004). *The Rapture Exposed: The Message of Hope in the Book of Revelation*. New York: Basic Books.
Ryn, C.G. (2003). 'The Ideology of American Empire', *Orbis*, 47(3), 383–97.
Scranton, P. (2002). 'Witnessing Terror, Anticipating War', in P. Scranton (ed.), *Beyond September 11: An Anthology of Dissent*. London: Pluto Press, pp. 1–9.
Stam, J. (2003). 'Bush's Religious Language', *The Nation*, 22 December, www.thenation.com/doc/20031222/stam/print, date accessed 24 November 2010.
Suess, P. (1998). 'Overcoming Evil: The Ambivalence of Biblical Notions of Salvation in History and the Present', *Concilium: International Journal of Theology*, 1, 46–55.
Thomas, S.M. (2005). *The Global Resurgence of Religion and the Transformation of International Relations: The Struggle for the Soul of the Twenty-First Century*. New York: Palgrave Macmillan.
Wallis, J. (2003). 'Dangerous Religion – Bush's Theology of Empire', www.informationclearinghouse.info/article5402.htm, date accessed 24 November 2010.

Walzer, M. (2004). 'Can There Be a Moral Foreign Policy?', in E.J. Dionne, J. Bethke Eshstain and K. Drogosz (eds), *Liberty and Power: A Dialogue on Religion and U.S. Foreign Policy in an Unjust World*. Washington DC: Brookings Institute, pp. 34–52.

Wink, W. (1999). *The Powers That Be: Theology for a New Millennium*. New York: Galilee Trade.

Notes

1. Journalist Juan Stam came up with the idea that evil is a theologically and morally loaded concept.
2. In the poem 'Word Terrorist', Cooke rejects his identity as a 'writa, poet, journalist, rhyma, chanta, Gleana Tursday columnist' and claims to be a 'word terroris – a dues-payin', cyard-carryin', executive memba of Al-Quaeda: Aggressive Lyricists Questioning Atrocious Unjustifiable Excesses, in Defence of America'.
3. 'If you can't ketch quaku, you ketch him shut'; literally, if you can't catch someone (Quaku) you can get his shirt (shut).

Part III
Ethical Issues in International Journalism

5
Saving or Drowning? The Paradox of Attempting Ethics in International News and Communication

Iman Roushdy-Hammady

The concept of ethics, though loaded with positive connotations, does not always yield the results aspired to when employed by the international media. This is because ethics in the international media are formulated socially and politically by powers and cultures of unequal weight in the global arena. As such, imposing one nation's standards on another, including exaggerating cultural contrasts, highlighting issues of assimilation and perceived loyalties, or even hurling accusations, becomes justified by an ethic of communication and global awareness. But more often than not, the resulting interventions tend to leave the targeted population with more suffering and greater ethical dilemmas. So, is it the absence of a common global ethics or rather the presence of multiple meanings and usage of this concept that is at issue? Using anthropological approaches, this chapter addresses this fundamental dilemma by looking at four different incidences in the Arabic and American media. The first is the airing of a female circumcision ritual from Egypt by CNN in 1994 and the repercussions that have followed. In this case the focus is on the challenging role of the global media to address critical issues entangled in politics, culture and history, the moral issues surrounding the exploitation of locals to achieve one's ends, and the mixing of political and humane messages that results in hurting the subjects one is allegedly trying to save. The second case is the commercial fashion advertising in popular American magazines in the framework of the wars against Iraq. Here the ethical issues crystallize in derogating the image of the *other* to gain political support of one's own people, to justify wars or to affirm one's superiority. The third instance is American government advertising on international Arabic television, and the use of the media by different US administrations to approach Arab, Arab-American and Muslim populations. On the one hand, the issue here is creating ethical dilemmas for ethnic populations between their countries of ancestry and their country of citizenship and, on the other hand, the great potential of the international media to restore relationships between hegemonic powers and global entities through ethical dialogues that recognize all players as equals. The fourth situation is the *problematique* of the Egyptian–Israeli peace treaty and naturalization efforts in the context of international news and the art of cinema. The ethical issues here are multilayered, given the complexity of Arab-Israeli relations, and the issues focus on the ethics of presenting and censoring or banning an art work of ethical value in the context of regional politics. Even though the focus on the media in these four examples assumes different contextual meanings, the examples provide a panoramic view of the different manipulations or justifications of ethics, which all lead to a richer understanding of the relationship between ethical interpretations, cultural contexts and political hegemony.

Drowning the drowned: the CNN story

The United Nations' International Conference on Population and Development (ICPD) was scheduled to take place in Cairo, Egypt from 5 to 13 September 1994. In the two months before this global event, the local and regional media were increasing awareness of the issues and the conference agenda through interviews with major local authorities, different TV programmes and newspaper coverage. The attention of most articles focused on the developmental issues which frequently came up in relation to population topics: birth control, family planning, female education, infant mortality and population growth. Receiving thousands of international guests, the media further emphasized the importance of the conference because of the anticipated revenues expected through tourism.

With the starting of the conference, the media reported on the daily sessions and portrayed the resulting local and global discourses and reactions to the topics raised, the most controversial of which were abortion, gay and lesbian rights, and under- and over-population in different regions in the world. The local interpretation of the sessions and action plan were highly political. For example, it did not go unnoticed that the conference was seeking solutions to boost population growth where birth rates were dropping, which was the case in many European countries, while all efforts were geared to curb populations in less economically advanced countries in the Middle East and Asia. The fact that the European countries were rich and overwhelmingly Christian, while the targeted countries in Asia and the Middle East followed diverse religions, made the ICPD acquire a negative identity in radical media discourses: as a weapon to eradicate non-Western populations.

During the heat of these discourses, the Pope left the Vatican on a mission. He was pictured in most Egyptian newspapers visiting the targeted countries in Asia and preaching against birth control. Local reactions to the Pope's visit were soon overshadowed by a piece of media coverage that shook Egypt and altered discourses on reproductive health and gender for years to come. The Cable News Network (CNN) aired a female genital cutting ritual from the fringes of Cairo.

Female genital cutting had been on the agenda of the conference and had been dealt with for years by local authorities and international health agencies. In the context of the ICPD, Mr Mubarak, the President of Egypt, was interviewed and asked about the country's efforts to combat this ancient tradition, which was seen by many activists as a violation of human rights, while others were concerned about the victims who suffered from the procedure's potential health complications. The President gave a brief answer indicating the country's successful efforts in limiting this practice to remote rural areas of the country.

CNN aired this interview and followed it with its report about a case of female genital cutting from around the city of Cairo. In addition to the CNN crew, the team comprised of two Egyptian cameramen and an Egyptian female social scientist affiliated with an American research institution in Cairo. The documentary captured the father of a ten-year-old girl taking her from a rural urban neighbourhood, where the girl was being celebrated, and going towards the local barber. At the barber's, the girl was placed on the table, held by her father to facilitate the procedure. Even though the girl knew it was 'her day' she screamed out of fear and pain 'have mercy on me', and viewers could hear voices trying to comfort her, saying 'shame, you are a big girl now, hold on', 'listen, the camera is filming you'. The screaming finally ended in faint weeping and the girl was taken back home after having gone through her rite of passage to prepare her for adulthood.

Already a controversial issue, sentiments against this procedure in Egypt arose as early as the 1930s and reached a peak in the 1950s, when the Ministry of Health finally issued a decree prohibiting the practice in 1959 (Moore *et al.*, 1997, p. 146). Most of the opposition came from doctors, who resented the medical complications and dangers for women's health, especially the fact that the procedure was usually performed by non-certified medical professionals; the other major group opposed to the practice was composed of different feminist activists, who saw the procedure as a violation of human rights and an effort to subjugate women. But some factions of populations in Africa who embraced this practice, regardless of their religion, saw it as a rite of passage to honour women.

A multilayered political reaction followed the CNN programme on female genital cutting. On one level, the CNN programme was considered a slap in the face, especially after the Egyptian President's reassurance that the phenomenon was restricted to remote areas of the countryside. All Egyptian elements involved in the making of the CNN documentary, including the father of the ten-year-old girl, were detained and questioned by state security agencies. On another level, the incident was seen as a conscious attempt to ruin the image of the country, especially while the proceedings of the conference were still in place. Other audiences found it shameful that the camera exposed the image of an Egyptian girl's body to audiences globally. Even though female genital cutting is an old African practice performed by Christians, Muslims and members of other religions across the entire continent alike, the Islamicists regarded it as another attempt by the US to exercise its supremacy and impose its hegemony over non-Western cultures. To put the matter into a more complex context, the ICPD occurred just three years after the 1991 Gulf War.

On Monday 12 September 1994, the popular weekly show *Hadith al-Madinah* (*The Talk of the City*), prepared and presented by Mufid Fawzi, was entirely devoted to the repercussions of the CNN documentary. The detainees reported about how they got involved in the documentary and wondered why this one was different from other collaborations they had had with CNN and other similar news networks. Some young media figures were asked to react to the event: 'So, if anybody comes and asks you to partake in a media project, would you do that automatically?' 'Well, I first have to figure out why I was chosen for the job, and what the purpose is of the show, and what that other foreign agency is trying to accomplish by doing so' (Fawzi, 1994). This answer provided a hint that the intentions of CNN seemed to be beyond merely drawing attention to the phenomenon of female genital cutting.

Other interviewees included Drs Samia Al-Saati and Farkhanda Hasan, two eminent women, a sociologist and a physicist,[1] respectively. They emphasized the importance of considering the cultural context of female genital cutting and the fact that it was not seen as a damaging procedure or an attempt to compromise the womanhood of a person, but rather to honour her. Dr Al-Saati brilliantly explained how strict laws and prohibitions were not the answer to the problem, as it had deep cultural roots that needed to be addressed through a comprehensive social and educational plan. Neither scientist showed any support for the idea that the father of the girl in question should be imprisoned, based on the fact that the procedure had been illegal since 1959, nor did they display any surprise that the father would gladly agree to have his daughter taped during the procedure, as for him, it probably felt like celebrating her birthday.

The camera then toured different slums and rural-urban areas, different festivities associated with the event were shown and women were asked about the procedure. The majority emphasized that it was a tradition to honour the girl. Needless to say, they referred to the procedure as 'circumcision' in the same way as they referred to the male procedure. The terms 'female genital cutting', 'infibulations' or 'mutilation' were foreign and incomprehensible to the population sector in question; as such, they were perplexed by the incarceration of the girl's father. Most importantly, none of them showed an awareness that the procedure was prohibited by law.

The interview with the girl's father, Ibrahim, in prison was moving. He had a rural background, modest education and was self-employed. He was perplexed at his incarceration for performing a traditional ritual to celebrate his girl's coming of age:

-So, Ibrahim, why did you do that?
-Did what, sir, I did nothing?
-How did you let the foreigners videotape your daughter?
-Why not? They promised they'd give me a video of her to show her mother and our folks!?
-Do you know you scandalized your daughter?
-Scandalized her? God Forbid! I wanted to celebrate her and give her something to cherish ...
-Do you see? ... [pointing at the playing video shot by CNN]. Is it ok for you to have your daughter exposed like that for publics and foreigners everywhere? (Fawzi, 1994)

There was an indication that Ibrahim partook in treason against the honour of his daughter, his country and the law. Ibrahim helplessly turned his hands in confusion, with tears showing in his eyes, uttering words like 'I just wanted to celebrate my daughter?!' (Fawzi, 1994)

A number of decisions were made following the airing of the CNN documentary, which turned female genital cutting into a high-profile issue on the agendas of different political, educational and health agencies. In the face of these events, the Ministers of Population and Health declared to the international community that they would enforce the 1959 decree to prohibit and eventually eradicate the practice. Yet, about a month after the conclusion of the ICPD, the Minister of Health authorized select public hospitals to perform the procedure medically. In the middle of the argument, the Grand Mufti announced the lack of strong supporting religious sources for the practice, which was performed in no Islamic country other than those in Africa, and said that its legality should be decided upon in consultation with medical experts. In July 1996, the new Minister of Health passed legislation to ban the procedure in public hospitals and to enforce legal penalties on individuals who performed it (Moore *et al.*, 1997, p. 148).

The debate around the topic included local and global academicians, politicians, local healthcare providers, religious groups, women's groups and the Grand Mufti, as well as local and global non-governmental organizations (NGOs), all discussing local and international legislation to protect the health of women and children. The only voices that did not make it to the debate were the pockets of population that actually practised female genital cutting.

CNN's attempt at drawing global attention to this practice was partly an ethical mission of the mass media to rescue populations who underwent it from medical and health damage. Nevertheless, to achieve its ends, it took advantage of a poor man and a number of others. Placing its documentary right after the interview with the Egyptian President was far from a coincidence, leaving the locals involved drowning in a sea of political entanglements. While addressing the issue, the supremacy of the singular perspective of the West prevailed in the arguments presented, at times characterizing the practice as barbaric and inhumane, yet not even mentioning that as far back as in the 1940s and 1950s, female genital cutting was an approved medical procedure in the US and England to eradicate masturbation, lesbianism and other sexual and medical conditions (including a number of psychological disorders such as hysteria) perceived as morally or physiologically deviant by the standards of the then-prevailing Western culture.

Covered or stripped? The *Vogue* story

The image of the Middle Eastern woman was made use of commercially during and in the aftermath of the 1991 Gulf War. Using *us-versus-the-other* portrayals, the Middle Eastern woman was unfavourably compared to her American counterpart in a Bijan perfume advertisement in *Vogue* magazine in 1992.² In this advert, the image of a veiled brunette, not necessarily an authentic Arab woman, was associated with qualities that appeared written in the lower corner of the image as 'quiet, composed, obedient, grateful, modest, respectful, submissive, and very, very serious'. Those qualities were visible in the portrayed face of the model, who was meant to represent the Middle Eastern woman. Qualities of obedience and submissiveness were especially catchy in the delivery of the message. On the other hand, the image of the American woman – where the adjective 'American' was implied by the presence of the American flag on top of the word 'woman' – was associated with adjectives indicating liberation and independence, expressed in the ad as 'bright, wild, flirty, fun, eccentric, tough, bold, and very, very bijan'.

In the winter of 1992, a group of American graduate students at Harvard University started a campaign against this advert by writing a petition and collecting signatures to express discontent with the presentation of the Middle Eastern woman's image. However, the people who wrote the petition saw in the advert more than simply a comparison between two women. The image of the American woman, holding the baseball bat, was regarded as being symbolic of holding a gun; together with the hat and the playful shouting gesture, this image could be saying something like: 'Be cool and support America in its war!'

The use of the image of the Middle Eastern woman in this case was extended to delivering a political message. Aside from the nature of the product advertised, the choice of a woman allowed for the possibility of using the veil as a political symbol, representing an entire nation. In fact, the veil is the item of clothing which has had the most influence on Western images of Middle Eastern women (Graham-Brown, 1988, p. 134). The veil has always been a source of challenge to the West and hence a subject of multiple interpretations throughout history. Even feminists indigenous to the Middle East were faced with a problem of interpretation early in the century: was the veil to be viewed as a symbol of male oppression of women or a crucial part of indigenous culture which was threatened by Western colonialism? In Algeria, for example, female dress became part of the national symbol and thus of defence against colonial rule. In the 1950s, the veil became a weapon of the oppressed in Algeria: 'hiding a face is also disguising a secret' (Fanon, 1986, p. 42). Algerian women used their traditional attire to conceal messages, guns and bombs under their veils. This image also has its extension nowadays, when veiled women are shown in the Western media in association with religious fundamentalism and fanaticism.

On the other hand, showing veiled Saudi women shopping on the streets of London reinforces an old orientalist rhetoric concerning the veil, as well as 'an image of the oppressive and fanatical religion, masking luxury, decadence and lasciviousness' (Fanon, 1986, p. 242).

The use of the veil, whether in the past or in the present, has been variably exploited in the Western media to express difference, imbuing messages laden with moral values and implicit value judgments. The opposite end of expressing difference in previous decades was non-covering. The peasant woman in the Middle East, due to her *otherness* to the Western gaze, was exploited in photography in this regard. While working in the field or filling water jars, women usually lifted their long dresses up to ease movement or to avoid getting muddy. Likewise, there was no social prohibition preventing a peasant woman from nursing her newborn publicly.

This image of exposing her breast to nurse was taken to the extreme in Western photography and film. In the late nineteenth century, a postcard made from a photograph of a veiled woman showing her breasts was entitled 'Scenes and Types – Arabian Woman with the *Yashmak* [covering]' (Alloula, 1986, p. 126). This photograph played out a general European belief that Arab women were more concerned with covering their heads (and faces) than their breasts. The postcard represented an exaggeration, putting the *other* in an inferior position, suggesting a lack of proper morals and appropriate standards of social conduct.

Whether in the past or now, the image of the Middle Eastern woman became commodified. This commodity was packaged to satisfy the market and solicit political support through the media. The dialectical problem between the veiling and the nude, the seen and the unseen has reflected the value system and the worldview of the West throughout history. While the ideal image of the Western woman was that of modesty and reserved sexuality in the late nineteenth and early twentieth centuries, the prevailing image of the Middle Eastern woman, even though covered, was that of exoticism and eroticism. Now, the almost nude *white* female body is publicly displayed in advertisements, photography and film, and, at times, is associated with women's liberation, as in the image of the singer Madonna. Therefore, the Middle Eastern woman and her modest dress are now used as a sign of submissiveness and backwardness, not to mention fanaticism in certain contexts: for example, in the contexts of the different wars against Iraq or of the Islamic movement.

So, what is too open and what is too closed? What is ethical and what is immoral in women's images? Difference is the answer. The Middle

Eastern woman is always conceived as *different* through the Western media. Whether covered or uncovered, there has always been something which rendered the image of the *other* woman morally different and, at times, inferior to the Western woman, unless of course that *other* woman blindly followed the example of her Western counterpart.

To be American, or not to be? The American government on Arabic television

The holy month of Ramadan is the hottest month of entertainment on Dish Network Arabic TV in the US (Roushdy-Hammady, 2006). In the Ramadan of 2007, there was something unusual that attracted my attention. I noticed for the first time that the US army advertised as sponsors for some popular entertainment programmes and shows. 'Go to www.usarmy.gov and see what the U.S. Army has for you' said one of the ads to encourage Arab Americans, especially those who were bilingual, to join the American army. Another commercial appeared at about the same time, being shown in-between a myriad of different programmes. It portrayed professional-looking women and men, seemingly of Arab heritage, interchangeably, while a male voice said assertively in modern standard Arabic: 'It is in your capacity to serve your country instead of working in a company; ... [then the speaker continues powerfully in English] ... CIA: the work of a nation, the center of intelligence.'

The advert continued running throughout the month of Ramadan and after, and became a common sight on the Arabic Radio and Television (ART) channels. Another phenomenon accompanied the appearance of these adverts. Short connection trailers, usually advertising the channel in question, were used to capture some aspect of the Arab life or scenes. The ART channels initiated a different approach, namely using Arab-American family-oriented trailers during different seasons in America. So, for example, the viewer would see children playing and making snow-angels during shows in the winter season. The effect of this on me as a viewer was supposed to bring me back to the US context. These adverts acknowledged the US to be the homeland for Arab Americans, a fact that used to be questioned in the American media during every period of political unrest involving the Middle East, such as 9/11 and the Gulf Wars (Roushdy-Hammady, 2006). Feelings relating to the issue of identities of Arab Americans surfaced during the presidential election campaign of 2008, which coincided with the events on Arabic TV described above. During that campaign, the opposition media questioned the heritage of the then presidential candidate Barack Hussein

Obama, his Arabic middle name and especially the presence of Muslim members in his family, as well as whether he lived for some time and was educated in Islamic countries. The fact that these elements were points of criticism, as well as a political weapon used in the opposition media to reduce the 'Americanness' of the presidential candidate, left the Islamic and Arab communities in a state of deep ambivalence over the question of their identity and the issue of secularism in American politics.

Addressing Arab Americans through their Arab satellite networks, urging them to serve their country – the US – and attempting to recruit them through the CIA and the army was a powerful statement of acknowledgement that stood in stark contrast with other forms of advertising to and the portrayal of Arabs in the American media and film, where Arabs had been mostly portrayed as the dangerous or simply different *other* (Roushdy-Hammady, 2006 and 2008).

Yet, while attempting to engage the Arab-American component of the US population, people who conducted the campaign assumed that population's undivided loyalty and support. Those expectations came at a time when the US was deeply entrenched in multiple Middle Eastern affairs and was heavily criticized in Arabic news and TV shows (Roushdy-Hammady, 2006). Appearing amidst those programmes, the aforementioned adverts acted not only as reminders of who one should be as an Arab American, but also as a medium of assimilation and distinction: disagreement with American policies in the Middle East should pose no obligation on you to oppose your country – the US – in its military and security undertakings.

To what extent media processes that aimed at the assimilation and engagement of Arab Americans actually caused a disruption in their ethnic identity, produced a shift in political elections, divided local Arab-American communities and changed its dialogue with the global Arab community is a matter of debate. Whatever the intent was, the consequences were complex, surpassed time and geographical framings and, due to the ethical issues involved, were hard to measure.

At the end of 2008, two events occupied the global media for a long time, until the inauguration of President Obama in January 2009: the throwing of shoes at the then President Bush and the Israeli attack on Gaza. Even though the two events seemed unrelated, their repercussions were not mutually exclusive for the Arab viewer, due to the absence of the American voice in the international media. The Arab street translated this unexpected absence of reaction as the Bush Administration's intentional response to the insult of the shoe throwing. Whether the

US media silence was interpreted as support for Israel or simply a case of the political laissez-faire doctrine, it left the Arab public with a sense of moral indignation against the Bush Administration:

> Yes, [Bush] acted nonchalant about the shoe throwing thing, and even took credit for it as a sign of democracy, which he introduced to Iraq. But he was insulted, and what an insult! Global!! and he knew we were all laughing at him, so he gave it back to the whole region ... 'Let them all suffer, those Arabs,' he is probably thinking; so, he is letting Israel butcher the Palestinians, and we are all here in disagreement and divided about what to do. Israel and Hamas are fighting, and the poor people are suffering. [Bush] did not even show up on TV once to even mention anything about it. What kind of morals does he have?! ... Even if these were a bunch of dogs dying, he should have reacted. After all, he is responsible for all this mess. (Part of a conversation between two men in the streets of Cairo, Egypt, 29 December 2008)

The image of the US and its political ethics in the Arabic media underwent a significant shift six days after the inauguration of Barack Obama as President. On 26 January 2009, *Al Arabiya* – a Dubai-based Arabic cable TV network – conducted the first formal interview with Barack Obama as President in the White House (Melhem, 2009). This interview took place as George Mitchell was on his way to the region to negotiate a ceasefire with Israel:

> Obama did not speak to Arab television during the election campaign ... We followed him ... and have tried many ways to talk to him, but he would not talk to us. Now we realize he was just waiting for the right time. (Muna Al-Shaqiqi, reporter and camera operator of *Al Arabiya*, 27 January 2009, cited in Ghazi, 2009)

The President attempted to undo the previous media image that had prevailed during the preceding administration. This old impression portrayed America as an enemy of Arabs and Muslims alike (Roushdy-Hammady, 2006). 'I have Muslim members of my family ... I have lived in Muslim countries' were the words Obama used, seemingly to rebuild bridges of communication and respect, and the recognition of Arabs and Muslims not as the *other* but rather as equals.

Obama managed to charm Arab audiences in his capacity as the President of a country of a global hegemonic order: to display the ability to listen as opposed to dictate. Firstly, choosing an Arabic television network to conduct the first interview with him after the presidential inauguration was in itself a sign of respect and honour to millions of Arabs. Secondly, he indicated interest in engaging in Arab and Muslim dialogues by choosing the same vocabulary used in an open letter addressed to him. The letter was published in the *New York Times* on the day of his inauguration and was initiated by the Conference of the Islamic Organization. It called on Obama to open 'a new page of partnership with the Muslim world':

> Obama's interview shows that the letter, which was on behalf of the Muslim world, had a positive effect on him ... Obama said that he wants to establish 'a new partnership with the Muslim world,' which were the exact same words used in the letter. ... The interview was a sufficient response to the open letter. It shows he cares a great deal about this subject matter. (Ghazi, 2009, p. 1)

These gestures had an effect on the reception of the interview's content. For example, Obama reiterated in the interview that Israel was an ally to the US, but also recognized that their friend would have to make hard choices to coexist in peace with its neighbours. His comments on Iranian politics included concerns over the country's possession of nuclear weapons and its threats to the security of Israel. Arab audiences and news analysts had for a long time interpreted similar messages in different contexts as pro-Israel and therefore anti-Arab or anti-Muslim. Obama framed the stand of the US on these two issues within an ethical context of respect and as an attempt to redefine America's position as that of a friend rather than an enemy. This approach invoked some recognition and understanding that each country had its own interests and had a right to protect those interests. Indeed, it seems to be reasonable to recognize that the process necessary to confront regional discord must recognize the interests of all parties involved and establish a dialogue accordingly.

While it is still too early to evaluate the Obama Administration's performance in terms of its policies towards the Middle East, this new approach at least seems to be in apparent contrast to the Bush Administration, which was mostly inclined towards the use of threats and force.

Arab-Israeli films: the paradox of the absent presence

Amidst all those events, art had its own ethical expressions on the big screen. In 2007, *The Band's Visit*, an Israeli film, told the story of an Egyptian orchestra of eight men that was invited to play at a cultural festival in Israel and ended up getting lost in an isolated desert town, where locals took the musicians into their homes and their burdened lives. Watching a screening in the US, I observed the audience's responses to the film. The movie was joyful, amusing and had humourous and funny plots, but plumbed a deeper philosophical terrain. The message of the film was that of the possibility of coexistence through remembrance, as well as cultural and human commonalities that melted down the politically enforced estrangement and distancing. In addition, it displayed the potential enrichment that each individual could offer other people on a personal level, and how the departure of the Egyptian band left both the locals and the visitors downhearted.

The film received the 2007 Israeli Film Academy Award and a great reaction at film festivals abroad. What was different about this movie was the fact that the cast included Arab Israelis as well as Israeli Jews and the script was trilingual: 20 minutes of the dialogue were in English and 18 minutes were reserved for both Arabic and Hebrew, while the rest of the 84-minute film was non-verbal acting (Kershner, 2007, p. 1).

Even though the film can be seen as an attempt by cinematic art to bridge the region's deep divides, the message of the film and the quality of its acting did not protect the film from falling prey to domestic and international strife. The movie was disqualified from being an official candidate for an Oscar nomination in the category of best foreign language film. Formally it was turned down because most of the dialogue was in English. The Israeli Film Academy instead chose to submit *Beaufort* for best foreign film. This film, which was all in Hebrew, was an anti-war movie, but it focused on a group of Israeli conscripts holding a post on a hilltop in Southern Lebanon shortly before Israel withdrew from that country in 2000. In addition, *The Band's Visit* was blocked from film festivals in the Arab world because it was an Israeli production. In one case the film was disqualified because of a rumour that the Egyptian actors' syndicate wanted officials to withdraw all Egyptian films from the Middle East International Film Festival held in Abu Dhabi in October 2007. 'Cairo's decision annoys me ... It's a great pity because we worked from the heart' (Saleh Bakri, Arab-Israeli actor from Haifa, cited in the *New York Times*, 31 October 2007).

A number of factors put this film in interlacing dilemmas. Firstly, the Israeli Film Academy's choice of *Beaufort* over *The Band's Visit* seems more political than technical. *Beaufort* highlights the role of the Israeli conscripts, while *The Band's Visit* sheds light on the interaction between Egyptians and Israelis. In fact, the beginning of the film sets up the Egyptian band members as the main players in the film. Secondly, even though officially Egypt is at peace with Israel, according to the peace treaty signed in 1979, different professional syndicates resist the normalization of relations. Thirdly, the Israeli population includes elements that were at one point in history referred to as Palestinians; these populations are now called 'Arab Israelis', as they reside within the State of Israel. Thus, while the film may be rejected in protest against Israeli politics in the region, the rejection simultaneously also includes those Arab elements whose identity is caught up in a number of social, political and ethnic entanglements. These multiple rejections portray a problem of evaluating a work of art – a dilemma stemming from the politics of the country of origin rather than from the work's artistic quality and moral value.

Reflections about ethics and the media

Returning to the main question, is it the absence of a common global set of ethics or rather the presence of multiple meanings and the usage of this concept that is at issue here? In the presentation and the analysis of the four scenarios in question, the aim was to illustrate the relationship between the event, the media, the surrounding historical context, political hegemonies and the web of ethical issues involved. American news and the use of its media, such as cinema, have for a long time emphasized differences when dealing with Arab and Muslim populations (Roushdy-Hammady, 2008, p. 282). Exoticism, coupled with different packaging of religion and culture, was used as a means to estrange these populations from a universal ethical system, associating them with moralities that were foreign and dangerous. Whether in the American-Arab, American-Muslim or Arab-Israeli contexts, these assumptions have long blinded audiences from seeing the commonalities between the different societies clearly present on a human level and thus forced viewers to see multiple conflicting ethical codes.

On the other hand, global and regional hegemonies have a long history of imposing their interests on others and framing those interests within ideological structures of justified ethics. Yet these hegemonies do not succumb to the same definitions of ethical moralities. As such, the hermeneutics associated with the action and meaning of 'suicide-bomber' in the Middle East context is transformed to 'martyrdom' in the American context (Roushdy-Hammady, 2006).

The examples here highlight that, because of the power imbalances, applying the same code of ethics to a more powerful opponent is less likely to happen. Multiple political events, especially the two wars against Iraq and the events of 9/11, as well as the subsequent local and regional political actions, do urge a re-examination of the Western image of the Arabs and Muslims with a focus on their human existential responses to unequal power weights. This may slowly incite an interpretive understanding of people's behaviour in the context of cultural, economic and political surroundings, rather than continuing the shallow blame on cultural, religious and moral differences. Global film industries are slowly coming to terms with these realizations, although they are still hampered by a host of local, regional and global political problems. Conversely, the current use of the Arabic media to address Arab and Muslim populations by the Obama Administration, in an atmosphere of mutual respect, understanding and recognition of human existentialist responses and interests, evokes a new hope as the media turn to recognize and, perhaps, participate in creating of a new global system of media ethics that is applied in all directions equally – regardless of the hegemonic weight of each country.

References

Alloula, M. (1986). *The Colonial Harem*. Minneapolis, MN: University of Minnesota Press.
Corbey, R. (1988). 'Alterity: The Colonial Nude', *Critique of Anthropology*, 8(3), 75–92.
Fanon, F. (1986). *Black Skin, White Masks*. London: Pluto Press.
Fawzi, M. (1994). *Hadith al-Madinah* [*The Talk of the City*], television programme, Cairo, Egypt, Channel 1.
Ghazi, J. (2009). 'Eye on Arab Media: Obama Charms Arabs on TV', *New America Media*, 28 January, http://news.newamericamedia.org/news/view_article.html?article_id=bf6a7564935c4d10e193fc0808dcf00d, date accessed 23 November 2010.
Graham-Brown, S. (1988). *Images of Women: The Portrayal of Women in Photography of the Middle East 1860–1950*. New York: Columbia University Press.
Kershner, I. (2007). 'Israeli Film about Harmony in the Mideast Provokes Off-screen Discord', *New York Times*, 31 October, www.nytimes.com/2007/10/31/movies/31band.html, date accessed 23 November 2010.
Koestler, A. (1941). *Darkness at Noon*. New York: Macmillan.
Kolirin, E. (Screenwriter/Director) and Dulac, S. (Co-director). (2007). *The Band's Visit*. Israel: July August Productions, Sophie Dulac Productions. US: Sony Pictures Classics (Distributors).
Melhem, H. (2009). 'President Obama's Interview with Al-Arabiya Arab TV Network', *Al Arabiya*, 26 January, www.huffingtonpost.com/2009/01/26/obama-al-arabiya-intervie_n_161127.html, date accessed 23 November 2010.
Moore, K., Randolph, K., Toubia, N. and Kirberger, E. (1997). 'The Synergistic Relationship between Health and Human Rights: A Case Study using Female Genital Mutilation', *Health and Human Rights*, 2(2), 137–46.

Roushdy-Hammady, I. (2006). 'Sheer and Opaque Screens. The Medical Ethnography of Arabic Television: A Phenomenological Quandary of Communal Memory, Suffering and Resistance', in A. Nikolaev and E. Hakanen (eds), *Leading to the 2003 Iraq War: The Global Media Debate*. New York: Palgrave Macmillan, pp. 165–80.

——. (2008). 'Some Reflections on Arab Cinema', in S. Akhtar (ed.), *The Crescent and the Couch: Cross-currents between Islam and Psychoanalysis*. New York: Jason Aronson, pp. 267–82.

Schivone, G.M. (2007). 'The Responsibility of the Intellectual. An Interview with Noam Chomsky', *Arts and Opinion*, 6(6), www.artsandopinion.com/2007_v6_n6/chomsky-4.htm, date accessed 23 November 2010.

Notes

1. Dr Hassan later became Secretary-General of the National Council for Women.
2. The ad can be found in the April 1992 issue of the magazine (182(4)) on pp. 22–3.

6
Identities, Ethics and International Communication in the French Context

Élisabeth Le

It has become a truism to say that the development of the Internet, along with other technologies of communication, has transformed our world into a global village where information presented by a national media *a priori* for its national audience can be easily and rapidly accessed by readers and listeners in a very distant part of the world. Thus, information that would normally be expected to conform to national standards of ethics is being received in other societies, each with its own specific combination of ethics rules. This is especially true for quality news media, whose regular audience may extend far beyond their national borders. Therefore, the issue arises as to how national media, engaged willingly or not in international communication, are able to conciliate the local with the universal.

Reflecting on a world where universal concern and respect for legitimate differences may clash, Appiah writes:

> [W]e cosmopolitans believe in universal truth, too, though we are less certain that we have it all already ... One truth we hold to, however, is that every human being has obligations to every other. Everybody matters: that is our central idea. And it sharply limits the scope of our tolerance ... One distinctively cosmopolitan commitment is to *pluralism*. Cosmopolitans think that there are many values worth living by and that you cannot live by all of them. So we hope and expect that different people and different societies will embody different values. (But they have to be values *worth* living by.) (2006, p. 144)

Furthermore, in response to the sensitive issue of potential conflict between different cultural standards of ethics, some have advocated the development of *universal communication ethics*. In his theoretical justification for such an ethics, Christians concludes that: 'the socially responsible media are brought to judgment before the ultimate test: do they sustain life, enhance it long term, contribute to human wellbeing as a whole?' (2005, p. 12). In their ethnographic study, Rao and Lee (2005) identify four core principles that international political journalists from Asia and the Middle East report using in their day-to-day work and recognize as both important and possibly universal: the respect of others (that is, the idea of compassion and humanism); tolerance for religious and cultural diversity; telling the truth with restraint (for example, to respect or protect someone's privacy); and freedom and independence (especially from governments). Finally, in his 11 recommendations for a research agenda in media ethics, Christians includes the following: 'democracy as a political philosophy ought to be the framework for understanding the media' (2008, p. 7). He adds that 'communication ethics is the foundation of genuine democracy' (p. 8). The standpoints given above underline three crucial and interlocking concepts in international communication ethics: pluralism, concern for everyone's well-being and democracy.

This chapter examines how argumentative strategies followed by the French quality daily *Le Monde* in its editorials published from 1999 to 2001 combine the newspaper's various sociocultural identities with national and universal ethical values. After a short presentation of *Le Monde* and its editorials, the theoretical framework of this study is explored and is followed by the definition of the corpus. The questions of human rights, of the French national motto and of different *Le Monde* identities are then examined from the viewpoint of official texts and through the analysis of *Le Monde*'s editorials on European and other international issues. Finally, the conclusion looks at *Le Monde*'s use of its sociocultural identities from an ethical angle.

Le Monde and its editorials

Founded in 1944 by Hubert Beuve-Méry, *Le Monde* kept its distance from the government. It adopted positions that reflected a type of humanism and linked the defence of freedom and democratic values with social justice; it also regarded money with suspicion because of its possible corrupting effect. Audience studies conducted in 1955 and later showed that *Le Monde* was read by right-wing and left-wing people, business leaders and union members. By the end of the 1960s, when Beuve-Méry retired, *Le Monde* had become the most influential French daily. In the 1980s, because of its leftist orientation, it started losing some of its audience and was hit by successive crises that brought it close to bankruptcy, but it remained a reference newspaper.

Le Monde made its code of ethics public in *Le style du Monde*, a brochure published in 2002. In the declaration of its principles (pp. 6–7), *Le Monde* claimed its independence and its pluralism, and it stated that it did not impose any editorial line on its journalists and respected the plurality of their opinions provided they did not go against the newspaper's values. Concerning these values, the newspaper fosters those contained in the French Republic's motto, *Liberty, Equality, Fraternity*; in particular, it champions justice and solidarity, and condemns racism and exclusion. It promotes openness and international cooperation, and is against nationalism and isolationism. *Le Monde* positions itself as an international newspaper and it states that most events cannot be understood solely in a national framework: they have to be placed in their international setting. *Le Monde* informs but does not claim to be neutral: it takes positions in its editorials and also in the analyses and comments of its journalists. The articles must present a solid argumentation and avoid a polemical and sarcastic attitude, as well as personal attacks. They must not take a peremptory tone and avoid 'giving lessons'. A mediator, nominated by the newspaper's director, makes sure that journalists are aware of readers' concerns and that readers understand journalists' choices, and he or she is responsible for the implementation of the journalistic rules as covered in *Le style du Monde*. These rules constitute a reading contract with *Le Monde*'s audience.

Le Monde's daily editorials express the newspaper's position on notable events. The draft editorials may be revised without their authors' consent for reasons of form or content by the executive director or the editorial director. In their conciseness, editorials '*n'hésite[nt] pas à porter la plume dans la plaie*' (that is, literally 'are not reluctant to stir [or stick] the pen in the wound') (*Le Monde*, 2002, p. 59). A study on the genre of *Le Monde*'s editorials published from 1999 to 2001 has revealed them to be:

> [S]hort argumentative texts that are developed by a media presenting itself as a national, European and international social actor ... Editorials are addressed to recognized institutional actors on the national, European and international levels both directly (by their directives) and indirectly (through the effects of the media persuasive skills on the general audience). (Le, 2010, p. 42)

Depending on their directives' addressees, *Le Monde*'s editorials belong to the domains of national, European (that is, the European Union [EU] area) or international (that is, non-European) communication. This chapter is concerned only with the latter two areas.

Theoretical framework

A larger general project, from which this chapter originates, is rooted in a constructivist approach according to which individual and collective identities can be discovered through the study of messages and relationships within social groups (Hecht *et al.*, 2003; Simon, 2004). It was conducted in an interdisciplinary framework that is both media-centric and society-centric and stems from linguistics and communication studies. The linguistic part associates genre studies (Askehave and Swales, 2001) and critical discourse analysis (Wodak and Meyer, 2001). As for the communication component, it combines the interactionist-systemic orchestra model (Mucchielli and Guivarch, 1998, pp. 37–9) with the cascading activation model (Entman, 2004).

Both the linguistic and the communication parts of the framework are anchored in a coherence analysis of the editorials that reveals their textual information hierarchy (Le, 2009). This recurrent coherence analysis brings to the fore themes, that is, points of departure for the argumentation, and macrostructures, that is, points of arrival of the argumentation and information most likely to remain in the long-term memory of its readers (van Dijk, 1980), for each paragraph and for the entire text. This coherence analysis thus exposes for each text its grid of hierarchized information in which other types of analysis can be grounded. The main elements in this grid (that is, themes and macrostructures) can also be used in the construction of *methodical* (as opposed to *intuitive*) summaries at the paragraph and text levels. The editorials given as examples in this chapter are presented using this procedure.

The analysis of *Le Monde*'s messages and interactions, both within its editorials (in the *media-centric* approach) and thanks to its editorials (in the *society-centric* approach), that is, realized within the linguistic and communication framework, makes it possible to examine the newspaper's identities.

In Simon's (2004) integrative approach to identity, based on sociologically-oriented perspectives as well as European and North American psychologically-oriented perspectives, identity is considered from a micro-level (that is, the individual person), the macro-level (that is, in reference to a social group), and the meso-level that links the micro- and macro-levels. In this theory, individual and collective identities make each other possible and serve as each other's background in defining where one belongs or does not belong and in providing people with respect and with a place from which to look at the social world and interpret it meaningfully.

Corpus

The above theoretical framework was applied to a corpus of 150 editorials that were published from August 1999 to July 2001, a period characterized by important identity issues at the national, European and international levels. During this time, *Le Monde* experienced a significant institutional malaise due to important structural changes (Éveno, 2001), and a number of politicians and journalists accused *Le Monde* of abuse of its power (Poulet, 2003).

The corpus is composed of four groups: 1) all 38 editorials published during that time period about internal politics whose topic was linked to a top front-page article in the same-day issue; 2) all 33 editorials on Russia; 3) all 26 editorials about the EU and dealing with institutional matters or relations with other states; 4) all other remaining editorials, 53 of which were randomly chosen and, therefore, arguably reflected the overall distribution of topic categories during that period (24 on internal politics; 24 on external politics; 5 on European politics).

Human rights, *liberty, equality, fraternity* and identities in the French context

As mentioned above, *Le Monde* expressly declares its allegiance to the French Republic motto *Liberty, Equality, Fraternity*. The meaning of this motto is closely linked to the Declaration of the Rights of Man and the Citizen (1789). The Declaration is explicitly referred to in the Constitution of the Fifth Republic (1958) and its first article states:

> Les hommes naissent et demeurent libres et égaux en droits. Les distinctions sociales ne peuvent être fondées que sur l'utilité commune.
> [Men are born and remain free and equal in rights. Social distinctions may be based only on considerations of the common good.]

In adding fraternity to liberty and equality, the republican motto meant that 'the Rights of Man were by no means exclusively a charter for individualism but also an instrument for rooting out special interests ... and a promise of civic unity' (Ozouf, 1996, pp. 85–97). It was understood that the third principle, *Fraternity*, 'was the highest and most comprehensive: the one that summed up, subsumed, and transcended the other two, that was capable of knitting the Revolution's partial truths together to form the basis of a common religion' (Ozouf, 1996, p. 100). However, it was not until the Third Republic (1870–1940) that *Fraternity* acquired its canonical meaning – that of solidarity.

The sociocultural values of liberty, equality and fraternity in France result not only from their inclusion in the national motto but also from their connection with the Declaration of the Rights of Man and the Citizen. As stated in its Preamble, the Declaration was placed by French people *'au commencement de leur nature politique* [at the basis of their political nature]'[1] and was used as the foundation for the constitution. Thus, in the hierarchy of principles and rules, it was established that principles of natural law would be at the top and just below would come the constitution, each article of which was to result from one of these principles. Liberty and equality, understood with the concept of fraternity, were thus made into cornerstones of French society and, because they were considered the principles of natural law, cornerstones of all other societies as well.

In practice, human rights are called upon differently. Their promotion and protection is officially emphasized on the French Foreign Ministry website, and a number of French intellectuals have been rather active in this domain since the Dreyfus affair[2] at the end of the nineteenth century. It was in the name of human rights that in 1979 the French journalist Jean-François Revel first talked about a *droit d'ingérence* (right to interfere) in cases of foreign humanitarian crises, and this 'right' became a *devoir d'ingérence* (duty to interfere). However, the activism of French intellectuals in this domain has not always been looked upon favourably outside as well as inside France. In 2000, when Hubert Védrine, French Minister of Foreign Affairs, wrote against attempts to convert the world to norms of Western democracy with the use of various means of pressures and sanctions,[3] he was partly referring to the demands of some French intellectuals.

With the combination of its explicit reference to *Liberty, Equality, Fraternity* (and therefore to human rights) and its proclaimed independence, it is implied that *Le Monde* incarnates a specific individual interpretation of what being *French* means; that is, the positions it takes vis-à-vis those it interacts with in France would express *its individual identity* (its *Le-Monde-ness*) in relationship with their *collective identity* (*French-republic-ness*). While *Le Monde*'s allegiance to the values of liberty, equality and fraternity undoubtedly strongly associate the newspaper with France, it also makes it more than just French. Indeed, *Le Monde*'s allegiance to the French republican motto automatically implies its adherence to values that are emphasized in the Preamble of the European Charter of Fundamental Rights (2000):

> Conscious of its spiritual and moral heritage, the Union is founded on the indivisible, universal values of human dignity, *freedom, equality and solidarity*; it is based on the principles of democracy and the rule of law. It places the individual at the heart of its activities, by establishing the citizenship of the Union and by creating an area of freedom, security and justice. (Emphasis added)

These values are also emphasized in Article 1 of the Universal Declaration of Human Rights (1948):

> All human beings are born *free* and *equal* in dignity and rights. They are endowed with reason and conscience and should act towards one another in a spirit of *brotherhood*. (Emphasis added)

Thus, when *Le Monde* bases its argumentation on the values of liberty, equality or fraternity, it can choose in which French, European or world sphere it situates itself and, thus, which other – *individual* or *collective* – identity (that is, French-republic-ness, European-ness or universal-ness) it will add to its *Le-Monde*-ness to persuade its audience of the righteousness of its position on a particular issue under discussion. This is illustrated in the next section with editorials on European and foreign issues.

Le Monde's editorial positions and European/international communication

Le Monde's editorials on European and foreign issues are messages from French editorialists to French nationals, but they are also messages sent to foreign nationals in the European and international spheres, as indicated by the editorials' genre analysis (see the quote from Le, 2010, p. 42, cited above). Editorials on European and foreign issues are examined below from the standpoint of what types of values they emphasize and what types of identity they portray.

Le Monde's editorials on the EU

The analysis of all 98 editorials on Europe (that is, bearing on the institutions or other topics) published from April 1999 to August 2001 (here we refer to the number of articles analysed in Le, 2002) revealed that *Le Monde*'s reliance on values mostly (62 per cent) relates to the category of the EU's external relations and that these values are almost half the time (48 per cent) seen as goals to be achieved. These values correspond to the respect for international law in order to guarantee liberty, the respect for plurality to provide equality, and the exercise of solidarity, that is, fraternity. Indeed, the type of Europe *Le Monde* supports is a Europe that is more than an economic community but is instead a political Europe capable of functioning as a world power, with its own currency and its own system of defence independent of the US:

> Après l'euro, l'armée: au moment où l'Union européenne accepte de s'ouvrir à de nouveaux membres, au risque de se diluer, à terme, dans une zone de libre-échange, elle se dote – ou tente de se doter – des deux attributs de l'Europe-puissance, une manière de faire contrepoids aux tendances qui conduiraient à la limiter à une Europe-espace.
> [After the euro, the army: at the time when the European Union agrees to admit new members, and thus takes the risk of getting weakened, into a free-market zone, it is acquiring, or trying to acquire, two attributes of a Europe-power, as a way to counteract the tendencies that would limit it to a Europe-space.] (*Le Monde* Editorial, 1999, p. 13)

Le Monde's argumentative use of identities in promoting this *Europe-puissance* (Europe-power) is illustrated in such editorials as 'L'Europe politique existe [There is a Political Europe]' (2 February 2000, p. 15), 'L'Europe et la Serbie [Europe and Serbia]' (12 October 2000, p. 19) and 'L'Europe des maladroits [Clumsy Europe]' (24–25 June 2001, p. 14).

'L'Europe politique existe [There is a Political Europe]' declares the existence of a political Europe based on the EU's decision, notwithstanding the absence of any clause to that effect in the European treaties, that a Member State's sovereignty is limited in the following manner: it may not include in its government members of an extreme right party even if electors have voted for this party in *democratic* (that is, legal) elections. If a Member State (Austria in this specific case) decides to go against this principle, it will be politically isolated within the EU. In other words, *Le Monde* supports the EU's position that tools of democracy (such as elections) cannot be used as a way for movements considered as non-democratic (for example, those of the extreme right) to exercise power. In concluding that Austria should choose to follow the EU and not accept the entry of Jörg Haider's party into the governmental coalition, *Le Monde* uses a universal principle (democracy) to build European-ness. In this editorial, it applies the top-down principle stated in the Preamble of the Declaration of the Rights of Man and the Citizen that natural law supersedes all other principles and rules; in other words, elections, which are supposed to be tools of democracy, are not *ethically* valid when used for non-democratic purposes. In this perspective, *Le Monde*'s position could be found unethical only if its evaluation of the danger for democracy presented by the presence of an extreme right party in a government were contested.

In 'L'Europe et la Serbie [Europe and Serbia]', a similar type of reasoning is brought to the international level, although in a slightly subdued manner (see the description of the genre of *Le Monde*'s editorials above). A general principle is posed in the first paragraph: it was a moral, political and strategic priority to remove Slobodan Milosevic because of his leading role in ten years of destruction in the Balkans. The second paragraph poses the premise of the argumentation: in cancelling its sanctions against Serbia, the EU could not set as a condition to have all existing problems solved, because this condition would have been impossible to fulfil. However, in view of the refusal by Serbian leaders to examine Serbia's responsibility in the Balkans and in the absence of a disavowal of the Greater Serbia ideology, *Le Monde* pronounces its sentence: not to have reminded Belgrade of the EU's democratic principles before it cancelled its sanctions was either an error or naiveté. In other words, *Le Monde* reminded the EU of a universal principle that it should follow in its construction of a European identity.

In both these cases, if one sides with *Le Monde*'s evaluation of the state of democracy within a specific part of the EU or outside of the EU (a manifestation of *Le-Monde*-ness), the newspaper's position can be seen as a form of 'solidarity with the oppressed', the manifestation of its will to have everyone enjoy freedom and equality 'without distinction of any kind, such as race, colour, sex, language, religion, political or other opinion, national or social origin, property, birth or other status' and without 'distinction ... made on the basis of the political, jurisdictional or international status of the country or territory to which a person belongs' (Universal Declaration of Human Rights) – that is, as an expression of universal-ness. However, if one disagrees with this evaluation by *Le Monde*, it can be thought of as a form of ideological expansionism – that is, something associated with the French Revolution – a form of French-Republic-ness.

'L'Europe des maladroits [Clumsy Europe]' does not call on universal-ness for the construction of Europe. Paragraph 1 defines what the issue is – the lack of vision of the future of Europe after its enlargement and the timorousness of its members' political leaders, including those in France. This is illustrated in paragraphs 2, 3 and 4, which each report a recent misstep in the European construction: the Irish *no* to the Nice Treaty, Romano Prodi's minimization of it, and Willem Duisenberg's doubts on the success of the euro. Finally, the last paragraph reveals the threat inherent to the problem that has just been exposed: the growing risk of seeing Europe as simply a free economic market zone (*une zone de libre-échange*) from the Atlantic to Russia (*une Europe-espace*) under the political influence of the North Atlantic Treaty Organization (NATO), completely in line with the wishes of George W. Bush, instead of a European power (*l'Europe-puissance*). In this editorial, *Le Monde* addresses not only the Irish electorate, the President of the European Commission and the President of the European Bank, but also the entire European political class to oppose the US President's vision for Europe. In other words, *Le Monde* makes an appeal to non-French Europeans for a type of Europe that corresponds to its own perspective (its *Le-Monde*-ness) and to the French perspective (its French-Republic-ness) insofar as the EU should be independent of the US.

The three examples above show that in promoting its own concep-tion of Europe and displaying its *Le-Monde*-ness (its individual identity), *Le Monde* uses its universal-ness (its most collective identity) to build a European-ness (France's collective identity at the European level) for France; moreover, it uses its French-Republic-ness (its individual iden-tity at the European level) to build a European-ness for the EU.

Le Monde's editorials on international issues

The semantic analysis of all editorials on Russia in combination with Entman's frame analysis (Entman, 2004, p. 24) uncovered the newspaper's remedies to the problems it perceived: Russia had to reform its economy and break the FSB's (the Russian Federal Security Service) control over the country, and the West had to be realistic and make sure human rights were respected (Le, 2006, p. 113).

As pointed out above, human rights in France owe their value not only to the 1789 Declaration and its character as the constitutional law but also to their link with the national motto, in particular with the value of fraternity (or solidarity). The question of humanitarian intervention, that is, solidarity with those whose human rights are violated, is a topic not infrequently addressed in *Le Monde*'s editorials. 'Nord-Sud: la fracture [North-South: The Split]', published a few days after the arrival of the UN multinational force in East Timor (23 September 1999, p. 16), is presented below in detail to show the argumentative strategy in favour of humanitarian intervention. Another editorial, 'Ingérence en Tchétchénie [Interference in Chechnya]' (7 October 1999, p. 17), reinforces this position.

The paragraph analysis of 'Nord-Sud: la fracture [North-South: The Split]' pays particular attention to the themes and macrostructures within each paragraph of the editorial. In the first paragraph, *Le Monde* acknowledges the existence of a dangerous and unhealthy split between North (rich Western states) and South (a number of African, Asian and Near-East states) that had been visible for some years but that opened up at the 54th session of the UN General Assembly. This split is defined by the positions taken by the North and South towards the right of intervention on humanitarian grounds (respectively, for and against). These positions are exposed in the second paragraph for the North and in the third paragraph for the South, which criticizes the intervention by NATO in Kosovo and the UN intervention in East Timor. In the fourth paragraph, *Le Monde* explains how these two interventions differ (the NATO intervention in Kosovo was decided against Serbia's will and without the agreement of the UN, while the UN intervention was agreed upon by Indonesia and decided by the Security Council) and takes note of the South's mistrust of the UN. *Le Monde* agrees with the South that the North does not use the same moral criteria in its reactions to politically strong states (for example, Russia and China). In the fifth and final paragraph, *Le Monde* uses this criticism of the South against the North to imply that the North undermines its own position by its attitude. From the beginning of the editorial up to this point, the editorial's argumentation has been developed in a rather well-balanced manner: the opposing positions have been outlined and reason and fault have been found in both. In the remainder of the fifth paragraph, *Le Monde* adds to this balance (which gives an impression of objectivity) the weight of the universal (and therefore not objectionable) principle of peaceful settlement of conflicts, and concludes in the last sentence, which has no explicit addressee and thus appears to be addressed to all, that no good arguments can be found against the right to intervention on humanitarian grounds.

At the text level, two text themes assert the opposition between rich Western states and a number of African, Asian and Near-East states. The argumentation itself is presented in four macrostructures. The Northern (the Western) position is examined in a positive light; it is followed by criticisms of the North's attitude (as formulated by the South in two successive macrostructures), criticisms to which *Le Monde* partly subscribes. This development is concluded in the text macrostructure: no good arguments can be found against the right to humanitarian intervention. Thus, while the editorial gives first the impression that it deals with a general world issue (North vs. South), the development of the argumentation shows that in fact it is the North (more precisely, its attitude as opposed to its positions) that is discussed. In this light, the conclusion takes a more defined meaning: *Le Monde* categorically tells the West that it does not have any good argument not to intervene. The specific cases at which this view was directed were China (Tibet) and Russia (the Second Chechen War had just begun).

The combination of the paragraph and text level analyses reveals how the editorial, under the guise of generality, objectivity and with the weight of universal principles – which are also embodied in the French Republic's motto – leads its readers to agree with *Le Monde*'s instruction to the West, a position that is far from being generally accepted: that the West must intervene whenever the humanitarian situation makes it necessary, regardless of the political weight of the involved state. In other words, *Le Monde* promotes its *Le-Monde*-ness within France and across the world using its French-republic-ness and universal-ness.

'Ingérence en Tchétchénie [Interference in Chechnya]' specifically calls for a humanitarian intervention in Chechnya. The editorial is divided into three parts at the macro-level. The first part aims to demonstrate how Russians bomb villages, their defenceless populations and destroy their homes. The second part poses more than it demonstrates a succession of 'facts': for less reprehensible actions in East Timor, Indonesia was subject to economic sanctions; during the war in Kosovo, Westerners took action against Serbia; for two years the Chechen President had been wanting to discuss the question of uncontrolled Chechen Islamic groups, albeit unsuccessfully; and the Kremlin never gave any evidence as to any Islamists' involvement in the Moscow explosions. In other words, the point of the second part is to state the Western double standard in terms of human rights and the Kremlin's false reasons behind its attacks on Chechnya. In the third part, *Le Monde* reveals what it holds to be the Kremlin's real reasons for this war: a revenge for the humiliating defeat of the Russian army in 1996; the war takes the attention away from the financial scandals in Moscow; and it destroys a people that Russians have been trying to dominate for centuries. *Le Monde* concludes with a directive: the right of interference should be brought up, even if only rhetorically, against the

Russian attacks in Chechnya. In summary, as in the preceding example, *Le Monde* uses universal principles (such as peace and solidarity) to promote its own position regarding Chechnya based on its individual evaluation of the political situation in the Kremlin.

The two examples above show that in its defence of human rights, *Le Monde* manages to be more than merely French (it actually purports to be universal) by being more French than even the French people and government (that is, even more respectful of French values). In other words, *Le Monde* as an individual media outlet (with its own *Le-Monde*-ness) uses its universal-ness to remind France of its own values and simultaneously uses its French-Republic-ness to remind the world of *universal* values.

Le Monde's use of its sociocultural identities and ethics

In the five editorials chosen to illustrate *Le Monde*'s European and international communication, the newspaper's argumentative strategies have rested on principles stemming from the fact that any two or three of its four possible identities (that is, *Le-Monde-ness*, French-Republic-ness, European-ness and universal-ness) can participate in the construction of any other of them. In this reciprocal and circular process, any combination of the four above-mentioned options is possible. Ironically, the common part between *Le Monde*'s four identities (i.e., their basic values of human rights) makes it relatively easy to criticize any editorial by saying that it is either too (or not enough) '*Le Monde*', French, European or universal, whatever identities *Le Monde* is actually using in its argumentation. This also explains how the same editorial can be seen at the same time as *very French* (displaying French-republic-ness) outside of France and *very Le Monde* (displaying *Le-Monde*-ness) within France while it may have intended to represent a *European* or even a *universal* perspective.

In all types of argumentation, principles of higher value are used to guide reasoning (Perelman and Olbrechts-Tyteca, 1988, pp. 99–103) and, as noted above, individual and collective identities (that imply adherence to specific values) are in constant dialectic relationship with each other. In this sense, *Le Monde*'s editorials do not present any specificity. What is *special* about them is their capacity to call upon universal principles that are also strongly perceived to be associated with national values, and thus to take advantage of the strong ethical appeal represented by the universalism of these principles to promote individual or national interests. It is true that if a principle is recognized as universal, it has the potential of being called upon anywhere. However, because of the special traditional rapport between *Liberty, Equality, Fraternity* and general human rights, *Le Monde*'s editorials may be especially effective at combining *Le Monde*'s French, European and world interests and presenting *Le Monde*'s specific type of nationalism (its *Le-Monde*-ness) as 'universal'. This would partly explain how *Le Monde*'s discourse – and, more generally, French discourse – may have been unofficially accused of *ideological imperialism* more than once.

By definition, *Le Monde*'s editorials aim to convince their readers of the righteousness of their positions. When considering these editorials from an ethical perspective, two elements need to be differentiated – their stated positions and their argumentative strategies. As to their positions, the concepts of pluralism as well as concern for everyone and democracy (which are key concepts for ethical international communication) are officially acknowledged in *Le Monde*'s values document and observed under the vigilance of the *Le Monde*'s mediator. Thus, notwithstanding possible occasional unethical positions, what appear to be really at stake are the types of argumentative strategies that are followed. When does a specific argumentative strategy become unethical? In *Le Monde*'s case, it would seem that the greater danger would lie in calling upon universal principles under the identity of universal-ness to promote *Le-Monde*-ness. In other words, it would be like saying 'do as I say not because *I* say it but because *my* point of view reflects *universal* principles that must be followed by everyone' while one is *really meaning* 'do as I say because my own specific point of view must prevail'. The specific danger for *Le Monde* in this respect is the ease with which it can go from the latter to the former type of reasoning because of how its identities overlap.

In practice, as indicated by the results of the analysis of the complete corpus, *Le Monde* is against the world's political unipolarity and it wants the world to be transformed by a more active, independent and powerful EU thanks in great part to the leading role of France and its values. Furthermore, *Le Monde* sets itself as the defender of human rights and wants the West – or more precisely Europe and therefore France – to follow its lead. But the violence of its criticism of Russia, undeniably based on 'universal' values but also on issues of self-insecurity (Le, 2006, p. 163), rhetorically impedes the return of Russia as a power figure on the international stage, and thus in fact supports a bipolar world – US/EU – in which the EU-associated France would play a crucial role.

In summary, the principles of liberty, equality and fraternity, whether framed in terms of one or other of *Le Monde*'s four identities

(*Le-Monde*-ness, French-Republic-ness, European-ness and universal-ness), appear to have been extensively used to pursue French objectives: they supported positions that promoted France in Europe and around the world. In terms of argumentative strategies, the four editorials that pertained to questions of human dignity ('L'Europe politique existe', 'L'Europe et la Serbie', 'Nord-sud: la fracture' and 'Ingérence en Tchétchénie') called on *Le Monde*'s universal-ness, while the editorial bearing on strategies for the construction of Europe ('L'Europe des maladroits') was based on the newspaper's *Le-Monde*-ness and French-republic-ness. While the value of human dignity can undoubtedly be considered at the universal level, practical strategies for political constructions vary according to specific contexts. Thus, although French national values (liberty, equality, fraternity) have been called upon as universal values for national aims, the five editorials given as examples in this chapter do not appear to display any unethical strategy according to *Le Monde*'s French understanding of the top-down application of natural law (as stated in the Preamble of the Declaration of the Rights of Man and Citizen). However, these strategies certainly rested on *Le Monde*'s individual political assessments of the specific situations in question, and in this way were open to political criticism.

In conclusion, this chapter has shown how the close connection between the French national motto and principles embedded in the Declaration of the Rights of Man and Citizen, the European Charter of Fundamental Rights and the Universal Declaration of Human Rights allows *Le Monde* to shift from one sociocultural identity to the other, and how the skilled handling of these sociocultural identities promotes specific positions favouring a national perspective in an international setting. Ethical questions raised by *Le Monde*'s editorials on European and foreign issues concern not only their stated positions but also the identity standpoints from which these positions are presented. If the content of the French national motto facilitates *Le Monde*'s identity shifting, it also makes it easy for *Le Monde*'s detractors to accuse it, rightfully or not, of power abuse.

References

Appiah, K.A. (2006). *Cosmopolitanism. Ethics in a World of Strangers*. New York: W.W. Norton & Company.
Askehave, I. and Swales, J. M. (2001). 'Genre Identification and Communicative Purpose: A Problem and a Possible Solution', *Applied Linguistics*, 22(2), 195–212.
Christians, C.G. (2005). 'Ethical Theory in Communications Research', *Journalism Studies*, 6(1), 3–14.

———. (2008). 'Media Ethics on a Higher Order of Magnitude', *Journal of Mass Media Ethics*, 23, 3–14.
Entman, R.M. (2004). *Projections of Power*. University of Chicago Press.
Éveno, P. (2001). *Le journal Le Monde*. Paris: Odile Jacob.
Gauchet, M. (1989). *La révolution des droits de l'homme*. Paris: Gallimard.
Hecht, M.L., Jackson, R.L. and Ribeau, S.A. (2003). *African-American Communication: Exploring Identity and Culture*, 2nd edn. Mahwah, NJ: Lawrence Erlbaum.
Le, E. (2002). 'The Concept of Europe in *Le Monde*'s Editorials', *Journal of Language and Politics*, 1(2), 279–325.
———. (2006). *The Spiral of 'Anti-other Rhetoric'. Discourses of Identity and the International Media Echo*. Amsterdam: John Benjamins.
———. (2009). 'Why Investigate Textual Information Hierarchy?', in J. Renkema (ed.), *Discourse, of Course*. Amsterdam: John Benjamins, pp. 111–24.
———. (2010). *Editorials and the Power of Media*. Amsterdam: John Benjamins.
Le Monde (2002). *Le style du Monde*. Paris: Le Monde.
Le Monde Editorial. (1999). 'L'Europe-puissance', *Le Monde*, 12–13 December, p. 13.
Mucchielli, A. and Guivarch, J. (1998). *Nouvelles méthodes d'étude des communications*. Paris: Armand Colin.
Ozouf, M. (1996). 'Liberty, Equality, Fraternity', A. Goldhammer (trans.), in P. Nora (ed.), *Realms of Memory*, vol. 3: *Symbols*. New York: Columbia University Press, pp. 77–114.
Perelman, C. and Olbrechts-Tyteca, L. (1988). *Traité de l'argumentation*, 5th edn. Brussels: Éditions de l'Université de Bruxelles.
Poulet, B. (2003). *Le pouvoir du Monde*. Paris: La Découverte.
Rao, S. and Lee, S.T. (2005). 'Globalizing Media Ethics? An Assessment of Universal Ethics among International Political Journalists', *Journal of Mass Media Ethics*, 20(2–3), 99–120.
Simon, B. (2004). *Identity in Modern Society: A Social Psychological Perspective*. Oxford: Blackwell.
Van Dijk, T.A. (1980). *Macrostructures*. Hillsdale, NJ: Lawrence Erlbaum.
Wodak, R. and Meyer, M. (eds). (2001). *Methods of Critical Discourse Analysis*. London: Sage.

Notes

1. Necker, J. (1792). *Du pouvoir exécutif dans les grands États*, in *Œuvres complètes* (1821), Paris, vol. VIII, p. 320 (as cited in Gauchet, 1989, p. iv).
2. In 1894, Dreyfus, a Jewish officer in the French army, was wrongly condemned to a life sentence on charges of treason. Thanks to the involvement of a number of French intellectuals, he was pardoned by the President of the Republic in 1899, his process was reviewed in 1904 and he was rehabilitated in 1906. This affair profoundly divided French society at the time.
3. '*Tribune du Ministre des Affaires Étrangères, M. Hubert Védrine*' in *Le Monde Diplomatique* (December 2000). *Le Monde Diplomatique* is a monthly publication on foreign affairs that is distinct from *Le Monde*.

7
The Dilemmas of War and Peace Reporting

Richard Lance Keeble

According to the most recent authoritative source, the Stockholm International Peace Research Institute's annual report for 2008, world military spending had reached $1.2 trillion by 2007.[1] This represented a six per cent increase in real terms over the previous year and a 45 per cent increase over the ten-year period since 1998. The US, responsible for around 80 per cent of the increase in 2005, accounts for some 45 per cent of the world total, distantly followed by the UK, China, France and Japan, each with four to five per cent of the world share.

Not surprisingly, given these figures – and the spread of conflicts across the globe – warfare and its coverage in the media have been the focus for a massive amount of research. Equally, the ethical dilemmas facing media workers covering conflicts have been explored at length. But this chapter aims to achieve something new: to synthesize a theoretical analysis (based on a wide range of sources) with an approach which draws on an exploration of many of the practical dilemmas involved in the reporting of conflict. The theoretical analysis also helps to problematize the field radically and to draw attention to the marginalized concepts and principles of peace journalism.

The corporate media have, globally, too often banged the drums of wars; here the crucial role of the media in promoting the resolution of conflict is explored. Most of the current debate over conflict reporting concentrates on the corporate media; here attention is given to the potential of the alternative media to provide a more ethical and human-focused journalism. All these issues are explored through a Socratic question-and-answer format. The listening-questioning approach lies at the heart of ethics. The intention is to open up the issues to a range of responses, to acknowledge the complexity of the issues and to also subject my own views to constant questioning.

How important is it for mainstream and alternative journalists to understand the complex underpinnings of US/UK military strategy?

It is clearly crucial for all journalists to understand the nature of US/UK military strategy – essentially operative since the early 1980s – if they are to be effective in challenging military and government myths and misinformation. There are three major strands to the strategy, all of which are conducted simultaneously – each accompanied by a particular form of media coverage. Firstly, the most important strategy is conducted in complete secrecy away from the glare of the media. Take for instance, the US/UK post-2001 occupation of Afghanistan. This 'secret conflict' has involved:

- the targeted assassinations in both Afghanistan and over the border in Pakistan of alleged Taliban leaders;
- night raids by the CIA and some of its 56,000 Special Forces (such as the Green Berets and Navy SEALs);
- secret detention and torture centres;
- the secret building of around 400 massive military bases across the country to reinforce the occupation (Engelhardt, 2010);
- many disappearances; and
- Pakistani military offensives against the Taliban and al-Qaeda, instigated by Washington, which have claimed thousands of lives and displaced more than a million people in the north-western tribal areas (Gopal, 2010).

The second strategy is known in militaryspeak as 'Low Intensity Conflict': this involves the day-to-day grind of long-drawn-out engagement, occasional small-scale skirmishes with the enemy (sometimes involving pilotless drones), the taking out of snipers and the removal of roadside bombs. The regular reporting of British soldier casualties ('our Heroes') and moves to inaugurate peace discussions with certain Taliban leaders are part of the sporadic coverage of this low-intensity conflict in the mainstream media.

Finally, there are the occasional manufactured, media-hyped 'operations' such as attack on Musa Qala in Afghanistan in December 2007, and the operation dubbed 'Moshtarak', launched in March 2010. In these operations, the nation with the largest and most heavily resourced fighting force in history has faced a comparatively small movement – though one which is highly skilled in guerrilla tactics – in one of the most impoverished countries in the world. These operations are then spectacular, essentially PR events providing the theatre in which the US and its allies can claim their so-called 'victories'. The origins of these manufactured 'operations' lie in early 1980s, when the UK military adventures in the Falklands (1982) and those of the US in Grenada (1983), Panama (1989) and Iraq (1991) all bore the hallmarks of the new military/media strategies:

- They were all quickie attacks. The Libya bombings (deliberately aimed at assassinating the President, Colonel Gaddafi) last just 11 minutes. All the others were over within days.
- They were all largely risk-free and fought from the air. All resulted in appalling civilian casualties. For instance, Colin Powell (1995, pp. 525–6) estimated in his account of the 1991 Iraq conflict that 250,000 Iraqi soldiers were killed. In contrast, the US-led forces lost just 353 soldiers: only 46 of these were actually killed in combat, and of those 52 per cent died in 'friendly fire' incidents (Keeble, 1997, p. 159). Casualty figures were covered up and the military hardware was constantly represented as 'precise', 'surgical', 'modern' and 'clean'.
- Following the end of the Cold War and the demise of the 'great enemy', the Soviet Union, the military industrial complex needed the manufacture of 'big' enemies to legitimize the continued massive expenditure on weapons of war. Thus, the massive displays of US/UK force bore little relation to the threats posed.
- Central to the new strategies was the demonization of the leaders of the 'enemy' states, such as 'mad dog' Gadaffi, 'drug trafficker' Noriega of Panama and 'new Hitler', 'Butcher of Baghdad' Saddam Hussein of Iraq.
- As the links between mainstream journalists and the secret state grew during the 1980s, so the warfare conducted by the state became increasingly secretive. By 1991, the military could fight a war in front of television cameras 24/7 and yet in almost total secrecy.

However, the mainstream media's pro-war consensus appeared to fracture during the 2003 invasion of Iraq.

Why was this? And in the context of the debate over press freedom, how significant was it?

All the invasions of the 1980s were celebrated in ecstatic language throughout the mainstream media in the UK. And following the collapse of the Berlin Wall in 1989, the media consensus of opposition to the Russian 'bear' shifted its focus to the new bogeyman – Saddam Hussein (significantly, allied to the West during its war with Iran in 1980–8). The consensus remained firm even during the 'humanitarian' NATO attacks on Serbia in 1999. Only the *Independent on Sunday* expressed opposition, and only days after the bombing ceased, the editor, Kim Fletcher, was sacked.

In 2003, with significant opposition to the rush to war being expressed by politicians, lawyers, intelligence agents, celebrities, religious leaders, charities and human rights campaigners – together with massive street protests – both nationally and internationally, the breakdown in Fleet Street's consensus was inevitable. Significantly, an International Gallup poll in December 2002, barely noted in the US, found virtually no support for Washington's announced plans for war in Iraq carried out 'unilaterally by America and its allies' (Ismael and Ismael, 2004).

On 15 February 2003, just days before the launch of the US/UK attacks on Iraq, an estimated two million people protested on the streets of London in the largest demonstration ever seen in the UK. Here was clearly a market that Fleet Street could not ignore. Yet still the vast bulk of Fleet Street backed the invasion of Iraq (though columnists and letter-writers were divided). Rupert Murdoch's mass-selling *The Sun, News of the World, The Times* and *Sunday Times* (along with virtually all his other global media outlets) newspapers were gung-ho backers of the military action. The views of *The Independent*, prominently carrying the critical views of foreign correspondent Robert Fisk, were the most hostile. Following the massive global street protests on 15 February, the *Independent on Sunday* editorialized: 'Millions show this is a war that mustn't happen' (Keeble, 2007, pp. 208–9).

The Guardian did not criticize military action on principle, but opposed the US/UK rush to war and promoted a wide range of critical opinions. Yet, significantly, its sister paper, *The Observer* (generally regarded as a liberal, left-of-centre newspaper, famous for its brave opposition to Britain's invasion in the Suez Crisis of 1956) was one of the most vociferous supporters of the military action. As Nick Davies comments in his wide-ranging critique of *The Observer*'s pro-war shift under editor Roger Alton: 'this flagship of the left was towed along in the wake of a determinedly right-wing American government: on this crucial, long-running story, the essential role of journalism to tell the truth was compromised' (2008, p. 331).

The tabloid newspaper *The Mirror* was also 'anti' in the run-up to the conflict (perhaps more for marketing reasons, since the rival

Murdoch press was always going to be firmly for the invasion), with the veteran dissident campaigning journalists John Pilger and Paul Foot given prominent coverage. But then, after Editor-in-Chief Piers Morgan claimed his paper's stance attracted thousands of protesting letters from readers, their opposition softened. Meanwhile, the mid-market *Daily Mail* managed to sit on the fence, mixing both criticism of the rush to military action with fervent patriotic support for the troops during the conflict.

The pro-war bias was not limited to the mainstream press. A major survey by researchers at the Universities of Manchester, Liverpool and Leeds, published in December 2006, found that in considering the 'humanitarian' rationale for the invasion, more than 80 per cent of mainstream media coverage (both print and broadcast) mirrored the government position, while less than 12 per cent challenged it. 'Most reports (54 per cent TV and 61 per cent press) making substantial reference to the WMD rationale for war reflected and reinforced the coalition argument by, for example, relaying the coalition's claims in unproblematic terms' (Robinson *et al.*, 2006).

Did the journalists embedded with the military during the 2003 invasion of Iraq forfeit their independence?

Both the US and the UK have deployed forces virtually every year since 1945 – most of them in secrecy away from the glare of the media (Peak, 1982). But at various moments the US/UK choose to fight overt, manufactured wars. We, the viewers and readers, have to see the spectacle. It has to appear real. During the first Gulf War, the pooling system was used to keep correspondents away from the action (Keeble, 1997, pp 109–26; McLaughlin, 2002, pp. 88–93). And since most of the action was conducted over the 42 days from the air, with journalists denied access to planes, the reality of the horror was kept secret.

In contrast, during the 2003 conflict, journalists were given remarkable access to the 'frontlines'. And the frontline images and reports from journalists who were clearly risking their lives aimed to seduce the viewer and reader with their facticity; the correspondents were amazed at their 'objectivity'. Yet beyond the view of the camera and the journalist eye-witnesses, with the war unproblematized, the essential simulated and mythical nature of the conflict lay all the more subtly and effectively hidden (Keeble, 2004; Hammond, 2007). Moreover, military censorship regimes always serve essentially symbolic purposes – expressing the arbitrary power of the army over the conduct and representation of war.

Most of the critical mainstream coverage highlighted the information overload. However, as David Miller commented: 'It is certainly true to say that it is new to see footage of war so up-close but it is a key part of the propaganda war to claim that this makes it "real"' (2003, p. 1).

Some 775 journalists were embedded with military units, including 128 from the UK media (such as the *Western Daily Press*, *The Scotsman*, *Manchester Evening News*, *Ipswich Evening Star* and *Eastern Daily Press*). Some 70 per cent of embeds were from the US national media and were 10 per cent from the US local media, while 85 were women (11 per cent of the total). In all, 352 slots were with the army, 214 were with the marines, 124 were with the navy, 71 were with the air force and 15 were with special operations (Seib, 2004, p. 53).

Ron Schieffer, Vietnam reporter for the Forth Worth *Star-Telegram* (and later CBS News correspondent), welcomed the system: 'I think putting reporters with the military gave the reporters a better chance of coming to know the military and I daresay it gave the military a chance to have a better understanding of what the press does. So I think it was good for both sides' (Sylvester and Huffman, 2005, p. 20). According to Phillip Knightley:

> The idea was copied from the British system in World War I when six correspondents embedded with the army on the Western front produced the worst reporting of just about any war and were all knighted for their services. One of them, Sir Phillip Gibbs, had the honesty, when the war was over, to write: 'We identified ourselves absolutely with the armies in the field.' The modern embeds, too, soon lost all distinction between warrior and correspondent and wrote and talked about 'we' with boring repetition. (2003, p. 7)

As *The Times* media commentator Brian MacArthur reported: 'Embeds inevitably became adjuncts to the forces' (2003, p. 20). An analysis commissioned by the Ministry of Defence of newspaper content produced by embeds found that 90 per cent of their reports were either positive or neutral (Miller, 2004).

Some 5,000 journalists were in the Gulf region to cover the hostilities. Of these, 2,000 were in Kuwait and on ships with the US and UK naval task forces in the Arabian Gulf; 290 were in Baghdad; 900 were in Northern Iraq with Kurdish fighters; while the rest were in Jordan, Iran, Bahrain and at the Allied Central Command in Doha, Qatar (Milmo, 2003). Here there was little consistent challenge to the dominant military agenda. On one occasion *New York* magazine writer Michael Wolff dared to break ranks and ask the provocative question: 'Why are we here? Why should we stay? What's the value of what we're learning at this million-dollar press center' (Wolff, 2003, p. 6). He was soon to pay the price for his daring. Fox TV attacked him for lacking patriotism and after right-wing commentator Rush Limbaugh gave out his email address, Wolff received 3,000 hate messages in one day.

Unprecedented access to the 'frontlines' was the carrot, but the stick was always on hand. Fifteen non-Iraqi journalists were killed, two went missing and many unilateral non-embeds were intimidated by the military. Had there been the same death rate as for journalists during the Vietnam War, there would have been 3,000 killed. As John Donovan (2003) argued, 'coalition forces saw unilaterals as having no business on their battlefield'. Unilateral Terry Lloyd, of ITN, was killed by marines who fired at his car; Reuters camera operator Tara Protsyuk and Jose Couso, a cameraman for the Spanish TV channel Telecino, died after an American tank fired at the 15th floor of the Palestine hotel in Baghdad while Tayek Ayyoub, a cameraman for Al-Jazeera, died after a US jet bombed the channel's Baghdad office. In all, seven journalists were killed in US attacks.

A major report by the Committee to Protect Journalists, *Permission to Fire*, blamed the US army for a breakdown in communication with the media and claimed the attack on the Palestine Hotel could have been avoided. Yet an investigation by the US military, released in November 2004, failed to explain why troops were not made aware that the hotel was widely used by journalists (Tomlin, 2008). The killings of journalists by US forces in Iraq continued relentlessly, even after the official ending of hostilities by President Bush on 1 May 2003. By March 2009, the number of journalists killed in Iraq had increased to 139, plus an additional 51 media support workers, according to the Committee to Protect Journalists.[2] We will never know how many Iraqi journalists perished during the 2003 invasion. For most of the Western mainstream media, they are non-people.

Were the media right to agree to the news blackout over Prince Harry's deployment to Afghanistan in 2008?

During the Falklands conflict of 1982, Prince Andrew, the Duke of York, served on the aircraft carrier *HMS Invincible*. No media blackout was necessary. There were no suggestions that his presence on the frontline was putting the lives of other soldiers at risk. It was very different in 2008. Then, the media – following an agreement between the Ministry of Defence and the Society of Editors – simply kept quiet over Prince Harry's deployment to Afghanistan's Helmand province in December 2007. Amazingly, in this age of transparency, tabloid hysteria and surveillance, when it seems that hardly any secrets can be held for any length of time, the global embargo lasted ten weeks!

On 26 December, eight days after Harry had been deployed, the Ministry of Defence received a call from US broadcast channel CNN, saying they were planning to run the story. After a short discussion they quickly fell into line (Green, 2008). A soldier also approached *The Sun* with photographs of Harry witnessing the beheading of a live goat during Christmas Day celebrations – but this, of course, never saw the light of day. Thus, while an Australian women's magazine, *New Idea*, first leaked the story on 7 January 2008, the global embargo was not lifted until Matt Drudge's notorious US gossip website, the *Drudge Report*, spilled the beans on 28 February.

So poor Harry had to quit the front (supposedly for the safety of the soldiers around him) – and the international media went immediately bananas. The BBC *Ten O'Clock News* devoted its first 15 minutes to the story, while *The Sun* carried nine pages of coverage (plus a big poster pullout of the handsome 'hero'), *The Mirror* 14 pages and the *Daily Mail* ten.

What do we learn from the 'Warrior Prince' saga? Perhaps more than anything else, does it not illustrate the extent to which over the decades since the Falklands War, the global media (despite all the dire warnings about Internet freedoms) have been seduced into embarrassing levels of complicity by the military and political elite? In 2005, the British media had similarly exposed themselves to international ridicule when they respected a Downing Street request not to reveal Prime Minister Tony Blair's holiday location for 'security reasons' – even though a US-based agency was regularly filing exclusive pictures from the location and a Google search could easily identify it.

Moreover, did not the media chiefs who backed the Harry embargo expose themselves to allegations that they had signed up to nothing more than a sophisticated PR stunt that ultimately served to lend legitimacy to a conflict and a royal family – both of which should be subject to rigorous critique? In short, the 'Hero Harry' story was deflecting attention away from the real Afghan news – that this was a highly controversial, expensive war, leading to massive civilian casualties. According to John Tulloch (2008), the coverage provided crucial *good news* to the media from an essentially *bad news* conflict.

Ultimately, the 'Hero Harry' coverage could only further damage the public's trust in the media, since people would be left thinking: 'If the media can shroud Harry's frontline fun and games in secrecy, what other more important secrets are they hiding away?'

Do mainstream media reports sanitize war?

On the one hand, journalists argue that the public simply does not have the stomach for seeing horrific images of warfare: their self-censorship is a response to these perceptions. On the other hand, the media is criticized for presenting a sanitized view of war. Anti-war campaigners argue that showing the *brutal and horrific realities* will jolt people out of their apathy; others argue that journalists have a professional responsibility to show *the truth*, however unsettling it may be. And, according to Miles Hudson and John Stainer, modern mass media coverage of war has proved an 'enormous bonus to mankind': 'Could the carnage on the Somme, Passchendale or Verdun possibly have continued if it had been witnessed nightly in millions of European sitting rooms? The answer must be that it could not' (Hudson and Stainer, 1997, p. 315).

Martin Bell, the white-suited BBC war correspondent turned independent MP, has called for the 'journalism of attachment', arguing that the media are increasingly failing in their representation of 'realworld violence'. Broadcasters were becoming more concerned with ratings than with the truth:

> Some images of violence – as for instance most of the pictures of both the market place massacres in Sarajevo – are almost literally unviewable and cannot be inflicted on the public. But people have to be left with some sense of what happened, if only through the inclusion of pictures sufficiently powerful at least to hint at the horror of those excluded. To do otherwise is to present war as a relatively cost-free enterprise and an acceptable way of settling differences, a one-sided game that soldiers play in which they are seen shooting but never suffering. The camera shows the outgoing ordnance but seldom the incoming. (Bell, 1998, p. 21)

Veteran war correspondent and Middle East specialist Robert Fisk agrees. In an interview with Amy Goodman, for the *Democracy Now!* radio show and website, he commented:

> If you go to war, you realize it is not primarily about victory or defeat, it is about death and the infliction of death and suffering on as large a scale as you can make it. It is about the total failure of the human

spirit. We don't show that because we don't want to. And in this sense journalists, television reporting, television cameras are lethal. They collude with governments to allow you to have more wars because if they showed you the truth, you wouldn't allow any more wars. (Fisk, 2005)

Criticisms of the media's sanitizing of wars have tended to focus on the coverage of the 1991 Gulf War. This was largely represented as a Nintendo-style, bloodless conflict fought by the 'heroic' allies with 'surgical', 'precise', super-modern weaponry. Shots from video cameras on missiles heading towards their targets (shown on television and reproduced in the press) meant viewers actually 'became' the weapons. These images, which were constantly repeated, came to dominate the representation of the Gulf conflict (and later the Kosovo War). As Kevin Robins and Les Levidow comment:

It was the ultimate voyeurism: to see the target hit from the vantage point of the weapon. An inhumane perspective. Yet this remote-intimate kind of watching could sustain the moral detachment of earlier military technologies. Seeing was split off from feeling: the visible was separated from the sense of pain. Through the long lens the enemy remained the faceless alien. (1991, p. 325)

Also during the Kosovo War, many critics argued that the media failed to convey its real horror. According to Phillip Knightley (2000, p. 505), between 10,000 and 15,000 civilians were killed, while thousands were traumatised and left jobless in terrible poverty (Chomsky, 1999; Hammond, 2000; Hammond and Herman, 2000). But these figures were rarely reported. When refugee convoys were bombed by NATO jets, they were 'mistakes' (rather than moral outrages) or blamed on Milosevic. The BBC's veteran war correspondent Kate Adie, however, prefers to stress the importance of the journalist's self-censorship when covering scenes of appalling violence: 'I've seen things I would never put on the screen. It is immensely upsetting to see humans dead on-screen or alive being mistreated. A corpse is OK if it is not being interfered with. If it is kicked or bits are being removed, that is not acceptable.' She had once witnessed an infant crucifixion but would never screen it (Methven, 1996, p. 1).

The issues are yet further complicated since complex historical, political and ethical factors so often collide in the coverage of wars. The significance and power of images, together with attitudes towards taste, can change over time. For instance, John Taylor highlights the way in which Eddie Adams's now famous picture of General Loan summarily executing a Vietcong suspect in a Saigon street on 1 February 1968 appeared when its moral and political dimension was acceptable to journalists. But this picture was 'universally rejected and published only in an obscure little magazine', probably because in 1962 the war in Vietnam was too small or viewed too favourably for hostile coverage (Taylor, 1998, p. 22).

How important is peace journalism as a critique of mainstream coverage of wars?

Too much mainstream journalism is clearly *war journalism*, being violence- and victory-oriented, dehumanizing the enemy and prioritizing official sources. I have always been committed to peace journalism. In the early 1980s, for instance, I launched the group *Journalists Against Nuclear Extermination* (JANE) to campaign for peace through the National Union of Journalists. And similar preoccupations have been ever-present in my journalism and academic writing and practice since then. My PhD dissertation (published as *Secret State, Silent Press: New Militarism, the Gulf and the Modern Image of Warfare* in 1997) examined the press coverage of the 1991 Gulf War. But it was essentially a protest (in appropriate academic prose) at the unnecessary massacres inflicted on defenceless Iraqis by the US-led coalition – and the way the mainstream media hid the reality of that horror behind the myth of heroic, precise warfare.

For me, it has always been clear that some of the most important responsibilities of the journalist are to promote peace, dialogue and understanding; to confront militarism in all its forms – and the stereotypes and lies on which it is based. And yet, while the mainstream media is awash with debates over citizen journalism and the impact of the Internet on traditional routines and professional values, little is heard beyond a select group of activist reporters and academics about *peace journalism*.

One of the most original contributions to the debate regarding its practical and theoretical aspects appears in *Peace Journalism* by Jake Lynch and Annabel McGoldrick (2005; see also Lynch, 2002 and 2003). Drawing particularly on the peace research theories of Professor Johan Galtung (1998), they argue that most conflict coverage, thinking itself neutral and objective, is actually war journalism. It is violence- and victory-orientated, *dehumanizing the enemy,* focusing on *our* suffering, prioritizing official sources and highlighting only the visible effects of violence (those killed and wounded and the material damage).

In contrast, *peace journalism* is solution-orientated, giving voice to the voiceless, *humanizing the enemy*, exposing lies on all sides, highlighting peace initiatives and focusing on the invisible effects of violence (such as psychological trauma). Dotted throughout the text are comments from practising journalists and advice from the authors. For instance, in order to resist war propaganda, they advise journalists:

- to be on the lookout for shifting war aims;
- to avoid repeating claims which have not been independently verified;
- to avoid demonizing a person or group;
- and to remind their audience of when war propaganda turned out to be misleading.

In its handbook on reporting crises, the Institute for War and Peace Reporting (IWPR) stresses six core duties for responsible peace journalists: to understand conflict, to report fairly, to present the human side, to cover the background and the causes of conflict, to report on peace efforts and to recognize the media's influence (2004, pp. 202–4). Journalists also have a responsibility to know international humanitarian law. As the IWPR comment:

> seeing an army shell a church or other historic site which is sheltering civilians is bad enough; but understanding that such an attack represents a violation of the Geneva Conventions raises it to another level of importance – elevating what may seem a routine article into a breakthrough report on a major shift in the tactics and implications of the conflict. (2004, p. 179)

It is also important to note that some researchers, such as Lynch and McGoldrick, focus in their studies almost entirely on the mainstream media and thus fail to acknowledge the contribution of campaigning, alternative media (such as those linked to radical left, feminist, environmental and human rights causes) to the promotion of peace journalism (Keeble, 2010).

What are the implications of the Universal Declaration of Human Rights for war and peace journalism?

Much of the theorising on peace journalism sees it as an aspiration – focusing too much on the journalist as professional producer. But do we not need a radical transformation of journalism theory, moving away from the concept of the audience as a passive consumer of a professional product to seeing the audience as producers of their own (written or visual) media? Hartley even suggests that Article 19 of the Universal Declaration of Human Rights of 1948 proclaims, in effect, the *right to journalism*, since it stresses that everyone has the right not only to seek and receive but to *impart* (in other words communicate) information and ideas:

> The UN Declaration of journalism as a human right is aspirational; a challenge to action, not a description of facts. It represents an ideal type of liberal democratic politics. If it is to mean anything in practice it needs to be championed, extended, used and defended. (2008, p. 42)

The very definition of 'journalist' can now be expanded to include a far wider range of communicators within the public spheres – such as political activists in the peace movement who often double as media activists. Take, for instance, *IndyMedia*.[3] It emerged during the 1999 'Battle of Seattle', when thousands protested in the streets against the World Trade Organization and the impact of global free trade relations – and were met by armoured riot police. Violent clashes erupted with many injuries on both sides. In response, 400 volunteers, rallying under the motto 'Don't hate the media: be the media', created a site and a daily news sheet, the *Blind Spot*, which reported news of the demonstration from the perspective of the protestors. Today, there are more than 150 independent media centres in around 45 countries across six continents. They publish in English, Spanish, German, Italian, Portuguese, French, Russian, Arabic and Hebrew and in all media – print, video, audio, website and photo.

In the UK, *Peace News* (for non-violent revolution) comes as both a hard-copy magazine and a lively website[4] combining analysis, cultural reviews and news about the extraordinarily brave activities of peace movement internationally. Not only does its content differ radically from the mainstream, but in its collaborative, non-hierarchical structures and sourcing techniques, *Peace News*, like other alternative media operations, challenges the conventions of mainstream organizational routines.

In April 2010, the website *Wikileaks*, as part of its campaign to expose the 'brutal face' of US imperialism, revealed a secret video showing members of the US air crew laughing at the dead after an air strike that killed 12 people, including two Iraqis working for Reuters news agency. Members of Fit Watch, a group protesting at the forward intelligence teams (Fits), the police units that monitor demonstrations and meetings, similarly combine political and media activism in their 'sousveillance' – the latest buzzword for taking videos and photographs of police activities and then uploading them onto the Web. They are part of a growing international media activist and protest movement. In Palestine, for instance, B'Tselem, the Israeli human rights group, gave video cameras to 160 citizens in the West Bank and Gaza, and their shocking footage of abuses by Israeli settlers and troops was broadcast on the country's television as well as internationally.

Campaigners in the UK and the US who upload images of police surveillance or brutality onto YouTube, or citizens who report the activities of protest movements via blogs, Twitter and websites in authoritarian societies such as China, Burma, Iran and Egypt, can similarly be considered participants in the alternative media sphere. As Stuart Allan stresses, commenting on the role of citizen blogs during the 2003 Iraq invasion:

> these emergent forms of journalism have the capacity to bring to bear alternative perspectives, contexts and ideological diversity to war reporting, providing users with the means to connect with distant voices otherwise being marginalised, if not silenced altogether, from across the globe. (2006, p. 111)

Indeed, with the global rise of citizen journalism committed to conflict resolution, there are reasons for optimism.

References

Allan, S. (2006). *Online News: Journalism and the Internet*. Maidenhead: Open University Press.
Bell, M. (1998). 'The Journalism of Attachment', in M. Kieron (ed.), *Media Ethics*. London: Routledge, pp. 15–22.
Chomsky, N. (1999). *The New Military Humanism: Lessons from Kosovo*. London: Pluto Press.
Davies, N. (2008). *Flat Earth News*. London: Chatto & Windus.
Donovan, J. (2003). 'For the Unilaterals, No Neutral Ground', *Columbia Journalism Review*, May/June, 35–6.
Engelhardt, T. (2010). 'Numbers to Die For', www.tomdispatch.com/post/175228/tomgram%3A_engelhardt%2C_numbers_to_die_for__/, date accessed 23 November 2010.
Fisk, R. (2005). 'War is the Total Failure of the Human Spirit', www.democracynow.org/2005/10/20/robert_fisk_war_is_the_total, date accessed 23 November 2010.

Galtung, J. (1998). 'High Road – Low Road: Charting the Course for Peace Journalism', *Track Two*, 7(4). http://ccrweb.ccr.uct.ac.za/archive/two/7_4/p07_highroad_lowroad.html, date accessed 23 November 2010.

Gopal, A. (2010). 'Afraid of the Dark in Afghanistan', http://www.tomdispatch.com/dialogs/print/?id=175197, date accessed 23 November 2010.

Green, C. (2008). 'The Warrior Prince and the Reporters', *The Independent*, 10 March, p. A24.

Hammond, P. (2000). 'Reporting "Humanitarian" Warfare: Propaganda, Moralism and Nato's Kosovo War', *Journalism Studies*, 1(3), 365–86.

——. (2007). *Media, War and Postmodernity*. London: Routledge.

Hammond, P. and Herman, E.S. (eds) (2000). *Degraded Capability: The Media and the Kosovo Crisis*. London: Pluto Press.

Hartley, J. (2008). 'Journalism as a Human Right: The Cultural Approach to Journalism', in M. Loffelholz and D. Weaver (eds), *Global Journalism Research: Theories, Methods, Findings, Future*. Oxford: Blackwell, pp. 39–51.

Hudson, M. and Stanier, J. (1997). *War and the Media*. Stroud: Sutton Publishing.

Institute for War and Peace Reporting (2004). *Reporting for Change: A Handbook for Local Journalists in Crisis Areas*. London, Washington, Johannesburg: IWPR.

Ismael, T.Y. and Ismael, J.S. (2004). *The Iraqi Predicament: People in the Quagmire of Power and Politics*. London: Pluto Press.

Keeble, R. (1997). *Secret State, Silent Press: New Militarism, the Gulf and the Modern Image of Warfare*. Luton: John Libbey Media.

——. (2004). 'Information Warfare in an Age of Hyper-militarism', in S. Allan and B. Zelizer (eds), *Reporting War*. London: Routledge, pp. 43–58.

——. (2007). 'The Necessary Spectacular "Victories": New Militarism, the Mainstream Press and the Manufacture of the Two Gulf Conflicts 1991 and 2003', in S. Maltby and R. Keeble (eds), *Communicating War: Memory, Media and Military*. Bury St Edmunds: Arima Publishing, pp. 200–12.

——. (2010). 'Peace Journalism as Political Practice: A New, Radical Look at the Theory', in R. Keeble, J. Tulloch and F. Zollmann (eds), *Peace Journalism, War and Conflict Resolution*. New York: Peter Lang, pp. 49–67.

Knightley, P. (2000). *The First Casualty: The War Correspondent as Hero and Myth Maker from the Crimea to Kosovo*, 2nd edn. London: Prion.

——. (2003). 'Turning the Tanks on the Reporters', *The Observer* (Business), 15 June, p. 7.

Lynch, J. (2002). *Reporting the World*. Taplow: Conflict and Peace Forums.

——. (2003). 'Reporting the World and Peace Journalism', *Peace News*, December–February, p. 27.

Lynch, J. and McGoldrick, A. (2005). *Peace Journalism*. Stroud: Hawthorn Press.

MacArthur, B. (2003). 'Changing Pace of War', *The Times*, 27 June, p. B20.

McLaughlin, G. (2002). *The War Correspondent*. London: Pluto Press.

Methven, N. (1996). 'Gruesome TV News Reports Should Be Cut, Says Kate Adie', *Press Gazette*, 11 October, p. 1.

Miller, D. (2003). 'Embedding Propaganda', *Free Press*, special issue, June, p. 1.

——. (2004). 'The Domination Effect', *The Guardian*, 8 January, p. A24.

Milmo, C. (2003). 'One Death a Minute: Toll of the Booming Arms Trade', *The Independent*, 10 October, p. A10.

Peak, S. (1982). 'Britain's Military Adventures', *Pacifist*, 20, 10.
Powell, C. (1995) *Soldier's Way*. London: Hutchinson.
Robins, K. and Levidow, L. (1991). 'The Eye of the Storm', *Screen*, 32(3), 324–8.
Robinson, P., Brown, R., Goddard, P. and Parry, K. (2006). 'Media Wars: News Performance and Media Management during the 2003 Iraq War', www.esrcsocietytoday.ac.uk, date accessed 23 November 2010.
Seib, P. (2004). *Beyond the Front Lines: How the News Media Cover a World Shaped by War*. New York: Palgrave Macmillan.
Sylvester, J. and Huffman, S. (2005). *Reporting from the Front: The Media and the Military*. Oxford: Rowman & Littlefield.
Taylor, J. (1998). *Body Horror: Photojournalism, Catastrophe and War*. Manchester University Press.
Tomlin, J. (2008). 'US Short on Answers', *Press Gazette*, 18 April, p. 8.
Tulloch, J. (2008). 'Soldiers and Citizens: The Press, the Military and the Breaking of the "Military Covenant" in the Iraq/Afghan Conflicts', talk at University of Lincoln, 2 April.
Wolff, M. (2003). 'I Was Only Asking', *The Guardian*, 14 April, p. 6.

Notes

1. See www.globalissues.org/article/75/world-military-spending for these details.
2. See http://cpj.org/reports/2008/07/journalists-killed-in-iraq.php.
3. Available at www.indymedia.org.
4. www.peacenews.info.

Part IV
International PR and Public Communication

8
Ethics, Cultures and Global Social Marketing Health Campaigns

Terry L. Rentner and Lara Lengel

Social marketing and public relations (PR) disease prevention and health promotion campaigns are designed to improve the lives of individuals and entire societies. With such altruistic motives, how can these campaigns be anything but in the best interests of all? However, like any campaign designed to influence a particular audience, there are ethical dilemmas involved. For example, while a campaign claims to address a particular social good, might there be underlying motives? Is there a point when campaigns serve needs and goals of campaign implementers more than those of targeted audiences? Can campaigns impede the agency and autonomy of individuals? Perhaps most importantly, *how* is the social good – in this case an intended outcome of a health promotion campaign – defined and *who* is involved in defining it?

There is much work to be done in order to examine these questions, to assess ethical concerns in existing social marketing health campaigns and to develop and sustain more ethical campaigns in the future. There are numerous types of social marketing and PR health campaigns, from HIV prevention to seatbelt safety. Here, alcohol health promotion campaigns in several global contexts are analysed because, despite the plethora of studies of such campaigns in the US and a few studies in Australia, Europe and New Zealand, there are no studies specifically analysing ethical considerations of these campaigns.[1] This study fills the gap in this particular area of health campaigns research, illuminates key ethical considerations involving identity, culture, power, history, values, beliefs and social norms in all health campaigns, and highlights the need for more research in this important area of ethics and international communication.

Before analysing alcohol health promotion strategies, it is important to contextualize and operationalize the concept of social marketing.

Research psychologist Wiebe (1952) is credited with launching the concept of social marketing when he concluded that marketing techniques used in traditional advertising campaigns could be applied to campaigns deemed beneficial to society. Two decades later, the term 'social marketing' was introduced in a *Journal of Marketing* article (Kotler and Zaltman, 1971) and its definition and application have continued to evolve since then. A recent definition is 'a process that applies marketing principles and techniques to create, communicate, and deliver value in order to influence target audience behaviors that benefit society' (Kotler and Lee, 2008, p. 7). Grounded in exchange theory, social marketing attempts to exchange one type of behaviour for another that is more positive.

Early applications of social marketing techniques can be traced back to family planning campaigns implemented in the US in the early 1970s. At the same time, immunization, family planning and nutrition campaigns were implemented in Africa, Asia and South America. By the early 1980s, the dip in the economy and the conservative mood in the US led campaign planners to abandon the focus on changes needed in the social and physical environment in favour of campaigns emphasizing individual behaviour, lifestyle and choices (Walsh *et al.*, 1993). The explosion of social marketing campaigns occurred in the late 1980s and early 1990s, and was credited to organizations such as the World Bank and the US Centers for Disease Control and Prevention. Most campaigns have focused on health issues such as HIV/AIDS, smoking, heart disease, and alcohol and other substance abuse, but more recent social marketing campaigns have expanded into areas such as the environment (recycling, fuel efficiencies) and community (voting, volunteering).

The implementation of social marketing campaigns generally follows the format of typical marketing or PR plans: understanding the problem through research, identifying target audiences, and developing goals and objectives. Targeting, or segmenting the audience, is key to developing effective messages. Campaign planners try to pinpoint barriers preventing target audiences from achieving desired behaviours, identify potential benefits of adopting the desired course of action and account for competing types of human conduct (Kotler and Lee, 2008). Once target audiences are identified, objectives are developed to increase knowledge or change attitudes, behaviours or beliefs. This is followed by a positioning statement on how campaign planners want target audiences to see desired behaviours relative to competing ones and the implementation of the marketing mix strategies (Kotler and

Lee, 2008). Ideally, this is followed by evaluation at the completion of the campaign (see Rentner, 2006).

A façade of altruism?

On the surface, social marketing campaigns appear to be altruistic, informing target audiences on improving their lives or how their actions will benefit society. Who can argue with that logic? For example, how could campaigns designed to reduce alcohol consumption be deemed anything other than good for a society?

Nevertheless, criticism of social marketing ranges from a lack of solid research assessing campaigns to claims that the definition itself is too ambiguous and all-encompassing (Smith, 1997). Even more pressing than these criticisms are greater concerns about serious ethical issues, which centre on the question of who benefits from the changed behaviour. Salmon argues that social marketing efforts, by their very nature of changing behaviours, 'compromise certain values and interests, often individual freedoms, in order to promote values and interests deemed more socially, economically or morally compelling by the organization sponsoring the change effort' (1989, p. 20). For example, while framing smoking on aeroplanes as a major health risk, the underlying motive of the airline industry to enact a smoking ban was motivated by profit, attributed to attempts at reducing costs of maintaining cabin air quality. Salmon (1989) further argues most social marketing campaigns are created by groups who possess social power and resources as opposed to groups who are socially, culturally or economically disadvantaged.

The ethical concerns presented here focus primarily on the impact of social marketing campaigns aimed at such disenfranchised groups. Targeting populations is in itself an ethical dilemma in that social marketing prevention and intervention messages ignore other groups, such as those branded hard to reach or as having special needs (Guttman and Salmon, 2004). The act of segmenting and targeting populations also creates a moral dilemma in that campaign planners may decide that it is not economically feasible to target messages towards groups who are considered 'low risk' and are therefore less valued. At the opposite end of the spectrum, if messages are aimed at the general population, then those at low risk are also being asked to modify or change a type of behaviour (Guttman and Salmon, 2004). This may perpetuate negative misconceptions that more people are engaging in unhealthy practices than actually are and therefore stigmatizing a certain population.

Exchange theory, the foundation of social marketing, presents additional ethical issues. Targeted groups are asked to exchange an unhealthy behaviour for a healthier one deemed more socially acceptable. The question becomes *who* decides what is socially acceptable?

Another ethical concern with social marketing campaigns is the personal responsibility model of health communication. As mentioned earlier, the late 1970s and early 1980s brought about a cultural shift in the US from social marketing campaigns aimed at the social structure to campaigns aimed at the individual. Critics of social marketing point out that such campaigns are 'politically compatible with the "ideology of individualism"; the paradigm that considers individual rather than social structure, as the appropriate focus of public health efforts' (Guttman and Salmon, 2004, p. 542). In 2006 the Drinks Industry Group of Ireland conducted a campaign focused on public attitudes towards alcohol misuse. The study of 1,062 adults aged 18 and over found that 31 per cent of respondents blamed drinkers themselves for alcohol misuse compared with only 7 per cent blaming alcohol adverts and 3 per cent blaming the alcohol industry (*Barkeeper News*, 2006).

Putting responsibility on the individual can also prompt perceptions of personal failure. Non-compliance with messages could be interpreted as laziness and irresponsibility, and result in individuals being labelled as a societal burden (Guttman and Salmon, 2004). The shift to personal responsibility from structural responsibility also ignores limitations for those wanting to change, such as limited information or financial resources. Thus, one may want to change the behaviour, but social and economic conditions render this shift impossible.

Potential for unintended consequences is another ethical concern of social marketing and PR health campaigns. These range from over-use of fear appeals to the creation of social gaps where messages reinforce gender, class or cultural stereotypes. For example, a needle exchange social marketing campaign aimed at those with drug addictions might nurture the perception that drug abuse only takes place in urban slums, ignoring the larger problem of drug abuse at all societal levels. In another example, an alcohol reduction message aimed at college students may reinforce the perception that all college students drink, while ignoring the large number of adults who regularly participate in heavy, episodic drinking.

Ethical concerns of social marketing campaigns exist across cultures as well. Such campaigns may disregard how a culture's history, language, values and beliefs affect how messages are perceived (Rentner and Lengel, 2009). For example, messages may place an emphasis on long-term gains for a culture that prefers the status quo or may even challenge a group's values (Flora, Schooler and Pierson, 1997). Guttman and Salmon present eight ethical considerations in public health communication campaigns, the first of which is '"targeting" and "tailoring" public health messages to particular population segments' (2004, p. 531). This consideration is important to draw attention to a key ethical problem in social marketing health campaigns, namely questionable levels of sensitivity to the cultures of targeted audiences. We hope this research can inform assessment of alcohol-reduction campaigns in other nations and regions, with a view to upholding sensitivity to difference and to *the other*. Here we draw upon cultural studies scholarship on identity, ethics, difference and the complexity of culture. We are informed by the body of research on international PR ethics that highlights the 'central role that culture, power, and identity play' in campaign communication practice (Curtin and Gaither, 2008, p. 1), the importance of culture more broadly and the constitution of *the other*.

Kellner argues that situating *the other* emerges from 'boundaries and borders of class, gender, race, sexuality, and the other constituents that differentiate individuals from each other and through which people construct their identities' (1997, p. 12). *Otherness*, Nakayama notes, 'is neither simplistic, nor monolithic'; rather, it is 'coalitional' and requires us to bring cultural codes, norms and contexts into question as we analyse intercultural interaction (1994, p. 162). As *otherness* is complex, nuanced and blurred by hegemony, communication that overcomes the positioning of *self* and *other* is uncommon. This is the case with much mediated communication and one-to-many communication practices, such as those inherent in social marketing and PR health campaigns. Until recently, many campaigns have increased boundaries and borders of difference, mainly through lack of attention to difference. Thus, they establish a binary opposition of *self-other*, where the *self* is the dominant culture and *the other* is 'unspoken and invisible' at the margins of 'predominantly white aesthetic and cultural discourses' (Hall, 1996, p. 114). The *other* is, instead, spoken for and visible only if situated as exotic or unusual (Lengel, 1998).

Questioning structures and hierarchies of power

Public relations scholarship has been questioned for its inability to consider the standpoint of *the other*. In their study of international PR ethics, Curtin and Gaither (2005) chronicle the critical turn in PR scholarship. They note that more than a decade ago, scholars (Roth *et al.*, 1996) first questioned structures and hierarchies of power as well as tendencies to conform to hegemonic norms, and 'challenged public relations practitioners and scholars to examine international public relations ethics by assuming the standpoint of "the other"' (Curtin and Gaither, 2005, p. 1). The authors call for a 'comprehensive ethical theory that accounts for diverse cultural values, the role of relative power in relationships, and fluid, often conflicting identities' (p. 3).

Breaking down hierarchies of power in social marketing campaign communication and establishing ethical relationships between campaign producers and their targeted audiences can be informed by Habermas's discourse ethics. For example, Choi (2005) analyses Habermas's (1984) requirements for ethical dialogue within the scope of PR ethics. For Habermas, ethical dialogue must provide 'participants an equal chance to attend the discourse and all ideas being open to challenge and discussion' (Choi, 2005, p. 6). Participants must also engage in dialogue 'free of manipulation, domination, or control' and have 'equal power to influence others' (p. 6). Often there is unequal participation in mainstream social marketing health campaigns. For example, in a study of substance-related problems in Australia since the 1960s, Rankin argues that there have been 'important failures and missed opportunities' in reaching audiences outside the dominant culture: 'The greatest failure has been our inability as a nation to work effectively with Aboriginal and Torres Strait Islander peoples so that they, too, can achieve the same aspirations and have the same benefits as their fellow Australians, most importantly lives not shortened unnecessarily by social and economic deprivation and the ravages of substance use' (Rankin, 2003, p. 261).

Only recently have there been social marketing anti-alcohol and anti-drug campaigns directed to Native American (Ching, 2005; Rentner and Lengel, 2009), Latina and Latino and African-American audiences in the US, despite the fact that all three cultural communities have the highest fatality rates from drink-driving and underage drinking.

Historically, nineteenth-century temperance efforts in America and Europe focused solely on white audiences, most notably the emerging middle class. In his study of temperance, gender and middle class ideology, Martin (2008) analyses temperance discourses directed specifically at women's intemperance which, although addressed far less frequently than men's alcohol abuse, ranked as a greater moral and ethical crisis. Temperance reform and media discourses alike positioned women alcoholics in the 'vice of groups far removed from the respectable middle class' – a collective *other* that included immigrants, the working class and African Americans (who were often simultaneously situated as a criminal *other*) (Martin, 2008, p. 34). In this case, as Stuart Hall argues, *the other* is established within a 'singular and unifying framework based on the building up of identity across ethnic and cultural difference' and 'culturally, this analysis formulated itself in terms of a critique of the way Blacks were positioned as the unspoken and invisible "other" of predominantly white aesthetic and cultural discourses' (1996, p. 114).

Class and culture have been foci of other international and cultural differences in alcohol use and abuse. For example, Figueriedo and Venâncio note that Portuguese and Brazilian urban upper classes were known to engage in moderate drinking: 'Such temperance, however, did not thrive in more popular quarters. The consumption, especially of sugarcane aguardente, was widely spread among the large population of slaves and poor mixed-breed people' (2003, p. 167).

The white aesthetic and cultural discourses were evident in the anti-alcohol campaigns in the twentieth century that continued to focus on the white middle-class male majority. 'Until recently,' Britt (2004) notes, 'white male populations have dominated studies of substance abuse, with little focus on gender, ethnicity and etiologic variations. These cultural biases and the emphasis on majority American values and lifestyles may contribute to the presence of substance abuse behaviors in the African-American community.'

Despite the white male middle-class dominance of substance abuse studies and anti-alcohol health campaigns, 'perhaps no other group in history has received more attention for its alcohol use' than Native Americans (Abbott, 2003, p. 446). Again, *the other* emerges only as a point of difference from cultural and societal norms of the white middle-class, predominantly male population to whom most temperance literature, reform and health campaigns have been directed. Abbott argues that 'embedded in the discourse about the role of alcohol in Native societies is the assumption that Indian drinking was and is qualitatively different from that of non-Indians' (2003, p. 446). Indeed, early European settlers did comment on the perceived addiction of Native Americans to alcohol; however, Abbott suggests that 'it is important not to accept the judgments of these observers at face value. In looking at alcohol use, misuse, and control, it is important to question the cultural biases and to examine the historical contexts in which alcohol consumption, alcohol control, and alcohol rhetoric occurred'. Indeed, alcohol consumption for Native-American communities, as well as African-American and Latino communities, 'became an outlet for numbing the experience of cultural dislocation, epidemic disease, and European conquest' (2003, p. 446).

The most successful, ethical responses to disease prevention and health promotion give an equal, if not dominant, voice to those in the target communities so that they can take on leadership roles in the design and implementation of culturally appropriate health campaigns. Abbott notes that 'a number of Native groups, both on-reservation and off, have developed recovery strategies that speak to Native American needs, cultures, and experiences' (2003, p. 449) (see also Rentner and Lengel, 2009). Many campaigns, particularly those ignoring identity markers of intended audiences, are less successful. This is certainly the case with many international social marketing campaigns targeted at developing countries in the late 1960s and early 1970s, particularly in the area of family planning programmes implemented in Colombia, India, Jamaica, Kenya and Sri Lanka (Walsh et al., 1993). Emerging from frustrations with ineffective clinically-based family planning services, early social marketing health promotion techniques included mass mediated messages combined with the distribution of contraceptives through pharmacies and community shops (Walsh et al., 1993). While these campaigns were credited with advancing social marketing, ethical concerns about relationships between the *self* (intersecting hierarchies of power constituted by government, corporations and development organizations) and *other* (targeted audiences, particularly those in less developed and newly industrializing countries) went largely unnoticed. Research in the decades that followed has critiqued the often destructive attitudes and practices of those who designed and conducted those health promotion programmes (Kapoor, 1999) and has highlighted problems associated with the Western dominance and, consequently, planned dependence-creation inherent in such campaigns. Despite the awareness that this research has raised about how such campaigns further marginalize an already disenfranchised *other*, ethical challenges have increased due to disconnects between research, policy and practice, as well as ongoing dissent among stakeholders and vast budget cuts and shifts in governmental funding.[2]

Ethical challenges are also on the increase in alcohol harm reduction programmes in locations such as Europe and Australia where there are increasing incidences of high-risk consumption and alcohol-related deaths, particularly among young people. In Sweden, 39 per cent of 15-year-old males and 38 per cent of 15-year-old females reported being drunk every time or almost every time they drank (Rehnman, Larsson and Andreasson, 2005). These findings prompted campaigns targeted to young adults, with varying levels of effectiveness. For example, researchers at Birmingham and Bath Universities assessed attitudes about drinking of 18 to 25-year-olds after they viewed 216 alcohol print and broadcast advertisements (Szmigin *et al*, 2008). Researchers concluded that youth audiences, to whom the print and broadcast adverts were targeted, did not see their cultures and behaviours reflected in the campaign. Specifically, television adverts showing young people injuring themselves or smearing vomit in their hair were viewed as 'laughably unrealistic' (*BBC News*, 2008).

The ethical concerns of such a campaign include stereotyping an entire population, presenting incorrect or exaggerated information to illustrate a point and over-using fear as a strategy. For example, car crashes were seen as unrealistic because youth respondents stated that they used designated drivers. Because these adverts were seen in print and on television, they also had unintended consequences, such as the perpetuation of attitudes held by older adults that all 18 to 25-year-olds drank excessively, or the emotional distress incurred by younger children who viewed the graphic and violent adverts.

The researchers did find that alcohol played an important role in forming group identity and that alcohol-related stories were a catalyst in bringing different social groups together (Szmigin *et al.*, 2008). However, UK government bodies that have produced literature and campaigns tended to constitute alcohol as an individual rather than a social problem. The ethical concern here is one of blaming the victim. Government and health officials not only put blame on the individual, but also the responsibility to 'fix the problem' without taking into account the challenges facing those wanting to change their behaviour. Thus, one may want to change, but socioeconomic conditions inhibit this shift.

It appears that this series of adverts lacked solid research that would have helped campaign planners better understand their targeted youth audience. The *other*, as described earlier, has not had an equal chance to participate in campaign development. Instead, these campaigns, which the UK government stated were to encourage young people to consider the grave consequences of drinking, had little or no effect on its intended audience.

While the UK programme focused its youth alcohol reduction campaign on the personal responsibility model of health campaign development, another programme emphasized an environmental approach that included policy development. The Beer Campaign, a community-based programme involving information and training of parents, police and shopkeepers, sought to limit the easy access teenagers under the 18-year-old age limit had in obtaining alcohol in Stockholm. Researchers used an experimental design with an intervention area and a comparison, or control group, area. Results showed that the perceived availability of alcohol by teenagers did not change (Rehnman, Larsson and Andreasson, 2005). Failure to change this perception may be attributed to lack of attention to the target audience. That is, social marketing efforts posit audience segmentation as critical, and a failure to include targeted audiences in various stages of programming raises many concerns.

Another consideration in the Stockholm campaign involves the cost-effectiveness of implementing the programme. The intervention area, which provided the information and training of parents, police and shopkeepers, achieved the same results as the control group, which only used surveillance and sanctions. The intervention area had higher costs in educating and training groups but yielded no significant differences from the control area that used established tactics (surveillance and sanctions). The ethical dilemma social marketing campaign designers face is in deciding when a campaign becomes cost-ineffective and therefore that resources are no longer used effectively for that population. This could result in a population being automatically eliminated from the intervention because they may be seen as hard to reach, at lower risk or not economically feasible to warrant an intervention. While the study mentioned above concluded that the campaign did not significantly reduce alcohol availability to Swedish teenagers, it did show some potential that more surveillance and enforcement by the police and the alcohol licensing board might have a positive impact (Rehnman, Larsson and Andreasson, 2005).

Let us recall Rankin's (2003) argument on missed opportunities. One of these missed opportunities involves the impact on the consequences of high-risk drinking among young men and women. A series of Australian national campaigns that targeted high-risk drinking among teenagers were implemented from the late 1980s to the mid-1990s. Evaluation of these campaigns showed a significant increase in awareness during the time the campaigns ran. A few years after the campaigns ended, surveys indicated that without campaign reinforcement messages, drinking levels among new teenagers returned to earlier levels (Carroll, 1998).

An ethical issue involved in the Australian campaigns is one that affects many campaigns – the sustainability of changed behaviours. As this case illustrates, once campaigns conclude, so do their long-term effects. The question becomes whether or not it is ethical to implement a behaviour change campaign with no maintenance component, that is, changed behaviours need reinforcement or individuals may fall back into their previous behavioural patterns. This is supported by Prochaska and DiClemente's (1983) stages of change model that lists maintenance as the last of five steps an individual must achieve in order for a behaviour change to occur. Arguably, it is unethical for campaign planners to induce change without providing ongoing support and tools necessary to maintain the change, especially for campaigns targeting youth audiences. Planners must include maintenance programmes in their budgets or the entire campaign itself is an ethical question mark. On the other hand, campaign planners may argue that they simply do not have the budget or other resources to maintain these campaigns in the long term.

Nationality, ethnicity and campaign effectiveness

The World Health Organization evaluated the implementation of a six-year plan (1992–8) in the European Union (EU) to prevent and reduce the harm caused by alcohol. Realizing one message does not fit all, campaign planners took into account differences in consumption levels across EU Member States. Ten strategies based on five ethical principles for the reduction of alcohol consumption and addiction formed the framework for the interventions in each country. Results showed that Italy, Poland and Spain had achieved the European target of a 25 per cent reduction (World Health Organization, 2000). Eleven other countries also reduced their overall alcohol consumption, but another 11 did not meet this goal (World Health Organization, 2000). Without access to the particulars of each campaign, it is not possible to speculate about the challenges each campaign encountered. However, this study does point to the importance of understanding cultural, ethnic and national differences when formulating social marketing campaigns, as evidenced both by the campaigns that succeeded and those that failed.

What's missing?

The international alcohol harm reduction campaigns presented here ignored a critical component in campaign development – keen awareness of the social norms of particular cultures. Social norms, as presented by Berkowitz and Perkins (1986), are embedded in one's *perceptions* of reality and not in *reality* itself. This theory can best be understood as an environmental approach that documents behaviours through survey research and then tries to reinforce correct attitudes through PR and social marketing campaigns. For instance, knowledge of peer influences, which may be based on perceived rather than actual behaviours, could help in setting up a new direction for social norms programmes.

Social marketing programmes, using social norms theory as a foundation, have been successful in many US college campuses (Rentner, 2007; 2008) and are starting to make headway internationally. In the UK, for example, the Sefton Primary Care Trust and the Centre for Public Health at Liverpool John Moores University conducted a study among teenagers to better understand the attitudes and norms of this population. The results provided a foundation for the development of its first social norms campaign (Lightowlers, Morleo and Harkins, 2009).

Kotler and Lee (2008) and other leading social marketing researchers point out that many ethical concerns can be avoided if each step of the development process includes consideration of 'issues of diversity and pluralism amidst mounting social and economic disparities within and across nations' (Guttman and Salmon, 2004, p. 533). Implementing social norms theory in social marketing campaigns is certainly not the magic bullet in solving the problem of alcohol misuse, but it does provide new possibilities for addressing the ongoing ethical issues presented here.

What else is missing? While important efforts have taken place, more open, equal and meaningful dialogue is needed to address ethical challenges in social marketing and PR disease prevention and health promotion campaigns. For example, the Centre for Corporate Responsibility of the National College of Ireland and Ireland's International Centre for Alcohol Policies hosted an event called 'Alcohol Ethics and Society: An International Conference on Rights and Responsibilities'. The conference provided a 'framework for constructive dialogue' on the role of stakeholders in the 'sometimes contentious alcohol debate, identifying ethical principles that should guide them' (O'Connor and Grant, 2002, p. 3). Both this conference and this study point to the importance of dialogue to address inequities in health policy and social marketing campaign development.

Summary

While this study focuses on one specific health issue, it has wider implications for both practitioners and researchers of social marketing health campaigns. Ethical questions raised here serve as a foundation for further defining ethical guidelines in health campaigns, a very understudied area. Researchers can further explore these ethical dilemmas in a variety of campaigns to assess if and to what extent social marketing and PR campaigns are crossing ethical lines.

As more culturally sensitive social marketing health campaigns are developed, leading to more equal dialogue between those in the centre and those moving out of the margins, communication ethics must change, adapt and become more fluid, just as culture and cultural identity are fluid and ever-changing. Evanoff suggests that ethics must be fluid, addressing 'particular problems faced by particular people in particular situations. As new problems emerge, new ethical solutions must be found; we cannot simply fall back on past ethical traditions for guidance' (2005, p. 2). He argues that 'ethical systems can be both abandoned and created ... we are constantly in the process of creating new ethical norms to deal with emergent problems, such as advances in medical technology and increased contact across cultures. Rather than seeing ethics as fixed and unchanging, a communicative approach sees ethics as dynamic and creative' (p. 2). Ethics, within the scope of intercultural and international communication, 'can be associated with an ecological model of cultural development which recognizes that cultures may proceed along different lines of development but nonetheless co-evolve through communicative relations with other cultures' (p. 2).

Social marketing health campaigns must co-evolve through increased engagement, equal participation and dialogue, ideally through leadership and advisory roles by community leaders of the targeted population to ensure effective and sensitive campaign development, implementation and sustainability. Such involvement breaks down bipolar opposition between the normative, powerful *self* and the invisible *other*, and illuminates underlying motives of campaigns by institutions in power.

References

Abbott, K.A. (2003). 'Native American Drinking Patterns and Temperance Reform', in J.S. Blocker, Jr., D.M. Fahey and I.R. Tyrrell (eds), *Alcohol and Temperance Reform in Modern History*, vol. 2. Santa Barbara, CA: ABC-CLIO, pp. 446–9.

Al-Jenaibi, B. (2008). 'The Effects of Media Campaigns on Different Cultures', *World Academy of Science, Engineering and Technology*, 46, 49–52.

Barkeeper News (2006). '"Drinkers Themselves" and "Parents" Top Misuse Blames', www.barkeeper.ie/News_Item.asp?News_ID=399, date accessed 30 November 2010.

BBC News (2008). 'Young Ignore Alcohol Campaigns', http://news.bbc.co.uk/2/hi/uk_news/7801640.stm, date accessed 30 November 2010.

Beauchamp, D. (1976). 'New Ethics for Public Health: Developing a Fair Alcohol Policy', *Journal of Health Politics, Policy and Law*, 1(3), 338–54.

Beauchamp, D. and Steinbock, B. (1999). *Exploring New Ethics for Public Health*. Oxford University Press.

Berkowitz, A.D. and Perkins, H.W. (1986). 'Problem Drinking among College Students: A Review of Recent Research', *Journal of American College Health*, 35, 21–8.

Britt, A.B. (2004). 'African Americans, Substance Abuse and Spirituality', *Minority Nurse*, summer 2004, www.minoritynurse.com/substance-abuse/african-americans-substance-abuse-and-spirituality, date accessed 30 November 2010.

Broom, G.M., Casey, S. and Ritchey, J. (2000). 'Concept and Theory of Organization-Public Relations', in J.A. Ledingham and S.D. Bruning (eds), *Public Relations as Relationship Management*. Mahwah, NJ: Lawrence Erlbaum, pp. 3–22.

Casmir, F.L. (1997). 'Ethics, Culture, and Communication: An Application of the Third-Culture Building Model to International and Intercultural Communication', in F.L. Casmir (ed.), *Ethics in Intercultural and International Communication*. Mahwah, NJ: Lawrence Erlbaum, pp. 89–117.

Carroll, T.E. (1998). 'Social Marketing and Teenage Drinking: An Evaluation of Australia's National Drug Offensive Campaigns 1988–1995 and the Competitive Communication Environment Within Which They Operated', Doctoral thesis, University of Sydney.

Ching, C. (2005). 'Native, Youth-Driven Social Marketing Campaign for HIV Prevention', paper presented at the American Public Health Association 133rd Annual Meeting & Exposition, Philadelphia, December.

Choi, H.-L. (2005). 'An Alternative View of Public Relations Ethics: Taking a Critical Perspective', paper presented at the annual meeting of the International Communication Association, New York City, May.

Christakis, N.A. (1992). 'Ethics are Local: Engaging Cross-cultural Variation in the Ethics for Clinical Research', *Social Science and Medicine*, 35(9), 1079–91.

Christakis, N.A. and Levine, R.J. (1995). 'Multinational Research', in W.T. Reich (ed.), *Encyclopedia of Bioethics*, revised edn. New York: Macmillan, pp. 1780–7.

Curtin, P.A. and Gaither, T.K. (2005). 'Privileging Identity, Difference, and Power: The Circuit of Culture as a Basis for Public Relations Practice', *Journal of Public Relations Research*, 17(2), 91–115.

——. (2008). 'International Public Relations Ethics: A Cross-disciplinary Approach to the Challenges of Globalization, Identity, and Power', paper presented at the annual meeting of the International Communication Association, Dresden, Germany, May.

Cvetkovski F. and Fry, C.L. (2006). 'Science, Ethics and the Regulation of Alcohol and Other Drug Research', *International Journal of Drug Policy*, 17(5), 450–2.

Edgett, R. (2002). 'Toward an Ethical Framework for Advocacy in Public Relations', *Journal of Public Relations Research*, 14(1), 1–26.

Ellis, B.H. (2003). 'Mobilizing Communities to Reduce Substance Abuse in Indian Country', *Journal of Psychoactive Drugs*, 35(1), 89–96.

Evanoff, R. (2005). 'A Communicative Approach to Intercultural Dialogue on Ethics', *Human Dignity and Humiliation Studies*, www.humiliationstudies.org/documents/EvanoffInterculturalEthics.pdf, date accessed 30 November 2010.

Figueiredo, L.R.A. and Venâncio, R.P. (2003). 'Colonization, European, and Drinking Behavior among Indigenous Peoples', in J.S. Blocker, Jr., D.M. Fahey and I.R. Tyrrell (eds), *Alcohol and Temperance Reform in Modern History*, vol. 1. Santa Barbara, CA: ABC-CLIO, pp. 165–8.

Fillinger, T. (2007). 'Women's Health Undercut by Administration Policies', *Foreign Service Journal*, 84(6), 47–52.
Flora, J.A., Schooler, C. and Pierson, R.M. (1997). 'Effective Health Promotion among Communities of Color: The Potential of Social Marketing', in M.E. Goldberg, M. Fishbein and S. Middlestadt (eds), *Social Marketing: Theoretical and Practical Perspectives*. Mahwah, NJ: Lawrence Erlbaum, pp. 353–73.
Guttman, N. and Salmon, C.T. (2004). 'Guilt, Fear, Stigma and Knowledge Gaps: Ethical Issues in Public Health Communication Interventions', *Bioethics*, 18, 531–52.
Habermas, J. (1984/1981). *The Theory of Communicative Action: Reason and the Rationalization of Society*, vol. 1, T. McCarthy (trans.). Boston, MA: Beacon Press.
Hackley, C., Bengry-Howell, A., Griffin, C., Mistral, W. and Szmigin, I. (2008). 'The Discursive Constitution of the UK Alcohol Problem in Safe, Sensible, Social: A Discussion of Policy Implications', *Drugs: Education, Prevention & Policy*, 1561–74.
Hall, B.J. (1997). Culture, Ethics, and Communication', in F.L. Casmir (ed.), *Ethics in Intercultural and International Communication*. Mahwah, NJ: Lawrence Erlbaum, pp. 11–42.
Hall, S. (1996). 'Minimal Selves', in H.A. Baker, M. Diawara and R.H. Lindeborg (eds), *Black British Cultural Studies*. University of Chicago Press, pp. 114–18.
Kapoor, P. (1999). 'Ritual in Development Theory as Ritual in India: A Story about Women and Modernization of the Third World', in R. Sharma and P. Bilimoria (eds), *The Other Revolution: NGO and Feminist Perspectives from South Asia*. Delhi, India: Sri Satguru, pp. 95–121.
Kellner, D. (1997). 'Critical Theory and British Cultural Studies: The Missed Articulation', in J. McGuigan (ed.), *Cultural Methodologies*. Thousand Oaks, CA: Sage, pp. 12–41.
Kotler, P. and Lee, N.R. (2008). *Social Marketing: Influencing Behaviors for Good*, 3rd edn. Thousand Oaks, CA: Sage.
Kotler, P. and Zaltman. G. (1971). 'Social Marketing: An Approach to Planned Change', *Journal of Marketing*, 35, 3–12.
Lengel, L. (1998). 'Researching the "Other": Methodological Considerations of Feminist Ethnography', *Journal of Communication Inquiry*, 22(3), 229–50.
Lengel, L. and Martin, S.C. (Forthcoming). 'Gender and Critical Intercultural Communication', in R. Halualani and T. Nakayama (eds), *Blackwell Handbook of Critical Intercultural Communication*. Oxford: Blackwell.
Lightowlers, C., Morleo, M. and Harkins, C. (2009). *Understanding Young People's Alcohol-Related Social Norms in Sefton – Interim Report*. Liverpool: Centre for Public Health.
Martin, S.C. (2008). *Devil of the Domestic Sphere: Gender, Temperance and Middle Class Ideology, 1800–1860*. DeKalb, IL: Northern Illinois University Press.
McFarlane, D. (2006). 'Reproductive Health Policies in President Bush's Second Term: Old Battles and New Fronts in the United States and Internationally', *Journal of Public Health Policy*, 27(4), 405–26.
McKee-Culpepper, M. (2005). *Social Marketing Higher Education: Challenges and Issues in Creating a Social Marketing Campaign for Traditionally Underrepresented Groups*. Minneapolis, MI: University of Minnesota Press.

Mead, G.H. (1934). 'Play, the Game, and the Generalized Other', in C.W. Morris (ed.), *Mind, Self and Society from the Standpoint of a Social Behaviorist*. University of Chicago Press, pp. 152–64.

Miller, P., Moore, D. and Strang, J. (2006). 'The Regulation of Research by Funding Bodies: An Emerging Ethical Issue for the Alcohol and Other Drug Sectors?', *International Journal of Drug Policy*, 17(1), 12–16.

Nakayama, T. (1994). 'Show/down Time: "Race," Gender, Sexuality, and Popular Culture', *Critical Studies in Mass Communication*, 11, 162–79.

Nielsen, G. (1995). 'Bakhtin and Habermas: Toward a Transcultural Ethics', *Theory and Society*, 24(6), 803–35.

O'Connor, J. and Grant, M. (2002). 'Conference Overview', in *Alcohol, Ethics & Society: An International Conference on Rights and Responsibilities*. Washington DC: International Center for Alcohol Policies and Dublin: National College of Ireland, p. 3.

Olson, S.R. (1997). 'Encountering the Other: Ethics and the Role of Media in International and Intercultural Communication', in F.L. Casmir (ed.), *Ethics in Intercultural and International Communication*. Mahwah, NJ: Lawrence Erlbaum, pp. 123–52.

Parrott, R.L. (1995). 'Presentation of Content and Linguistic Considerations', in E. Maibach and R.L. Parrott (eds), *Designing Health Messages: Approaches from Communication Theory and Public Health Practices*. Thousand Oaks, CA: Sage, pp. 7–23.

Polonec, L.D., Major, A.M. and Atwood, L.E. (2006). 'Evaluating the Believability and Effectiveness of the Social Norms Messages "Most Students Drink 0 to 4 Drinks When They Party"', *Health Communication*, 20(1), 23–4.

Prochaska, J. and DiClemente, C.C. (1983). 'Stages and Processes of Self-change of Smoking: Toward an Integrative Model of Change', *Journal of Consulting and Clinical Psychology*, 51, 390–5.

Rankin, J.G. (2003). 'From Scrubland to Vintage Wine: Australia's Response to Substance-Related Problems in the Last 40 Years', *Drug and Alcohol Review*, 22, 255–62.

Rehnman, C., Larsson, J. and Andreasson, S. (2005). 'The Beer Campaign in Stockholm – Attempting to Restrict the Availability of Alcohol to Young People', *Alcohol*, 37, 65–71.

Rentner, T.L. (2006). 'Fighting Back with Facts: Case Study in Research and Evaluation', in D. Guth and C. Marsh (eds), *Public Relations: A Values-Driven Approach*, 3rd edn. Boston, MA: Allyn & Bacon, pp. 229–31.

——. (2007). 'Experiences in Effective Prevention', in W. Dejong (ed.), *Higher Education Center for Alcohol and Other Drug Abuse and Violence Prevention*. Washington DC: US Department of Education.

——. (2008). 'Integrating Social Norms Theory in Public Relations Campaign Development', in T.L. Hansen and B.D. Neff (eds), *Public Relations: From Theory to Practice*. Boston, MA: Pearson, pp. 195–208.

Rentner, T.L. and Lengel, L. (2009). 'Alcohol-Reduction Campaigns in Comparative Perspective', refereed paper presented at the 5th International Conference on the History of Alcohol and Drugs, University of Strathclyde, Glasgow, 28 June.

Roth, N.L., Hunt, T., Stavropoulos, M. and Babik, K. (1996). 'Can't We All Just Get Along? Cultural Variables in Codes of Ethics', *Public Relations Review*, 22(2), 151–61.
Salmon, C.T. (1989). 'Campaigns for Social "Improvement": An Overview of Values, Rationales, and Impacts', in C.T. Salmon (ed.), *Information Campaigns: Balancing Social Values and Social Change*. Newbury Park, CA: Sage, pp. 19–53.
Sheldon, T. (1996). 'Dutch Anti-alcohol Campaign is Under Attack', *British Medical Journal*, 313(7069), 1349.
Smith, W.A. (1997). 'Social Marketing: Beyond the Nostalgia', in M.E. Goldberg, M. Fishbein and S.E. Middlestadt (eds), *Social Marketing: Theoretical and Practical Perspectives*. Mahwah, NJ: Lawrence Erlbaum, pp. 21–8.
Starck, K. and Kruckeberg, D. (2003). 'Ethical Obligations of Public Relations in an Era of Globalization', *Journal of Communication Management*, 8(1), 29–40.
Szmigin, I., Griffin, C., Hackley, C., Bengry-Howell, A., Weale, L. and Mistral, W. (2008). 'Reframing "Binge Drinking" as Calculated Hedonism: Empirical Evidence from the UK', *International Journal of Drug Policy*, 19(5), 359–66.
Walsh, D.C., Rudd, R.E., Moeykens, B.A. and Moloney, T.W. (1993). 'Social Marketing for Public Health', *Health Affairs*, 12(2), 104–19.
Weber, M. (2002). 'Engaging Globalization: Critical Theory and Global Political Change', *Alternatives*, 27, 301–25.
Wiebe, G.D. (1952). 'Merchandising Commodities and Citizenship on Television', *Public Opinion Quarterly*, 15, 679–91.
World Health Organization, Regional Office for Europe. (2000). *Evaluation of the European Alcohol Action Plan, 1992–1999. European Alcohol Action Plan for 2000–2005*, Research Report. Copenhagen, Denmark.

Notes

1. This analysis draws from our own research, the few studies of ethics in public health communication interventions (Beauchamp, 1976; Beauchamp and Steinbock, 1999) and related work in PR and globalization (Starck and Kruckeberg, 2003), transcultural ethics (Christakis, 1992; Christakis and Levine, 1995; Nielsen, 2005) and ethics in international and intercultural contexts (Casmir, 1997; Hall, 1997; Olson, 1997). There are a small number of studies examining ethics in the regulation of alcohol and other drug research in global contexts (Cvetkovski and Fry, 2006; Miller, Moore and Strang, 2006).
2. See, for example, critiques of the enormous changes in US domestic and global reproductive health policies during the Reagan and Bush Administrations (Filinger, 2007; McFarlane, 2006).

9
An Ethical-Theory-Based Analysis of the Social Responsibilities of Three Global Corporations: ExxonMobil, Shell and Pfizer

Cornelius B. Pratt and Wole Adamolekun

A ubiquitous societal expectation of global corporations is that they engage in activities that indicate their acknowledgment of a broad spectrum of their stakeholders' interests – regardless of their product lines. Corporations that renege on their social responsibilities – and more so those without a compelling reason – tend to lose societal and stakeholder support or, as Davis noted more than three decades ago, their social power:

> Society gave business its charter to exist, and that charter could be amended or revoked at any time if that business fails to live up to society's expectations. Therefore, if business wishes to retain its present social role and social power, it must respond to society's needs and give society what it wants. (1973, p. 314)

Corporations that fail to meet such societal expectations are also deprived of the benefits associated with being good corporate citizens. Studies have reported that environmentally sensitive companies have better operational and financial outcomes than those with dismal environmental records, because consumers base their purchasing decisions or their support of an organization's mission on a firm's willingness to be socially responsible by, for example, protecting the environment as an indicant of its corporate social performance (Berman *et al.*, 1999; Bhattacharya, Sen and Korschun, 2008; Burke and Logsdon, 1996; Cochran and Wood, 1984; Falck and Heblich, 2007; Hart, 1995; Mohr and Webb, 2001; Pava and Krausz, 1996; Russo and Fouts, 1997; Sen and Bhattacharya, 2001; Sen, Bhattacharya and Korschun, 2006; Vafeas and Nikolaou, 2001; Waddock and Graves, 1997). Consequently, multinational enterprises acknowledge the interplay between social performance and ethics by asserting their 'moral responsibility to protect the physical environment and society in which they carry out their operations' (Eweje, 2006, p. 37).

Multinational corporations engage in the traditional conceptualization of corporate social responsibility (CSR) by which they use thought leadership, that is, offering knowledge and technology critical to resolving a specific global problem, or concrete action, that is, implementing a coordinated strategy for corporate engagement on a global scale, or both (Schwab, 2008). Even so, they are also active partners in political CSR – becoming politicized, assuming an enlarged political co-responsibility in their business environments and fulfilling responsibilities once regarded as strictly the domain of governments (Scherer and Palazzo, 2007; Scherer, Palazzo and Baumann, 2006; Scherer and Smid, 2000; Snow, 2006).

Other studies, however, did not find any relationship between social responsibility and corporate financial performance (Abbott and Monsen, 1979; Alexander and Buchholz, 1978; Aupperle, Carroll and Hatfield, 1985). Still others (such as McMillan, 1996 and O'Connor and Meister, 2008) reported mixed results, the neutral impact of CSR on financial performance (for example, McWilliams and Siegel, 2000) and, in certain conditions, negative effects (Sen and Bhattacharya, 2001).

The purpose of this chapter is fourfold. Firstly, it profiles and outlines behaviours of three global corporations within the social contexts of their programmed activities. Secondly, it applies classical ethical theories to analysing those behaviours. Thirdly, based on an analysis of the ethics of the companies, it prescribes four actions specifically for Nigeria and identifies how those actions could have broad implications for regulatory policies on corporate behaviours in developing countries. Such prescriptions are cast within the overarching framework of both the Sullivan Principles and the United Nations Global Compact. The Sullivan Principles require, among other things, that companies support economic, social and political justice wherever they do business, encourage equal opportunities at all levels of employment, including racial and gender diversity on decision-making committees and boards, and help improve the quality of life for communities, workers and children with dignity and equality. Like the Sullivan Principles, corporate adherence to the Global Compact, launched by the United Nations in 2000, is a voluntary demonstration of an organization's citizenship in a global economy through its support of core values in four areas: human rights, labour standards, the environment and anti-corruption (United

Nations Global Compact, 2008). Together, the Sullivan Principles and the Compact's ten universally accepted principles are frameworks that encourage companies to commit to responsible business practices and to a sustainable global economy. Finally, the purpose of this chapter is to identify a tentative research agenda as a basis for extending theory building to developing nations.

Three global corporations – and their social responsibilities

The selection of the three corporations for this case study was based largely on their impact on Nigeria, which has the world's tenth-largest proven oil reserves and where, collectively, the companies do most of their business in Africa. Additionally, all three are formidable organizations in their product lines. ExxonMobil is the world's largest oil-prospecting and oil-refining company, and Royal Dutch Shell PLC, parent company of Shell Petroleum Development Company of Nigeria Limited (SPDC), is the second-largest. New York-based Pfizer is the world's largest research-based biopharmaceutical company that develops, manufactures, promotes and markets prescription medications worldwide. Its revenue for 2008 was $48.3 billion; on 15 October 2009, it acquired Wyeth Pharmaceuticals, which had sales of $15.7 billion in 2008.

ExxonMobil's social responsiveness

Globally, ExxonMobil has had record levels of corporate earnings since 2005, enabling it to be increasingly philanthropic. In Nigeria it donates funds to women's groups and supports the disabled, sports and debate teams in schools, bringing the monetary value of its contributions to communities in which it operates *during the past decade* to $280 million (ExxonMobil, 2009). Given its global status, this figure – of which $3.2 million was contributed in 2006 and $8.4 million in 2005 – has been publicly criticized as paltry.

Perhaps because the lynchpin in the company's programmes in social responsiveness has been philanthropy, activities such as social reporting, community engagement and consultation have been minuscule. The company's programmes in Nigeria's Niger Delta region are inadequate and pale in comparison to the region's massive community needs that go far beyond funding school debate teams and donating resources to exclusive social clubs and women's groups; there are bigger issues of a crumbling infrastructure, low food productivity and a scarcity in the supply of drinking water and of electricity.

Shell's social responsiveness

To facilitate communications with its stakeholders and host communities, Shell signed 22 Global Memoranda of Understanding in 2006 and committed $53 million to various projects in basic services, community health, economic empowerment, human capital development and maintenance of community infrastructure, particularly generating plants. Additionally, Shell provided $110 million to the Niger Delta Development Commission (a government agency set up to ensure the rapid development of the area). In addition, the company has partnerships with: (a) organizations such as the United Nations Development Programme to use publications to create awareness of community development strategies; (b) the United States Agency for International Development (USAID) in its cassava enterprises initiative; (c) Africare on malaria, HIV/AIDS and other health programmes and facilities; and (d) Globacom Telecommunications on youth empowerment through the provision of phone kiosks to rural and urban users. Under the auspices of those partnerships, it has undertaken 131 projects at a cost of $53.3 million; 92 such projects were completed in 2005. Their purpose was to strengthen relations with key community stakeholders. The projects included local content initiatives through which the company transferred three oil rigs to indigenous interests. Others supported 89 basic services (such as classrooms, roads, jetties, and water and electricity supplies), implemented 36 economic empowerment projects (for example, microcredit schemes, income-generating projects for young people and women, agriculture and transportation) and four human capital development programmes (such as scholarships and training programmes), and established two community health projects (dealing with malaria and HIV/AIDS). It appears that Shell's best efforts to assuage hard feelings in communities over the company's apparent development lapses are being overshadowed by the absence of: (a) complementary government programmes in those communities; (b) the development initiatives of other oil companies; and (c) the availability of community-grounded programmes, from which residents could benefit. Shell's poor public perception and its publicly besmirched reputation are an albatross for the oil giant.

The industry in which Shell Nigeria operates has been analysed within the context of an interface between government policy and market forces, both of which have major implications for the industry's social responsiveness. Gbadamosi, Kupolokun and Oluleye (2008) made a strong case for fully liberalizing and deregulating the downstream petroleum sector in Nigeria, arguing that the Nigerian government's earlier control of the storage, distribution and transport infrastructure bred corruption, mismanagement and inefficiency in that sector. Yet, since deregulation in 2003, problems of communication, transparency, poverty, violence, vandalism and inequity are still apparent, raising critical questions about the true value of the industry's social responsiveness, not least that of an oil giant operating in Nigeria, the world's fourth-largest producer of oil.

Pfizer's social responsiveness

Pfizer Nigeria is a leading pharmaceutical organization that operated with relatively little public visibility in Nigeria until the effects of the Trovan drug trial on some Nigerian children in Kano, a northern state, became national news in 1996. The fallout from that trial led to both Nigeria's federal and Kano state governments pressing criminal and civil charges against the pharmaceutical behemoth.

Pfizer's business in Nigeria is in the retail and wholesale trading by which small manufacturing units compound and deliver drugs to consumers. Worldwide, the company operates 70 manufacturing units in 30 countries. This is consistent with the company's mantra: 'It is not acceptable that people should be stranded without healthcare.' However, using proactive communication and building enduring relationship with communities was not one of Pfizer's major strengths. Had it been so, its Trovan controversy would not have morphed quickly into a major crisis that tested the limits of the company's reputation. Pfizer would not have been pushed back on its heels – forced to defend itself from criticism of its failed clinical trial. In essence, then, the company bore the brunt of the complacency exhibited by some multinational corporations that tend to limit their major communications to their annual general meetings and to occasional advertisements of their products. In other words, the company could have used strategic communications to inform and educate its host communities about what it is that it does, why it does it, how it does it and how sensitive it is to the cultural, religious and social nuances of communities. Even though Pfizer insists that its business interests in Nigeria have 'provided significant benefit to some Nigeria's youngest citizens' (Stephens, 2007, p. A10), the legal battle over Trovan seems to contradict this notion. Pfizer further insists that its 1996 Trovan clinical test was conducted in a 'responsible and ethical way consistent with the company's abiding commitment to patient safety' (Stephens, 2007, p. A10). Media reports and coverage of the crisis were suggestive of the limits of Pfizer's community relations programmes. Regardless of the outcome of the Trovan lawsuit, the seeming absence of consistent (and sustained) communications by the company could determine the implications of the case for the corporate behaviour of multinational enterprises (MNEs) in developing nations. Even though Pfizer has an historical involvement in drug manufacturing, its CSR roles are not well known. Rather, what seem to be widely known are litigation and recriminations about the fallout from a botched trial. Yet, drugs produced by Pfizer have helped to save lives, have strengthened national wellness and have contributed in no small measure to community projects.

Classical ethical theories and global organizational behaviours

Each of the three corporations in this qualitative case study has had its behaviours challenged on both ethical and legal grounds. The British Royal Society, for example, argued that ExxonMobil spread 'inaccurate and misleading' information about climate change and that it had financed interest groups, such as the Competitive Enterprise Institute, the American Enterprise Institute, the International Policy Network and the Center for the Study of Carbon Dioxide and Global Change, to encourage them to misinform the public about the issue (Nocera, 2007; Timmons, 2006). Similarly, the Union of Concerned Scientists accused the company of not taking the threat of global warming more seriously and claimed that it was manipulating public opinion on the seriousness of the threat (Krauss, 2007, 2008).

Shell faced a major international environmental crisis in 1995 when its plan to sink an obsolete oil-storage facility – the Brent Spar – in the North Atlantic ignited the fury of non-governmental organizations (NGOs), particularly Greenpeace, and affronted the world conscience over its planned use of an ocean floor as a dumping ground for industrial waste. The company has also been criticized for its neutrality over the execution of Ken Saro-Wiwa, an anti-oil company social activist. SPDC continues to face ethical and legal challenges in its operations in Nigeria's Niger Delta, where charges have been based on environmental violations and devastation: gas flaring, high-pressure, above-ground pipelines that crisscross prime agricultural land, oil spillage, oil waste and flooding (Eweje, 2006). Victims of oil pollution have filed three lawsuits against Shell Nigeria and Royal Dutch Shell PLC, charging both companies with polluting drinking water and agricultural land (including fish ponds) in Oruma, a village in Nigeria's Niger Delta. The first of those lawsuits was heard at The Hague in December 2009. Thus, its reputation has been sliding so fast that 'BP Amoco is working hard in Angola to avoid Shell's errant ways in Nigeria' (Ruggie, 2002, p. 35). Both ExxonMobil and Shell, like much of the oil industry, are the target of charges stemming from environmental degradation and human rights abuses (Okeke, 2008).

If both oil companies were acting in accordance with teleological (or consequence-based) ethics, they would evaluate their decisions on at least two grounds: ethical egoism and utilitarianism. Were the companies' actions predicated more on their own self-interest (egoism) or on their desire to promote the best interests of most people, that is, on maximizing stakeholders' happiness or on minimizing their pain (utilitarianism)? On the other hand, to the degree that both companies violated their social trust, it is reasonable to conclude that they defied a sense of duty, that is, adherence to their obligation to society, rules, maxims or principles (all elements of deontology). The companies' actions cannot be justified by Aristotelian ethics by which their actions could be deemed virtuous, that is, exemplifying justice, temperance and courage in promoting societal well-being while avoiding extreme behaviours.

It is plausible that the oil companies were enamoured with ethical relativism, by which the morality of their actions did not blindly follow maxims or moral rules. Protestant theologian Joseph Fletcher (1966) argues that a morally justifiable action does not necessarily follow moral rules blindly but is based on love, sensitivity to situations and the moral sentiments of involved parties. Merrill takes issue with this moral reasoning, arguing that: 'When the matter of ethics is watered down to subjectivism, to situations or contexts, it loses all meaning as ethics' (1990, p. 169).

A key question that arises from the profiles of the social responsibility programmes of the three corporations is whether they apply the same CSR principles in a Third World nation as they do in both Europe and North America, or whether they subscribe to ethical relativism, justifying their actions on geographical and cultural grounds. A case study of the operations of a Canadian oil company in Sudan found that the lack of regulations of Canadian corporations abroad resulted in corporate actions incongruent with Canada's human security agenda (Blackwood, 2004). Yet a criterion of deontological ethics is that an act must be universalized as a measure of its ethicalness. It has been argued that differences in the institutional structures, political legacies and cultures of Europe and the US affect societal expectations of CSRs and are important in explaining the influence of NGOs in the policy-making process vis-à-vis CSRs (Doh and Guay, 2006). It is therefore plausible that, to a degree, existing legislation and regulatory processes, by which corporate conduct in the developing countries is determined, are primarily toothless. So, MNEs in those countries exhibit behaviours that are antithetical to the Sullivan Principles and to the United Nations Global Compact.

Pfizer Nigeria had been accused of using a meningitis epidemic in 1996 to push through a sloppily conducted drug study that contributed to the death of some and to infirmities in others. Its defence was that it was responding clinically to a meningitis outbreak in Nigeria. According to the charges filed in court, Pfizer made no effort to inform and educate the public, yet insisted that the 1996 Trovan clinical test was conducted in a 'responsible and ethical way consistent with the company's abiding commitment to patient safety' (Stephens, 2007, p. A10). The company could have offered a three-pronged argument: firstly, that its drug caused fewer deaths (five) than those caused by the use of the standard medication; secondly, that it did not knowingly administer an unsafe drug in a clinical trial – in fact, it had cautioned subjects through nurses and clinical technicians that there was a possibility of adverse effects from participating in the trials; and, finally, that the company was largely driven by a morally – and clinically – just cause: to stymie the devastating effects of a spinal disease. To stand idly by was unconscionable and an affront to its guiding principle on healthcare. It was better to attack a scourge than to do absolutely nothing. Drawing upon classical ethical theory, Pfizer adopted a utilitarian perspective: to seek the greatest happiness for the greatest number. But its actions were short on virtue ethics and on the three cardinal tests of deontology: that the moral rule on which it was based should: (a) be universalized, which means it should serve as a guide to every organization's conduct; that is, a standard should be applied that is universally valid and applicable to *all* organizations or doers; (b) treat people as ends in themselves, not as means to an end; and (c) apply voluntarily and autonomously to each organization without its being imposed by the state or by any extra-organizational interests.

On 30 July 2009, Pfizer reached an out-of-court settlement to pay $75 million to Nigeria's Kano state government. This settlement allocated $35 million to compensate victims and their families, $30 million to invest in healthcare initiatives in the state and $10 million to cover litigation costs incurred by the state. State government officials interpreted that settlement as the company's admission of culpability and Nigeria's federal government is still seeking about $6 billion in damages against the company.

Within the context of classical ethical theories, then, and to the degree that all three corporations promote more pleasure than pain (utilitarianism), even as they treat people as means rather than as ends, as in Pfizer's Trovan case (in violation of Kant's categorical imperative), the ethics of their practices raises serious implications for corporate communication geared towards building a corporate reputation of socially sensitive organizations. Similarly, to the degree that both oil companies will be hard-pressed to argue that their pricing practices, by which they accrue large profits, should serve as a guide for everyone's conduct, their corporate communication lacks conformity with deontological ethics. Does Pfizer's 1996 clinical drug trial in Nigeria constitute a breach of ethics, even though the survival rate for children given its experimental drug, Trovan, was higher than that for the control group?

SPDC's communications are too often restricted to official publications (such as annual reports) and rarely go through the various electronic and print media used to communicate the company's socially responsible practices broadly. Similarly, ExxonMobil's socially responsible programmes in Nigeria are limited to awarding scholarships, initiating community projects and offering donations to various causes. And the fact that its activities are mostly offshore, necessitating limited contact with communities, does not justify its failure to build broader relationships that could ensure successful and sustainable business associations and interactions.

Four prescriptions

The failure of all three companies to demonstrate consistently their adherence to the Sullivan Principles and to the United Nations Global Compact suggests four prescriptions, each of which has implications for communication management in MNEs. Firstly, MNEs, particularly in their operations in global environments, need to consider moving from the classic one-way communication model to expanding their communication programmes to emphasizing community participation and relationship-building – that is, encouraging communities to participate as investigators, planners, producers, performers and evaluators.

Such participatory communication has four strengths. Firstly, because it is embedded within locales, it is viewed as an active part of a civil society, enabling communities to participate extensively through using alternative media in public issues that are at the core of community well-being. Carpentier writes that: 'Alternative media are often part of large civil society networks, and act as meeting points and catalysts for a variety of organizations and movements' (2008, p. 241). Such media can be *the* standard medium for delivering and gathering corporate news.

Secondly, community participation helps MNEs delineate between participation *in* the communication process and participation *through* the communication process. Following Carpentier's assertion on the 'need to distinguish between participation *in* the media and *through* the media' (2008, p. 243), we define community participation *in* the corporate communication process as that which involves the exertion of community power and influence on the whole gamut of communication – from fact-finding to programme evaluation. This means that communities serve as corporate peers in focus groups, indepth interviews and on idea juries and advisory committees; they play vital roles in decision making on how and where programme evaluation will occur and on how results will eventually be used.

Participation *through* the communication process includes how communities, organized or otherwise, 'can communicate their views, represent themselves and enter into deliberations and debates in a series of mediated public spaces' (Carpentier, 2008, p. 243). They can use both mainstream and social-networking media such as Facebook and Twitter.

The third strength is that community participation acknowledges limitations in a process in which communication 'topics are chosen in the same way, by professional communicators, and targeted towards the apparent needs and interests of the audience' (Berrigan, 1979, p. 7).

The fourth strength is that it engenders relationship-building by providing immeasurable opportunities that nurture organization–public relationships and loyalties, both of which have major implications for effective communication management and its effect.

In summary, MNEs are mostly focused on using shop-worn, even though occasionally effective, communication methods in their relationships with communities. But ideally communities need to be continually reassured that corporate interest is indeed synonymous with community interest.

The preceding premise leads logically to the second prescription, which emphasizes the role of territorialized and extra-territorialized movements and organizations in requiring the modification of corporate behaviour, as has been the case in Nigeria's volatile Niger

Delta region. Such organizations and movements promote their vision of socially responsible business practices, take a seat at the negotiation table and begin to have major impacts on corporate management, strategy and governance (Doh and Guay, 2004, 2006; Doh and Teegen, 2002, 2003).

In Nigeria, NGOs and the media have organized themselves into a critical group of activists that persuades MNEs to be transparently responsive to the need of the communities in which they operate. They have accomplished this by using persistent media campaigns, by filing lawsuits and by encouraging similar interest groups to follow in their footsteps through offering awards and recognizing them publicly for their public support of responsible corporate management.

The third prescription is based on the prevalence of weak government legislation and enforcement that should be strengthened to assess punitive and compensatory damages against corporations that refuse to act responsibly. This possibility hinges on the expansion and sustenance of democratic governance in Nigeria and on the increasing realization by the MNEs that business cannot be conducted as usual. There are no specific regulations on CSR in Nigeria. What are found in the statutes are implied laws that seek to ensure that individual rights and freedoms are not violated. Recently, however, the Niger Delta imbroglio made legislation on CSR a compelling option for the country's federal government. Thus, both Nigeria's House of Representatives and the Senate are considering a draft bill on CSR entitled 'A Bill for an Act to Provide for the Establishment of the Corporate Social Responsibility Commission', which will control and regulate the activities of corporate organizations in Nigeria. It defines CSR as 'the obligation of an organization to seek actions that protect and improve the welfare of the society along with its interest' ('A Bill for an Act', n.d.). It seeks to ensure that corporations and companies accomplish the following:

- contribute to economic, social and environmental progress with a view to achieving sustainable development of the affected communities;
- respect the human rights of those affected by their activities in keeping with Nigeria's international *obligations* and commitments;
- encourage local capacity through close cooperation with the local community, including local business interests, as well as appropriately developing links between their corporate activities and the benefit of the communities;

- develop and apply effective self-regulatory practices and management systems that foster a relationship of confidence and mutual trust between enterprises and the societies in which they operate;
- support and uphold good governance principles and practice, and abstain from any improper involvement in local political activities.

Oversight will be provided by a Governing Board of the Commission, which will create a standard for CSR that is consistent with international standards and will integrate social responsibility into Nigeria's trade policies while respecting World Trade Organization rules.

However, given the present realities, this could be one of the solutions to the present challenges the oil-producing industry faces, because no self-respecting multinational company will wilfully violate the laws of the countries in which it operates.

The fourth prescription, and the least likely to occur, is an internal monitoring, or self-regulation, of corporate behaviour. This has yet to produce tangible results in Nigeria. Granted, global corporations had a good understanding of the interface between an environment conducive to business and its financial health. Therefore, it behooves corporations to explore avenues to project the very best in their practices as they acknowledge consistently the mutual dependence of their corporate interests and of those of their stakeholders.

Hartley (2005) analyses classic ethical violations, identifies paragons of good ethical practices and suggests four pointers for corporate behaviour modification: firstly, he recommends that multinationals eschew a heavy-handed stance in other countries, especially those in the Third World; secondly, being supportive of the host country will be compatible with the long-term interests of MNEs; thirdly, MNEs now have responsibilities as ambassadors of their countries of origin, whose images are affected by corporate practices; and, finally, non-management staff should increasingly resist the questionable standards of higher management. All of these actions can be internally accomplished by realigning corporate and community interests and monitoring them regularly.

Implications for a tentative research agenda for theory building

The Sullivan Principles and the United Nations Global Compact provide the framework for the equitable use of corporate resources in responding adequately to their responsibilities to communities affected by their operations in particular and to the global community in general. Together, they require that corporations, among other things: (a) support universal human rights; (b) promote equal opportunity; (c) respect the freedom of association; (d) fight corruption; (e) protect human health and the environment; and (f) improve community life. This chapter concludes that asymmetrical (and occasionally unethical) CSR communications with key publics and audiences justify developing a (prescriptive) template that ensures that global corporations with major operations in Third World countries can improve their community-oriented practices, communicate their programmes more effectively to their audiences and publics, and maximize their own benefits from their social programmes. The behaviours of the three companies profiled in this chapter suggest utilitarian considerations – that is, they acted according to Mill's (1861) principle of utility, by which morality is determined by the greatest balance of good over evil and by doer-receiver happiness as the end of human action. Almost equally, those behaviours raise questions that could be framed within Kant's categorical imperative, which requires actions to demonstrate clearly where corporate loyalties, duties and responsibilities lie, and that all rational human beings be treated as ends in themselves, not merely as means. Are these loyalties, then, conditioned by corporate duty to a dominant coalition, to a broad spectrum of stakeholders or to society at large?

It is hoped that corporate leaders would consciously and strategically employ best communication practices in running their organizations. In much of Africa, and particularly in Nigeria, most organizations tend to interpret the value of corporate communications within the context of crises management, far removed from their emerging ongoing role in relationship-building in terms of brand loyalty and reputation enhancement. ExxonMobil and Shell, for example, evaded their responsibility by using scapegoatism in their reactive denial strategies in their crisis responses to the Ogoni people (Olaniran and Williams, 2008). Similarly, the top 100 information technology companies in India tend not to use creative and proactive CSR on their websites (Chaudhri and Wang, 2007). Yet the growing literature in relationship management alerts us to the importance of the relations with publics in public relations (Johansson, 2007), of a broadened view of corporation–stakeholder interaction (Haas, 2003) and of interpersonal communication theory as a guide to managing relationships, analysing interactions and establishing mutual trust with and confidence in stakeholders (Coombs, 2001; Ledingham, 2003; Toth, 2000). This inconsistency is borne out by the growing evidence on the fallout from perfunctory, tactical communication, bereft of strong relationships, and by its consequences. As for entire CSR concept, it is left largely to multinational corporations, banks, telecommunications companies and growing national conglomerates. These multinational corporations are too cautious to communicate as much as they should, and their mode of communication is essentially targeted at the elites. The grassroots approach to communication, advocated by some of these companies, is more idealistic than pragmatic.

Several areas for research and, by extension, for theory-building are manifested in this CSR analysis. Firstly, what is the ethical rationale for the companies' approach to corporate communications? As Blackwood (2004) has reported, Canadian companies demonstrated double standards in their international operations, calling into question their undermining of, say, ethical universalism in their social responsibility programmes in Africa. Are such standards indicative of ethical relativism as the dominant ethical theory at play in the operations of MNEs in developing countries? In essence, what dominant ethical theory is manifested in the behaviours of MNEs in developing countries? Secondly, how does this rationale affect the perceptions of the corporate brand among key stakeholders? Thirdly, what dominant moral reason is indicated in ethical decision making associated with corporate operations, insofar as the latter affect other sectors of corporate behaviours and stakeholder relationships? Is such decision making consistent with, say, the three tests of deontology as outlined in this chapter? Fourthly, what core corporate values ensure that stakeholders will respond positively to corporate actions? Finally, what are the valid and reliable measures of CSR and its effects on corporate performance? The search for answers to those questions can be appropriately grounded in classical ethical theory, which can serve as the arbiter of corporate actions and conscience, and as the building blocks for theoretical searchlights on and guides to more CSR actions, particularly in fledgling, developing and emerging economies.

References

'A Bill for an Act to Provide for the Establishment of the Corporate Social Responsibility Commission (n.d.). Sponsored by Senator Uche Chukwumerije, Abia North, in the National Assembly of the Federal Republic of Nigeria.

Abbott, W.F. and Monsen, J.R. (1979). 'On the Measurement of Corporate Social Responsibility', *Academy of Management Journal*, 22, 501–15.

Alexander, G.J. and Buchholz, R.A. (1978). 'Corporate Social Responsibility and Stock Market Performance', *Academy of Management Journal*, 21, 479–86.

Aupperle, K.E., Carroll, A.B. and Hatfield, J.D. (1985). 'An Empirical Examination of the Relationship between Corporate Social Responsibility and Profitability', *Academy of Management Journal*, 28, 446–63.

Berman, S.A., Wicks, A., Kotha, S. and Jones, T. (1999). 'Does Stakeholder Orientation Matter? The Relationship between Stakeholder Management Models and Firm Financial Performance', *Academy of Management Journal*, 42, 488–506.

Berrigan, F.J. (1979). 'Community Communications: The Role of Community Media in Development', Reports and Papers on Mass Communication No. 90. Paris: UNESCO.

Bhattacharya, C.B., Sen, S. and Korschun, D. (2008). 'Using Corporate Social Responsibility to Win the War for Talent', *MIT Sloan Management Review*, 49, 37–44.

Blackwood, E. (2004). 'Globalization and Corporate Social Responsibility: The Need for Mandatory Regulation of Foreign Direct Investment in Conflict Zones', unpublished master's thesis, University of Calgary.

Burke, L. and Logsdon, J.M. (1996). 'How Corporate Social Responsibility Pays Off', *Long Range Planning*, 29, 495–502.

Carpentier, N. (2008). 'The Belly of the City: Alternative Communicative City Networks', *International Communication Gazette*, 70, 237–55.

Chaudhri, V. and Wang, J. (2007). 'Communicating Corporate Social Responsibility on the Internet: A Case Study of the Top 100 Information Technology Companies in India', *Management Communication Quarterly*, 21, 232–47.

Christians, C. (2004). 'Ethical and Normative Perspectives', in J.D.H. Downing, D. McQuail, P. Schlesinger and E. Wartella (eds), *The Sage Handbook of Media Studies*. Thousand Oaks, CA: Sage, pp. 19–39.

Cochran, P.L. and Wood, R.A. (1984). 'Corporate Social Responsibility and Financial Performance', *Academy of Management Journal*, 27, 42–56.

Coombs, W.T. (2001). 'Interpersonal Communication and Public Relations', in R.L. Heath (ed.), *Handbook of Public Relations*. Thousand Oaks, CA: Sage, pp. 105–14.

Davis, K. (1973). 'The Case for and against Business Assumption of Social Responsibilities', *Academy of Management Journal*, 16, 312–22.

Doh, J.P. and Guay, T.R. (2004). 'Globalization and Corporate Social Responsibility: How Non-governmental Organizations Influence Labor and Environmental Codes of Conduct', *Management International Review*, 44(2), 7–29.

——. (2006). 'Corporate Social Responsibility, Public Policy, and NGO Activism in Europe and the United States: An Institutional-Stakeholder Perspective', *Journal of Management Studies*, 43, 47–73.

Doh, J.P. and Teegen, H. (2002). 'Nongovernmental Organizations as Institutional Actors in International Business: Theory and Implications', *International Business Review*, 11, 665–84.

——. (2003). *Globalization and NGOs: Transforming Business, Governments, and Society*. Westport, CT: Praeger.

Eweje, G. (2006). 'Environmental Costs and Responsibilities Resulting from Oil Exploitation in Developing Countries: The Case of the Niger Delta of Nigeria', *Journal of Business Ethics*, 69, 27–56.

ExxonMobil (2009). 'ExxonMobil: Proudly Supporting Nigeria's Economic and Social Development', *The Guardian*, 2 December, pp. 32–3.
Falck, O., and Heblich, S. (2007). 'Corporate Social Responsibility: Doing Well by Doing Good', *Business Horizons*, 50, 247–54.
Fletcher, J. (1966). *Situation Ethics: The New Morality*. Philadelphia: Westminster Press.
Gbadamosi, R., Kupolokun, F. and Oluleye, O. (2008). *A Story of the Deregulation of the Nigerian Downstream Oil Sector*. Abuja, Nigeria: Petroleum Products Pricing Regulatory Agency.
Haas, T. (2003). 'Toward an "Ethic of Futurity": Corporate Social Responsibility in the Age of the Risk Society', *Management Communication Quarterly*, 16, 612–17.
Hart, S. (1995). 'A Natural Resource-based View of the Firm', *Academy of Management Review*, 20, 986–1014.
Hartley, R.F. (2005). *Business Ethics Mistakes and Successes*. Hoboken, NJ: John Wiley & Sons.
Johansson, C. (2007). 'Goffman's Sociology: An Inspiring Resource for Developing Public Relations Theory', *Public Relations Review*, 33, 275–80.
Krauss, C. (2007). 'Exxon Accused of Trying to Mislead Public', *New York Times*, 4 January, p. 7C.
——. (2008). 'Rockefellers Seek Change at Exxon', *New York Times*, 27 May, p. 1C.
Ledingham, J.A. (2003). 'Explicating Relationship Management as a General Theory of Public Relations', *Journal of Public Relations Research*, 15, 181–98.
McMillan, G.S. (1996). 'Corporate Social Investments: Do They Pay?', *Journal of Business Ethics*, 15, 309–14.
McWilliams, A. and Siegel, D. (2000). 'Corporate Social Responsibility and Financial Performance: Correlation or Misspecification?', *Strategic Management Journal*, 21, 603–9.
Merrill, J.C. (1990). *The Imperative of Freedom: A Philosophy of Journalistic Autonomy*, 2nd edn. New York: Freedom House.
Mill, J.S. (1861). *Utilitarianism*. London: J.M. Dent & Sons.
Moemeka, A.A. (1983). 'Radio's Role in Non-formal Education', *Prospects: Quarterly Review of Education*, 13, 517–27.
——. (2006). 'Radio Strategies for Community Development: A Critical Analysis', in A. Gumucio-Dagron and T. Tufte (eds), *Communication for Social Change Anthology: Historical and Contemporary Readings*. South Orange, NJ: Communication for Social Change Consortium, Inc., pp. 432–41.
Mohr, L. and Webb, D.J. (2001). 'Do Consumers Expect Companies to be Socially Responsible? The Impact of Corporate Social Responsibility on Buying Behavior', *Journal of Consumer Affairs*, 35, 45–72.
Murray, J. (2004). 'Corporate Social Responsibility: An Overview of Principles and Practices', http://digitalcommons.ilr.cornell.edu/codes/5, date accessed 1 December 2010.
Nocera, J. (2007). 'Exxon Mobil Just Wants to be Loved', *New York Times*, 10 February, p. 1C.
O'Connor, A. and Meister, M. (2008). 'Corporate Social Responsibility Attribute Rankings', *Public Relations Review*, 34, 49–50.

Okeke, C.N. (2008). 'The Second Scramble for Africa's Oil and Mineral Resources: Blessing or Curse?', *The International Lawyer*, 42, 193–209.

Olaniran, B.A. and Williams, D.E. (2008). 'Applying Anticipatory and Relational Perspectives to the Nigerian Delta Region Oil Crisis', *Public Relations Reviews*, 34, 57–9.

Pava, M.L. and Krausz, J. (1996). 'The Association between Corporate Social Responsibility and Financial Performance: The Paradox of Social Cost', *Journal of Business Ethics*, 15, 321–57.

Ruggie, J.G. (2002). 'The Theory and Practice of Learning Networks: Corporate Social Responsibility and the Global Compact', *Journal of Corporate Citizenship*, 5 (Spring), 27–36.

Russo, M. and Fouts, P. (1997). 'A Resource-based Perspective on Corporate Environmental Performance and Profitability', *Academy of Management Journal*, 40, 534–59.

Scherer, A.G. and Palazzo, G. (2007). 'Toward a Political Conception of Corporate Responsibility: Business and Society Seen from a Habermasian Perspective', *Academy of Management Review*, 32, 1096–120.

Scherer, A.G., Palazzo, G. and Baumann, D. (2006). 'Global Rules and Private Actors. Toward a New Role of the TNC in Global Governance', *Business Ethics Quarterly*, 16, 505–32.

Scherer, A.G. and Smid, M. (2000). 'The Downward Spiral and the U.S. Model Principles. Why MNEs Should Take Responsibility for the Improvement of World-wide Social and Environmental Conditions', *Management International Review*, 40, 351–71.

Schwab, K. (2008). 'Global Corporate Citizenship: Working with Governments and Civil Society', *Foreign Affairs*, 87(1), 107–18.

Sen, S. and Bhattacharya, C.B. (2001). 'Does Doing Good Always Lead to Doing Better? Consumer Reactions to Corporate Social Responsibility', *Journal of Marketing Research*, 38, 225–43.

Sen, S., Bhattacharya, C.B. and Korschun, D. (2006). 'The Role of Corporate Social Responsibility in Strengthening Multiple Stakeholder Relationships: A Field Experiment', *Journal of the Academy of Marketing Science*, 34, 158–66.

Shell (2005). *Shell Nigeria Annual Report – People and the Environment.* The Shell Petroleum Development Company of Nigeria: Lagos.

——. (2006). *Shell Nigeria Annual Report – People and the Environment.* The Shell Petroleum Development Company of Nigeria: Lagos.

Snow, C., Jr. (2006). 'Public Diplomacy Practitioners: A Changing Cast of Characters', *Journal of Business Strategy*, 27, 18–21.

Stephens, J. (2007). 'Pfizer Faces Criminal Charges in Nigeria', *Washington Post*, 30 May, p. A10.

Timmons, H. (2006). 'British Science Group Says Exxon Misrepresents Climate Issues', *New York Times*, 21 September, p. 2C.

Toth, E.L. (2000). 'From Personal Influence to Interpersonal Influence: A Model for Relationship Management', in J.A. Ledingham and S.D. Bruning (eds), *Public Relations as Relationship Management: A Relational Approach to Public Relations.* Mahwah, NJ: Lawrence Erlbaum, pp. 205–19.

United Nations Global Compact Office (2008). *Corporate Citizenship in the World Economy*, UN Publication No. DC2-612, www.unglobalcompact.org/docs/news_events/8.1/GC_brochure_FINAL.pdf, date accessed 1 December 2010.

Vafeas, N. and Nikolaou, V. (2001). 'The Association between Corporate Environmental and Financial Performance', *Advances in Public Interest Accounting*, 8, 195–214.

Waddock, S.A. and Graves, S.B. (1997). 'The Corporate Social Performance-Financial Performance Link', *Strategic Management Journal*, 18, 303–19.

10
Cultural and Historical Aspects of Media Transparency in Russia

Katerina Tsetsura

Media transparency is a building block for professional media development based on trust between the media and the audience (Tsetsura and Kruckeberg, 2009). Journalists must be open and thus transparent with their audiences (Kovach, 2001). Honesty, independence of opinion, fair judgment and other traditional news values are the main factors that define journalistic principles and media credibility. If one or several of these principles are violated, the audience has a right to know what influenced journalistic decisions (Craig, 1999, 2006, 2008). The absence of any direct and indirect influence is central to the concept of media transparency. A lack of disclosure of influences and constraints placed on journalists, editors and the media in general in which articles or programmes appear is often referred to as non-transparency (Tsetsura and Grynko, 2009). Publishing news in exchange for a payment or a favour compromises a traditional function of mass media in a democratic society and undermines the media's roles as gatekeepers (Boynton, 2007; Craig, 2007; Pasti, 2005).

Non-transparent practices exist worldwide (Tsetsura and Kruckeberg, 2009). Understanding how diverse information sources, such as public relations (PR) practitioners who work for organizations, can influence the news is at the heart of media non-transparency studies (Tsetsura and Kruckeberg, 2009; Tsetsura and Grynko, 2009; Klyueva, 2008). The growing amount of research on the topic (Kruckeberg and Tsetsura, 2003; Tsetsura, 2005a, 2005b; Klyueva, 2008; Tsetsura and Grynko, 2009) defined the phenomenon of media non-transparency as any form of payment for or influence on news coverage. Media non-transparency has also been known as cash for news coverage (Kruckeberg and Tsetsura, 2003), media bribery (Tsetsura, 2005b), envelope journalism (Shafer, 1990), paid news (Tsetsura and Zuo, 2009) and media opacity

(Tsetsura and Kruckeberg, 2009). Many practitioners use slang words to refer to this phenomenon: *zakazukha* in Russia (Holmes, 2001), *jinsa* in Ukraine (Tsetsura and Grynko, 2009) and *pay-for-play* in the US (Tsetsura, 2008). This chapter addresses the cultural and historical particularities of PR, specifically media relations, in Russia to address media non-transparency and to investigate why media non-transparency is so widespread in Russia.

The influence of journalism on the development of PR in Russia

Understanding the history of journalism in Russia is essential in order to understand how media practices developed in this country. Traditionally, freedom of the press has not been the first and foremost right of Russian citizens (McReynolds, 1991). The very first newspaper in Russia, *Sankt-Peterburgskie Vedomosti* (*Saint Petersburg Gazette*), was started by the order of Tsar Peter the Great and was transferred to the control of the state-run Academy of Sciences in 1703 (Zassoursky, 2004). Because of the political and economic changes, post-Soviet Russian journalism has undergone several crucial changes, but the challenges that it faced were still very much a part of the historical baggage (Ragozina, 2007). The post-Soviet media system, with a strong emphasis on economic independence and market orientation, contributed to the development of PR in Russia. The origins of Russian PR were in journalism, as the very first PR practitioners were journalists (Tsetsura, 2003) and PR theory and practice were built on journalistic traditions (Tsetsura, 2004).

Each of three major periods into which the history of Russian journalism can be divided has contributed to the unique development of journalism and PR in Russia (Cassara *et al.*, 2004). The three periods are divided up as follows: the first is the pre-Soviet period from the eighteenth to the early twentieth centuries; the Soviet period covers 1917 to 1985, which includes the Soviet contribution to the development of journalism and the beginning of the *perestroika* period; and finally there is the Gorbachev and post-Soviet period (1985 to 2000), during which there was free speech without regulation, rules or restrictions. Recently, a new period was identified as the Putin-era period, which covers the development of journalism from 2000 until the present day (Koltsova, 2006).

When the Bolsheviks came to power in 1917, a state monopoly on advertising was put in place to deprive the commercial press of its main source of income. The young Soviet government believed that a truly free press could only be formed without any capitalistic or market-driven principles and influences (Koltsova, 2006). However, before too long, the Soviet period of Russian journalism was characterized by a combination of extreme media control and censorship, and little attention to public opinion about the media (Koltsova, 2006). During the Soviet era, the mass media was treated as a means of mass information and propaganda, and the media's function was to report government news and to propagate socialist ideals (McNair, 1991).

A true rebirth of the principles of objectivity and openness in journalism happened when Gorbachev initiated the *Glasnost* campaign in 1984. The new information policy established the principles of freedom of information, pluralism of opinions and the open exchange of ideas among citizens (Zhirkov, 2001). Economic and political reforms led to a free market economy and opened doors to the development of all market-driven industries, including advertising, marketing and PR (Tsetsura, 2004). Journalists were the first in Russia to start working in the field of PR (Goregin and Nikolaev, 1996). The first and foremost function of these new PR practitioners was to deliver information to the mass media, in a manner similar to the Western tradition of media relations (Goregin and Nikolaev, 1996). And because these journalists knew how the media system worked in Russia, they were the best professionals for this new job.

As the markets developed in Russia, concerns over corporate ownership and the commercialization of journalism became inevitable. Pasti (2005) argued that journalists in the 1990s perceived journalism as a handy PR tool which could benefit influential groups rather than as an objective profession, an independent entity that served society. Harro-Loit and Saks (2006) demonstrated that the commercialization of journalism led to the blurring of borders between journalism and advertising in Eastern Europe. The continuing commercialization and economic pressures led to the reconceptualization of PR and journalism in Russia and to the rapid development of media non-transparency.

Understanding media non-transparency

Credibility in the media lies at the root of independent, objective and responsible journalism. But what exactly constitutes objectivity and how independent can the modern media, self-supported by advertisers' money in some countries and subsidized by governments in others, be? And what role does journalistic integrity play in the modern world of materialism? In the investigative report 'Money vs. Ethics: A Balancing Act' published by the International Press Institute in 2003, journalist Mike McGraw tried to answer these difficult but important questions. He provided specific examples of how media professionals could discredit themselves by accepting bribes from their information sources. He demonstrated that media bribery became one of the most difficult problems to overcome.

In the contemporary information era, editors, reporters and specialized journalists become increasingly dependent on their sources to provide them with accurate, up-to-date and relevant information that becomes the basis for news. This information is fast, detailed and current. Most importantly, this information is free. The journalists do not need to hunt for information any longer; they often only need to perform their gatekeeping role of deciding whether to distribute the information through the media channels and by so doing to set the agenda. And we, as a public, rely on journalists to decide what information is the most important, most newsworthy and most relevant for us out of the constant huge flow of information.

As such, we expect the media to follow several essential information gatekeeping principles: independence of opinion, fair and honest judging of facts and reporting, and freedom from outside non-media influences. Most importantly, we expect the media to separate for us on the pages of newspapers and magazines and during its radio and TV programmes which pieces are truly journalistic materials and which have a commercial or advertising character, that is, material paid for by sources of information. This is what we call a sense of ethical behaviour. A special case of media non-transparency has for a long time been at the centre of debates on the nature of the relationship between publicity materials and PR media relations practices. Offering services and paying cash for publishing publicity pieces, news releases and other types of materials often becomes standard practice in many countries (Kruckeberg and Tsetsura, 2003).

Media non-transparency is defined as any form of payment for news coverage or any influence on the editorial and journalistic decision-making process that is not clearly stated or identified in the final media product (Tsetsura and Grynko, 2009). Media non-transparency instances were found and identified in many countries (Kruckeberg and Tsetsura, 2003). Research shows that media non-transparency is a serious problem in the Eastern European countries, including Estonia, Poland, Russia and Ukraine (Tsetsura, 2005b; Pasti, 2005; Harro-Loit and Saks, 2006; Klyueva, 2008; Tsetsura and Grynko, 2009; Klyueva and Tsetsura, in press; Tsetsura and Zuo, 2009). A number of previous studies have showed that paying cash for news coverage and placing advertising in the media in exchange for news coverage, as well as providing gifts, free meals or free trips to journalists and editors in exchange for the publication of material in which real sources of influence are not disclosed, are practices that are present in much of the world. In most of the world, however, such practices of media non-transparency are condemned by both PR practitioners and journalists alike (Tsetsura, 2008).

Some critics advocate that such non-transparent media practices are part of the culture in some places around the world, but no studies have shown that culture has influenced the decision-making processes of journalists and PR practitioners in the case of media non-transparency. Professionals in some regions of the world emphasize that direct or indirect influences on the media are common practice in such countries as China and Russia (Tsetsura and Zuo, 2009; Tsetsura and Luoma-aho, in press). But almost 85 per cent of the professionals who are members of international organizations, including the International Public Relations Association, the International Press Institute and the International Federation of Journalists, from around the world condemn these practices as unprofessional and unethical (Tsetsura, 2008). Additional multi-year research into global media practices convincingly demonstrates that culture is not a factor that could predict the existence of media non-transparency (Tsetsura and Kruckeberg, 2003; Klyueva, 2008; Tsetsura and Grynko, 2009; Klyueva and Tsetsura, 2010). Rather, it is political, economic, historical and societal factors, as well as the level of professional development and the level of the development of ethical standards, that define whether media non-transparency practices are perceived as corrupt.

Black and white PR in Russia

The two terms 'black PR' and 'white PR' were first introduced in the late 1980s and early 1990s, and soon became very popular among professionals and scholars in Russia. According to the *black vs. white PR* view, ethics divides PR practices into *black* and *white*, or simply bad and good. Black PR is associated with manipulative techniques that are often used in political PR and political election campaigns (Tsetsura, 2003). White PR, on the other hand, presents a Western view of PR, which is rooted in the ethics-oriented *Excellence Project* (Maksimov, 1999). In many discussions about PR practices in Russia, PR scholars, practitioners and journalists often refer to the field in 'black' and 'white' terms.

Some scholars disagree that PR practices should be described as black and white (Klyueva and Tsetsura, in press). Instead of categorizing PR in such a way, they argue that black PR is not PR at all, but rather propagandistic effort (Tsetsura, 2003). They argue that the black-vs.-white-PR discussion takes place because the PR profession in Russia has been slow to adopt proper ethical standards (Tsetsura and Grynko, 2009). Some US scholars believe that black PR cannot exist because 'any misuse or abuse of public relations is a question, not of "bad" public relations of which only an individual practitioner can be held responsible, but rather such misuse or abuse becomes a question of unethical professional practice which is of collective concern and which must be [the] collective responsibility of all practitioners' (Kruckeberg, 1992, p. 34).

From the Western perspective, PR professional ethical standards are not followed in Russia. Some Russian professionals joined international PR associations – such as the International Public Relations Association (IPRA), the International Association of Business Communicators (IABC) or the Public Relations Society of America (PRSA) – and subscribed to the codes of ethics of these organizations. However, many of them found these rules and codes not particularly well suited for the Russian PR environment (Tsetsura, 2003). These professionals often consider Western ethical codes to be idealistic and inappropriate for Russian PR practices (Tsetsura, 2003). The main problem, however, lies in the fact that these Russian practitioners themselves actively argue for ethical PR in their everyday discourses and agree that they do not act ethically when they break PR codes of ethics (Klyueva, 2008; Pashentsev, 2002). Thus, the argument that Russian PR ethics are not the same as Western ethics becomes questionable: if Russian PR practitioners agree that, for instance, publishing press releases for money is wrong (Klyueva and Tsetsura, in press), how can this *wrong* practice be ethical (*right*) in their own eyes?

Many Russian PR scholars and practitioners are concerned with an existing practice of paying money to journalists and editors for publishing publicity materials. While such instances originally took place in Moscow and St Petersburg, now the problem is becoming more and more common in many other regions in Russia. This practice is often called *zakazukha*, a Russian slang word which means a material in favour of an organization written by a journalist and published on editorial pages but paid for by that organization. Usually, the payment goes in cash directly to a journalist or an editor.

In a classic experiment, Promaco Public Relations, a Moscow-based PR firm, showed that 13 out of 21 Russian national newspapers and magazines were ready to publish a fake press release (without even checking the facts), charging $200–2,000 for the service (Sutherland, 2001). In the Russian legal system, this unlawful activity is called hidden advertising.

Unfortunately, the law against hidden advertising is not enforced in Russia. Journalists who get paid, or PR professionals who pay for materials to be published, are not challenged legally for their wrongdoings. As a result of such non-enforcement, *zakazukha* is a common Russian PR practice, which creates a strong negative perception of the field in the country (Tsetsura, 2003; Tsetsura and Kruckeberg, 2004).

Zakazukha played a significant role in attracting the public's attention to the worldwide problem of media non-transparency: the phenomenon was publicly discussed at several international conferences of professionals working in PR and journalism. Many agreed that Moscow was probably an extreme case since it was often called a bribery capital, but Vuslat Doğan Sabanci, CEO of Hürriyet, Doğan Media Group, confirmed that anecdotal evidence of *zakazukha* existed in many other countries as well. In fact, examples of media bribery could be found around the world. Media bribery in Egypt was reported in *The Economist* (International, 2 September 2002) when Muhammad Wakil, a director of news for Egypt's state television monopoly, was caught taking a bribe to put a doctor on a popular chat show. As the investigation showed, Wakil had been charging 'clients' for years to appear on popular shows. The UK specialists often reported that trade magazines asked for 'colour separations' payments when they used a company's photo on their pages. Everybody also knew that certain make-up cosmetics brands were chosen for the front covers of some beauty magazines because those brands were the magazines' biggest advertisers.

One of the latest media non-transparency scandals in the US featured the well-known Ketchum PR agency and the Bush Administration. Ketchum received a contract to promote the No Child Left Behind (NCLB) government programme, an educational campaign vigorously advocated by the Republican Administration. It turned out that Armstrong Williams, a famous TV commentator, entrepreneur and founder of an advertising/PR firm, who actively supported the educational campaign and often discussed it in a favourable light in his programmes on American TV, was a subcontractor for Ketchum. His job, according to the contract, was to actively promote the NCLB's benefits and advantages.

Free Press, a non-government organization, demanded the launch of an investigation by the US Congress and the Federal Communication Commission to examine the conflict of interest situation in this case. When the scandal broke out in the middle of January 2005, Mr Williams issued an apology: 'I supported school vouchers long before the Department of Education ran a single ad on my TV Show.

I did not change my views just because my PR firm was receiving paid advertising promoting the No Child Left Behind.' Later, he said: 'I now realize that I have to create inseparable boundaries between my role as a small businessman and my role as an independent commentator' (Williams, 2005). It seems at the very least strange to hear a comment like this one from an experienced PR professional and, more importantly, from a famous journalist, who just at that time realized that he needed to create boundaries between the two roles.

The reaction from Williams's competitors was furious: Richard Edelman, President of Edelman PR, said: 'Ketchum's "pay for play PR" contract with the Department of Education has dealt a serious blow to our industry's effort to "clean up" its behavior.' He continued: 'This kind of pay for play PR takes us back in time to the days of the press agent who would drop off the new record album and $10 to the deejay.' Edelman urged Ketchum CEO Ray Kotcher to 'take steps to ensure that it never happens again' (Edelman, 2005). Ketchum's response shortly followed, and Kotcher said: 'We are certainly not pleased by this turn of events.' The client, the Department of Education, also reacted to the scandal. 'At this point, what I can say [is] that at a minimum, there were *errors of judgment* at the Department, and I am diligently working to get to the bottom of it all' said Education Secretary Margaret Spellings (McDonough, 2005, emphasis added).

In short, it seems that Russian PR people are not the only ones who violate professional codes of ethics. They generally agree that it is important to observe such codes, but they also argue that common perceptions of 'black PR' and widespread bribery make it difficult to practise 'white PR' in Russia (Pashentsev, 2002; Tsetsura, 2003). Some simply say that it is impossible to practice ethical PR because nobody pays for ethics (Maksimov, 1999). But these excuses are weak for two reasons: 1) the majority of Russian practitioners agree that ethics need to be taken into consideration while practising PR, particularly with regard to media transparency (Klyueva and Tsetsura, in press); and 2) Russian scholars and practitioners actively defend the principles of PR codes of ethics as a unifying element of international PR (Alyoshina, 1997; Egorova, 2000; Klyueva and Tsetsura, 2010; Konovalova, 2000; Lebedeva, 1999; Pashentsev, 2002; Tsetsura, 2008). This analysis suggests that the ethics of PR in Russia require more attention and further discussion and research.

Russian PR professional organizations as well as practitioners face the same problem as their counterparts in many other countries: accepted codes of ethics are not enforceable and thus are not practised (Tsetsura and Grynko, 2009). Although codes of ethics exist worldwide, specialists highlight numerous problems with their enforcement. One of the goals of PR practitioners and educators is to find better ways of enforcing such codes and of positioning the benefits of following ethical rules and standards. This goal can be quite challenging, especially for contemporary Russian PR practitioners; however, it is very important to continue promoting ethical practices for educational and professional communities in the name of a better future for Russian PR.

References

Alyoshina, I. (1997). *Public relations dlja menedgerov i marketerov* [*Public Relations for Managers and Marketers*]. Moscow, Russia: Gnom-press.
Boynton, L.A. (2007). 'Commentaries: Commentary 1. This PR Firm Should Have Known Better', *Journal of Mass Media Ethics*, 22, 218–21.
Cassara, C., Gross, P., Kruckeberg, D., Palmer, A. and Tsetsura, K. (2004). 'Eastern Europe, the Newly Independent States of Eurasia, and Russia', in A.S. de Beer and J.C. Merrill (eds), *Global Journalism: Topical Issues and Media Systems*. Boston, MA: Pearson, pp. 212–56.
Craig, D.A. (1999). 'A Framework for Evaluating Coverage of Ethics in Professions and Society', *Journal of Mass Media Ethics*, 14, 16–27.
——. (2006). *The Ethics of the Story: Using Narrative Techniques Responsibility in Journalism*. Lanham, MD: Rowman & Littlefield.
——. (2007). 'The Case: Wal-Mart Public Relations in the Blogosphere', *Journal of Mass Media Ethics*, 22, 215–18.
——. (2008). 'Journalists, Government, and the Place of Journalism across Cultures', *Journal of Mass Media Ethics*, 23, 158–61.
The Economist (International). (2002). 'Gamal, the Brisk New Broom; Egypt's Political Scandals', *The Economist* (London edition), 364(8289), 61.
Edelman, R. (2005, January 7). 'Pay for Play PR is Not On', *Richard Edelman Blog*, www.edelman.com/speak_up/blog/archives/2005/01/, date accessed 1 December 2010.
Egorova, A. (2000). 'International Public Relations: Order Out of Chaos. A Delphi Study Focusing on Russia', unpublished master's thesis, University of Lousiana, Lafayette.
Goregin, A.G. and Nikolaev, A.G. (1996). 'Evolution of Modern Russian Communication', *Communication World*, 13, 68–70.
Harro-Loit, H. and Saks, K. (2006). 'The Diminishing Border between Advertising and Journalism in Estonia', *Journalism Studies*, 7, 312–22.
Holmes, P. (2001). 'Russian PR Firm Exposes Media Corruption', *The Holmes Report*, 1(9), 5 March, www.holmesreport.com/story.cfm?edit_id=156&typeid=1, date accessed 1 December 2010.
Klyueva, A. (2008). 'An Exploratory Study of Media Transparency in the Urals Federal District of Russia', unpublished master's thesis, University of Oklahoma, Norman.

Klyueva, A. and Tsetsura, K. (2010). 'Ethicality of Media Opacity as a Predictor of Acceptance of Non-transparent Media Practices among the Romanian Media Professionals', paper presented at the 13th IPR International Public Relations Research Conference, Miami, FL, March.

——. (in press). 'News from Urals with Love and Payment: The First Look at Non-transparent Media Practices in the Urals Federal District of Russia', *Russian Journal of Communication*.

Koltsova, O. (2006). *News Media and Power in Russia*. London and New York: Routledge.

Konovalova E. (2000, April). 'A za PR otvetish' pered ... sovest'ju', *Sovetnik*, 4, 20–3.

Kovach, B. (2001) *Elements of Journalism: What Newspeople Should Know and the Public Should Expect*. Westminster: Crown Publishing Group.

Kruckeberg, D. (1992). 'Ethical Decision-Making in Public Relations', *International Public Relations Review*, 15, 32–7.

Kruckeberg, D. and Tsetsura, K. (2003). 'International Index of Bribery for News Coverage', Institute for Public Relations, http://www.instituteforpr.org, date accessed 23 November 2010.

Lebedeva, T.Y. (1999). *Public relations. Korporativnaya i politicheskaya rezhissura* [*Public Relations: Corporate and Political Directing*]. Moscow, Russia: MGU.

Maksimov, A.A. (1999). *'Chistye' i 'gryaznye' teknologii vyborov: Rossijskij opyt* [*'Clean' and 'Dirty' Election Campaign Technologies: Russian Experience*]. Moscow, Russia: Delo.

McDonough, S. (2005, January 28). 'Another Columnist was Paid to Help Bush Administration Agency', *Associated Press Newswire* (electronic version), http://global.factiva.com.ezproxy.lib.ou.edu/aa/?ref=APRS000020050128 e11s00imw&pp=1&fcpil=en&napc=S&sa_from=, date accessed 1 December 2010.

McGraw, M. (2003). 'Money vs. Ethics: A Balancing Act', *Global Journalist*, 1 April, www.globaljournalist.org/stories/2003/04/01/money-vs-ethics/, date accessed 1 December 2010.

McNair, B. (1991). *Glasnost, Perestroika, and the Soviet Media*. London and New York: Routledge.

McReynolds, L. (1991). *The News under Russia's Old Regime: The Development of a Mass-Circulation Press*. Princeton University Press.

Pashentsev, E.N. (2002). *Public relations: Ot biznesa do politiki* [*Public Relations: From Business to Politics*], 3rd edn. Moscow: Finpress.

Pasti, S. (2005). 'Two Generations of Contemporary Russian Journalists', *European Journal of Communication*, 20, 89–114.

Ragozina, I. (2007). 'The Status of Public Relations in Russia', unpublished master's thesis, East Tennessee State University, Johnson City.

Shafer, R. (1990). 'Greasing the Newsgate: Journalist on the Take in the Philippines', *Journal of Mass Media Ethics*, 5, 15–29.

Sutherland, A. (2001). 'PR Thrives in Harder Times', *Frontline, IPRA*, 23, 5.

Tsetsura, K. (2003). 'The Development of Public Relations in Russia: A Geopolitical Approach', in K. Sriramesh and D. Vercic (eds), *A Handbook of International Public Relations*. Mahwah, NJ: Lawrence Erlbaum, pp. 301–19.

——. (2004). 'Russia', in B. van Ruler and D. Vercic (eds), *Public Relations and Communication Management in Europe: A Nation-by-Nation Introduction to Public Relations Theory and Practice*. Berlin: Mouton de Gruyter, pp. 331–46.

——. (2005a). 'The Exploratory Study of Media Transparency and Cash for News Coverage Practice in Russia: Evidence from Moscow PR Agencies', *Proceedings of the 8th International Interdisciplinary Public Relations Research Conference*, University of Miami.

——. (2005b). 'Bribery for News Coverage: Research in Poland', *Institute for Public Relations Online: International Research*, www.instituteforpr.com/international.html, date accessed 1 December 2010.

——. (2008). 'An Exploratory Study of Global Media Relations Practices', *Institute for Public Relations Research Reports: International Research*, www.instituteforpr.com/international.html, date accessed 1 December 2010.

Tsetsura, K. and Grynko, A. (2009). 'An Exploratory Study of Media Transparency in Ukraine', *Public Relations Journal*, 3(2), http://www.prsa.org/prjournal/index.html?WT.ac=PRJournalTopNav, date accessed 1 December 2010.

Tsetsura, K. and Kruckeberg, D. (2004). 'Theoretical Development of Public Relations in Russia', in D.J. Tilson (ed.), *Toward the Common Good: Perspectives in International Public Relations*. Boston, MA: Pearson Allyn & Bacon, pp. 176–92.

——. (2009). 'Truth, Public Relations and the Mass Media: A Normative Model to Examine Media Opacity', *Proceedings of the 12th International Interdisciplinary Public Relations Research Conference*, University of Miami.

Tsetsura, K. and Luoma-aho, V. (in press). 'The Role of Trust and Innovation in Russian Journalism', *Ethical Space: The International Journal of Communication Ethics*.

Tsetsura, K. and Zuo, L. (2009). 'Guanxi, Gift-giving, or Bribery: Ethical Considerations of Paid News in China', paper presented at the Media Ethics Division of the AEJMC Annual Conference, Boston, MA, August.

Williams, A. (2005). 'My Apology', column in *Town Hall: Your Source for Conservative News, Cartoons, Issues, Blogs and Magazine*, 10 January, http://townhall.com/columnists/ArmstrongWilliams/2005/01/10/my_apology, date accessed 1 December 2010.

Zassoursky, I. (2004). *Media and Power in Post-Soviet Russia*. London: M.E. Sharpe.

Zhirkov, G.V. (2001). *Istoriya cenzuri v Rossii v IXX–XX vekah* [*The History of Censorship in Russia in the 19th–20th Centuries*]. Moscow: Aspect Press.

11
Visual Ethics in Public Relations: An Analysis of Latin American Government Websites

Melissa A. Johnson and Eileen M. Searson

The recent transition in many Latin American countries from authoritarian to democratic systems makes it timely to study the ethical aspects of public relations (PR) because of the implied link between democracy and more transparent forms of communication. New transparency and information access laws, neoliberal movements and increased international trade are factors that have driven PR growth in Latin America.

Latin American PR professionals may abide by the ethical codes of international as well as local professional organizations and associations. These codes focus on different facets of PR work. However, with the increased reliance on pictures and videos in Latin America and elsewhere, practitioners and scholars must also concern themselves with the ethical aspects of visual communication, referred to as visual ethics (Kienzler, 1997).

The purpose of this chapter is to explore the concept of visual ethics as it manifests itself on Latin American government organization websites via quantitative as well as qualitative content analysis of 50 sites. Our goals are to add to the body of knowledge of international PR ethics and to improve understanding of PR practitioners' ethical use of digital visual communication. At the end of the chapter, we propose two items that may be added to international PR codes of ethics or to those of Latin American and other professional associations.

PR ethics

Ethics is a concept based on an understanding of what is right or wrong. It is a foundation of the two-way symmetric model of PR (Bowen, 2004; Fitzpatrick and Gauthier, 2001; Grunig, and White, 1992; Marsh, 2001). In addition, because PR managers handle issues management and serve as the voices of their organizations, the PR function acts as the institution's ethical conscience.

Studies in PR ethics are generally based on philosophical principles of utilitarianism and deontology (Bowen, 2004; Marsh, 2001). Following a utilitarian approach may lead a practitioner to privilege what is best for the majority rather than what might be optimal for worthy smaller publics. For instance, while the liberalization of mining rights in Peru might be advantageous for multinational mining companies and the Peruvian economy, it could be detrimental for original landowners and village communities who will suffer the environmental impacts. Pratt (1991) found that situational ethics, a type of utilitarian ethics, is the primary choice among PR professionals.

Conversely, Kantian deontology focuses on the moral principles within the ethical argument rather than on outcomes. A Kantian underpinning could uphold the viability of a universal international code of PR ethics. Indeed, some scholars argue that a universal code for practitioners functioning in an international forum is possible (for example, Roth et al., 1996). However, a Kantian focus on universality collides with the international PR literature that emphasizes the impact of culture on PR decision making. With wide cultural variance worldwide, PR practitioners engaged in international practice may have trouble determining what everyone would agree on as universally best. For example, in an ethics survey of 573 PR officers in eight countries, El-Alstal (2005) found that while there was agreement about general values like honesty and accuracy, practitioners disagreed about practices surrounding media relations, such as gift-giving or buying meals.

Visual communication and visual ethics

Despite the attention paid to PR ethics, one area that has not been addressed in international PR is visual ethics. Kienzler said that visual ethics is concerned with 'the consequences of constructing a particular visual in a particular way' (1997, p. 172). Some visual communication practitioners, such as photojournalists, have codes of ethics (National Press Photographers Association, 2009) and scholars studying photojournalism and documentary filmmaking have also grappled with visual ethics (Butchart, 2006; Wheeler, 2002). Technical communicators have also been concerned with applied issues related to ethics and visual communication (Allen, 1996), as have experts writing about the responsibilities of graphic designers (Roberts, 2006). In addition, Borgerson and Schroeder (2002) argued for ethical choices in the visual representations used in marketing, although they did not propose a code of ethics.

However, we could find no explicit items dealing with visual communication in PR codes mentioned in the literature (for example, Skinner, Mersham and Valin's analysis of 17 codes of ethics). Further, visuals are not separately addressed in the international ethics codes of the International Association of Business Communicators (IABC), the International Public Relations Association (IPRA) or the Global Alliance. Given the reliance on visual communication by PR practitioners, we assert that codes of ethics should address visual ethics. Like technical communicators and photojournalists, PR practitioners are creators of visual representations. In digital communication, altering images is easy to do, and juxtapositions can create new visual realities that can violate norms of honesty, fairness and other tenets of professional PR codes.

According to Allen (1996), the major issues in visual ethics are selection, emphasis and framing. Like others (Newton, 2001; Wheeler, 2002), Allen noted that aesthetics must be balanced with ethics – in other words, improving the visual appeal may skew the truthfulness of the visual even if it were done merely to make a page more appealing. For example, it is generally acceptable in PR to remove a plant from a photograph if it looks like it is growing out of someone's hair, but it is not acceptable to add to a photograph someone who was not present at the time it was actually taken. Unfortunately for visual ethics, new technologies have increased the ability to create misleading photography and graphics. Another important consideration is that more elements do not necessarily equate with better overall communication with a target audience. There is a risk of visual clutter (Allen, 1996) taking into account the almost unlimited space on webpages compared with traditional communication tools like brochures or newsletters.

In summary, the deontological philosophical tradition supports the ideal of a universal code of ethics in international PR and the utilitarian foundation guides situationalism and cultural relativism. While other communication professions have explored visual codes of ethics, neither scholars nor practitioners have discussed visual PR ethics. The following section discusses the Latin American context in which we will explore visual ethics.

Latin American governments, transparency and website communication

The Latin American School of Public Relations is an approach to PR advocated by representatives of the Inter-American Confederation of Public Relations (CONFIARP) along with other practitioners and scholars (Molleda, 2000). The focus is on humanistic concerns and overall societal improvement through the contributions of PR practitioners and of the organizations for which they work. According to the Declaration of Principles, PR practice must be based on such principles as freedom, justice, harmony, equality and respect for human dignity (Molleda, 2000, p. 519). These ideals are also generally found in the Latin American PR ethics codes we analysed for this study. In practice, however, the ideals are challenged by practitioners who have been encouraged by their organizations to emphasize the needs of government celebrities or government organizations over the interests of stakeholders (Molleda and Moreno, 2008).

The late twentieth-century return to democracy in Latin America has increased the need for PR. According to Ferrari (2009), in many of the countries that were subject to military dictatorships in the 1960s and 1970s, PR was restricted and some university PR education programmes were closed. Conversely, despite political upheavals, other countries have upheld more sophisticated approaches to PR. For instance, Brazilian PR professionals must have a PR degree and be licensed by the states' regional councils. The Brazilian constitution emphasizes citizens' participation and access to information (Martell, 2007; Molleda, Athaydes and Hirsch, 2009).

While journalism and public communication in Latin America are not entirely free, there has been a twenty-first-century move towards more transparency in government communication. In recent years, Columbia, Mexico, Panama and Peru have passed transparency laws (Hughes and Lawson, 2005). These countries, along with Belize, Jamaica and Trinidad and Tobago, have also approved laws that give journalists and citizens the ability to obtain government information in a timely manner. In 2004, Ecuador passed the Organic Law on Transparency and Access to Public Information, and in 2008, both Chile and Guatemala passed transparency and access laws that became effective in April 2009 (Carter Center, 2009; Freedominfo.org, 2009).

Beyond laws, other recent Latin American government policies have also promoted Internet use by citizens. For instance, when the Argentinean government enacted policies to cut the price of leased telephone lines (the main avenue to Internet access) and reduced tariffs for local Internet dial-up calls, the number of Internet users in Argentina grew (Hawkins and Hawkins, 2003). In addition, Mexico's former President Vicente Fox (2000–6) launched an e-Mexico initiative early in his term that by 2002 had established more than 800 digital centres throughout Mexico to promote education, health and access to information (Freeman, 2002).

Although government websites serve a nation's citizens, the sites also reach stakeholders outside the nation. Government communication solicits external investment in the country, promotes tourism and trade, and creates a foundation for public diplomacy. Websites help to brand a nation (Fursich and Robins, 2002; Morgan and Pritchard, 2005) and a solid national brand could serve as a foundation for business and diplomatic objectives.

In general, many of the concepts espoused by the Latin American School of Public Relations and evident in new Latin American legislation are integral to international PR codes of ethics such as the IABC, the IPRA and the Global Alliance. PR associations in UN member countries have accepted the principles of the Code of Athens (El-Astal, 2005) adopted in 1965 by the IPRA. However, practitioners also consult codes devised by professional organizations in their own countries, such as the codes found in Argentina, Brazil, Colombia and Mexico. They focus on responsiveness to their stakeholders, openness to society at large, general humankind values and the obligation of maintaining professional expertise.

Research questions

Based on the literature in international PR ethics and visual ethics along with studies related to the Latin American government communication context, we selected several concepts to focus on in our analysis. Our research questions were as follows:

RQ1: What is the level of *visual honesty* in Latin American government websites?
RQ2: How *organization-focused* and/or *community/society-focused* are the websites?
RQ3: What *values* are displayed on the websites?
RQ4: How *responsive* are the websites to their users?
RQ5: How much technological and professional *expertise* is displayed on the websites?

Methodology

Sampling

Websites from the following ten countries were analysed for this research: Belize, Brazil, Chile, Colombia, Costa Rica, Ecuador, Honduras,

Mexico, Panama and Venezuela. Two lists of Latin American websites along with corresponding governmental hyperlinks posted on both the Latin American Network Information Center (LANIC) website (http://lanic.utexas.edu) and a website featuring a comprehensive global list of governmental websites (www.gksoft.com/govt) were combined to generate an initial sampling frame. From this list, five governmental sites were selected for each of the ten countries in a purposeful sampling design. Some hyperlinks were outdated or did not load properly, so those government organizations were accessed through hyperlinks posted on other sites or directly via the URL. For example, the President of Mexico's homepage linked numerous ministries and governmental offices. Given the technological challenges and inconsistencies among government websites, a non-probability sample with country quotas was the best choice for this exploratory study. This allowed us to scrutinize a wide range of types of government sites from a variety of countries.

Measures

As previously noted, in devising the code sheet, we reviewed codes of ethics from the Global Alliance, the IABC, the Code of Athens and five codes from professional PR or organizational communication associations in Latin American countries. In addition, we excerpted key companion concepts from the Latin American School of Public Relations (Molleda, 2000). In order to conduct a manageable study, we chose five concepts from these sources to operationalize. The variables were a combination of dichotomous nominal variables, other nominal variables and Likert scales. A few variables measured ratio-level data such as the number of website sections.

The first concept, *honesty*, was measured in several ways. We evaluated whether the sites contained seemingly authentic photos (that is, not staged), illustrations and graphics that appeared to be informational rather than exaggerated, and a real-time orientation. Also included were whether or not the sites featured a transparency policy and a feature for correcting errors. In support of Allen's (1996) observation that clutter can obscure the message, we coded for the amount of visual clutter on the websites on a 1–5 Likert scale, measured by assessing the amount of white space.

The next concept, drawn from the philosophies of the Latin American School of Public Relations and various codes of ethics, measured how *organization-* or *society-focused* the websites were. To measure this, researchers discerned the visual depictions of obligations to society – whether visuals were more organization- or community/society-focused, the types of national symbols and photographs included, and whether the website promoted responsible citizenship.

The third research question focused on *values*. These included traditional Latin American values such as family orientation, collectivity and respect. In addition, coders logged whether values of the new transparency and access laws and of the Latin American School of Public Relations philosophy were manifest, including societal harmony.

The fourth research question dealt with *responsiveness to target publics* (government organization stakeholders) via interactive website features and other means. Variables measuring responsiveness and interactivity included the appearance of interactive (two-way communication) features such as surveys, forums/blogs/chatrooms, spot polls or petitions. In addition, the authors noted the inclusion of contact email addresses, mailing addresses, telephone numbers, a search bar, a frequently asked questions section, the availability of page formatting for printing and a site map. Links to other sites were also included here because we characterized them as a service to viewers.

The fifth research question explored technological and professional *expertise*. Expertise-related variables included whether sites had a font-adjustment option, a notation of when the website was last updated, a privacy policy statement, legal information, a press room feature, the presence of a website hit counter and the availability of moving images (such as flash films, videos or YouTube links).

Results

Among the 50 government websites, 16 per cent were presidential sites, 16 per cent were offices or ministries of environment or agriculture, 14 per cent covered health-related issues, 12 per cent related to education, 10 per cent were in the areas of foreign affairs or external relations, 8 per cent explored tourism and the remainder were created for the other governmental bodies of countries. Five Brazilian sites and one other (12 per cent) were in Portuguese, 82 per cent were in Spanish, 30 per cent were in English and 2 per cent each were in French, Chinese and German. (Totals are greater than 100 per cent because almost a third of the sites were bilingual or multilingual.) Sites ranged in length from 2 to 23 pages, with a mean of 8.34 pages. The number of subsections ranged from none to 68, with a mean of 22.82.

Visual honesty

Sixty per cent of the sites included a transparency policy (asserting that the site upheld transparency regulations or the spirit of transparency). Fifty-two per cent of the sites appeared to be mostly or very visually honest and only 8 per cent appeared artificial or staged (we conceptualized candid photographs as more visually honest than posed photographs). Thirty-two per cent of the websites contained only candid photographs, 36 per cent contained both candid as well as posed shots, and 26 per cent had no candid pictures. Four per cent had no photos of humans and 2 per cent had no photos at all. None of the sites included a correction of an error feature at the time of our analysis.

As noted in the literature review, visual honesty has the potential to decrease with an increase in visual clutter. We rated 28 per cent of the sites highly cluttered or moderately highly cluttered, 42 per cent with generally equal amounts of design elements and white space, and 30 per cent as low or moderately low in visual clutter. A post hoc analysis of variable relationships showed that clutter was correlated with the presence of various pieces of contact information, update notations and privacy policies. Of course, government stakeholders benefit from such disclosure, especially when they can access large amounts of information. But subject matter should be displayed clearly, perhaps separating content into different pages when necessary.

Societal focus

Following the principles of the Latin American School of Public Relations and the societal orientation of the ethical codes, we were interested in whether sites tended to be society- and community-focused or whether there would be a more traditional focus on government personalities (such as presidents) and government organizations, in part to aggrandize their legitimacy. Ten per cent of the sites were rated mostly organization-oriented, 30 per cent were generally balanced and 60 per cent were mostly geared towards society. Similarly, text accompanying photos tended to be society-focused, with 64 per cent moderately high to highly oriented towards society, 22 per cent balanced between society and organization foci, and just 14 per cent being mostly organization-focused. As might be expected, the presidential sites tended to focus more on personalities than on societies, as did a few other types of sites as well. For instance, the Venezuelan Ministry of Tourism site featured numerous photographs of President Hugo Chavez.

Latin American values

Values are also central to most codes, although they can vary from deontologically-based items to those that are more culture-specific. We coded photos to see whether the three above-mentioned traditional Latin American values were present. We found that 24 per cent of the sites demonstrated a family orientation, 58 per cent showed emphasis on collectivism and 74 per cent expressed respect. An example was the Mexican Department of Health website, which had photographs promoting a 'family day'. The value of respect was illustrated by Panama's Ministry of Education website, which included a picture of several of the ministers of that department as well as their personal biographies. The Chilean Ministry of Economy website illustrated collectivity with the depiction of individuals working together, signifying people working in concert to build a better economy. The Latin American Public Relations School's value of harmony was also present in the visuals. About 72 per cent of the sites reflected societal harmony and 6 per cent portrayed some form of disharmony. In addition, 94 per cent of the sites promoted responsible citizenship. The qualitative data also suggested that the values of tradition and history were present in some websites. For instance, the Venezuelan presidential website featured many historic sepia-toned photos from 1870 to 1965, perhaps visually reinforcing the Chavez Administration's emphasis on the cult of Simón Bolivar. This accent was also clearly present on government website headers – 'Gobierno Bolivariano de Venezuela'.

In a post hoc analysis of the presentation of values on government websites, we found that images that were more society-focused were likely to demonstrate collectivity ($r = .355$, $p < .05$) or social concerns or harmony ($r = .621$, $p < .05$). Orientation towards society was also correlated with visual honesty ($r = .769$, $p < .05$). In short, many sites were clearly oriented towards society, collectivity and harmony (at least in the one-way communication present on the sites).

Responsiveness to stakeholders

Very few interactive features aimed at soliciting citizens' views were included on the government websites. For instance, only 10 per cent had surveys, only 4 per cent featured spot polls and only 2 per cent included petitions. However, 80 per cent of the sites employed links to other government websites, with the number of links per site averaging about 16 (ranging from 1 to 82). The types of link depended on the types of sites. For instance, airlines and travel agencies were linked to tourism sites, whereas health ministries tended to link to world health organizations. Ninety-eight per cent of the sites included an email address for stakeholders, with 90 per cent also featuring a regular mailing address and another 94 per cent highlighting a telephone number. In addition, 64 per cent used some form of search function, 54 per cent employed a site map, 24 per cent had a frequently asked questions section and 30 per cent used a feature that made the content easy to print. These were indicators that the site producers were respectful of the right to inquiry and possible questions of Web users. Some interesting examples included the page rating system on the Colombian Ministry of Environment website as well as the 'share your Belize story' and 'send us an online Belize postcard' sections on the Belize Tourism Board website.

Expertise

Our last research question evaluated the level of professional and technological expertise visible on the government websites. Most of the international and nation-specific PR ethics codes emphasize the burden on professionals to be experts in their discipline. We measured this with variables that assessed the types and number of useful features on the websites. In general, the sites proved to be visually strong: 98 per cent of the sites included photography and 58 per cent had moving images such as flash films, videos or YouTube links and excerpts. Ten per cent of the sites allowed font adjustment, while 24 per cent indicated when it was last updated, 56 per cent specified when the site was established and 12 per cent had visible hit counters. Other features included legal documents or other official factual elements such as treaties, decrees or the constitution (76 per cent), press releases (70 per cent), a daily agenda or calendar for the president or other officials (34 per cent), quotes from dignitaries (16 per cent), speeches (20 per cent) and interviews (14 per cent). Sixty-four per cent had a separate section for the press, 22 per cent had a privacy policy and 8 per cent mentioned a law or policy related to freedom of information. Our analysis of the relationships among various expertise variables revealed that sites that offered features like privacy policies or press rooms were more likely to include helpful options such as font adjustment, search functions or contact information. In general, Latin American government websites studied here demonstrated some sophistication, with an opportunity for further enhancement for most sites. However, it is important to note that sites experiencing technical difficulties could not be explored, so the sites studied are not necessarily representative of the technical level of sophistication of all government sites in the ten countries.

Conclusions and discussion

Societal focus and values

Except for a few cases, our study's findings did not support the views of PR practitioners interviewed by Molleda and Moreno, who found that: 'The professionals working in government offices complain about having to put the greater effort in promoting the personalities and actions of their organizations instead of communicating with the citizenry either through public information initiatives or education campaigns' (2008, p. 155). Perhaps other tactics such as media relations or producing controlled tools are more likely to support such a conclusion. However, some website content – such as presidential speeches – promoted public figures while also conveying information to citizens.

Responsiveness and expertise

The Internet is an important tool for Latin American governments to propagate their national identities (brands), serve their citizens and create an important foundation for international trade, tourism and investment. However, we observed a variety of technical flaws that could impede the process of achieving these objectives, including links to photo galleries that lacked any photos or had blurry pictures that may have been produced by amateur photographers or those without quality equipment. Mexico could be applauded for branding all of its government websites consistently. This strengthens the country's image, creates coherence and allows easy recognition among users.

While the Latin American and international codes of ethics emphasize PR expertise, one cannot state that a practitioner is unethical because of lack of expertise, especially when technologies or opportunities for professional training are limited. We anticipate that government websites will continue to improve over time. We would also encourage further longitudinal research to ascertain the growing sophistication and improvement in visual honesty and accessibility in the Web-based communication of Latin American governments.

As noted in the results section, despite Latin American codes of PR ethics stressing the importance of participation and free expression for citizens, there was a dearth of interactive mechanisms for them to do so. Some websites, such as the Chilean tourism site, required users to register. In PR, this is an evaluation technique for tracking site visitors. However, for some government agencies, this may not be appropriate because of exclusivity connotations, the impact on privacy or consumers' concern over follow-up commercial solicitations. In addition, ministries or government offices in former authoritarian regimes may determine that this is ill advised, given the need to build trust in current governments.

Visual honesty

In general, the websites analysed attempted visual honesty. Through our qualitative and quantitative analyses, we identified five features related to visual honesty, including types of photographs, the use of picture galleries, the use of archives, visual clutter and aesthetics. One challenge is that sometimes the most candid or honest photographs are not inviting. An example was the Belize Foreign Affairs website, which depicted several dignitaries sitting together but not looking at the camera and therefore not engaging the viewer of the photo. Tourism sites present other challenges to the concept of visual honesty because of the perceived need to feature the most pristine landscapes, exotic seascapes or other alluring attractions.

Secondly, photography galleries of presidents or other leaders (for example, the Chilean President's website) demonstrate reverence for tradition and history. However, they can also suggest an organizational focus, such as when photographs of the President's childhood are displayed instead of shots of the leader with citizens, acting on behalf of his or her country. In addition, the juxtaposition of old photos within new digital technologies provides an interesting message about the modern Latin American country that retains some of its traditions. Moreover, it is possible that some Latin American countries want to reinforce the message of their long histories and especially the rich cultures that had been present long before Europeans touched the soil of the continent.

Thirdly, archives (such as all press releases, speeches and videos) are website elements that constitute another aspect of the honesty concept. These are particularly important in Latin American countries that have dealt with *the disappeared*.[1] A visual history is an 'anti-disappeared' element. This aspect of visual honesty aligns with the movement by Latin American governments to be more transparent (and regulations to this effect in some countries). When a government official makes a statement, the organization-sponsored archive allows a citizen to check on the consistency of such statements and related policies.

Fourthly, like Allen (1996), we recognize that visual clutter can detract from visual honesty and mar accessibility. Latin American government communicators would be wise to ensure that there is ample white space on Web pages and that the entire site is organized clearly; our study identified this as a weakness. Government communicators are challenged to decrease clutter while producing substantive and technically sophisticated sites that encourage access to the organization.

Finally, we acknowledge the struggle between aesthetics and visual honesty as discussed by Newton (2001), Wheeler (2002) and others. Aesthetics attract, and might keep, a viewer at a site, especially at visually important sites like those that encourage tourism. Honest images must be balanced with the artistic training of photographers, writers and graphic designers.

Visual ethics

Do these Latin American government websites uphold elements of international codes of ethics or country-specific ones? With a few exceptions, most sites appear to strive for visual honesty and uphold the Latin American School of Public Relations touchstone of societal orientation. Values mentioned in some codes as well as in one of the codes of the Latin American School of Public Relations are also apparent in visuals – especially respect, societal harmony and responsible citizenship. Of course, these visual messages can also be used as propaganda by regimes wanting to avoid disharmonious actions such as strikes or protests.

Responsiveness to one's stakeholders is another key element of ethics codes and here the governmental sites we analysed get mixed reviews. While they feature few interactive mechanisms for users, they are still quite strong on including contact information and useful links. Finally, all ethics codes considered for this study celebrated professional expertise. We found a moderate level of expertise overall, but some countries had very sophisticated sites. This suggests that more professional training, larger budgets, more modern hardware and software, and other enhancements may be in order.

As noted at the outset of this chapter, visual ethics is not explicitly included in any of the PR codes that we reviewed. We recommend that professional PR associations may want to consider two possible additions, modified from the National Press Photographers Association's Code of Ethics. The first may be: 'Be accurate and comprehensive in the [visual] representation of subjects.' A PR code could also say: 'Be accurate and comprehensive in the visual representation of the organization and organizational stakeholders.' Another item from the photographer's code could be: 'Be complete and provide context when photographing or recording subjects. Avoid stereotyping individuals and groups. Recognize and work to avoid presenting one's own biases in the work.' The first two clauses of the latter item would be particularly suitable for the PR profession.

Finally, given the traditional PR debate over ethical relativism versus universal standards, we consider whether visual ethics is universal (deontological) or if it varies by culture (utilitarian). It is possible that this type of norm can be more universal than some other aspects of PR ethics, such as the way in which media relations are conducted in different cultures. Certainly, visual standards of honesty, respect and non-stereotyping should be upheld across cultures. As global audiences for digital communication tools will continue to grow, PR practitioners must find ways to communicate across cultures while still serving their constituents. Of course, some sites, such as those for ministries of education and health, can feature special sections for different populations (indigenous peoples, women, young people, etc.), but the burden of upholding universal visual ethical standards should not be reduced while conducting such targeted communications.

It appears that the twenty-first-century Latin American regulations, specifically regarding such values as transparency, social justice and honesty, mostly uphold the Kantian deontological tradition. But utilitarianism is more apparent in PR ethics code items that encourage responsiveness and expertise, the values that may be more context-specific.

The long and complex political history of Latin America, including the suppression of creative expression of indigenous groups, could create different expressive standards. A recently authoritarian nation may view *any* information distribution to the public as being responsive, while a long-term democracy would strive for more complete transparency. In addition, visual norms arising out of the artistic traditions of various Latin American cultures (such as Moche ceramics, Guatemalan weavings or Mexican murals) may be one reason for culture-specific visual expressive standards rather than a universal approach. One direction for future visual ethics research is to consider whether differences in cultural dimensions – such as power distance, masculinity-femininity, individualism-collectivism, uncertainty avoidance or long-term orientation (Hofstede, 2010) – may play a role in nation-specific visual ethics approaches.

References

Allen, N. (1996). 'Ethics and Visual Rhetorics: Seeing's Not Believing Anymore', *Technical Communication Quarterly*, 5(1), 87–105.

Borgerson, J.L. and Schroeder, J.E. (2002). 'Ethical Issues of Global Marketing: Avoiding Bad Faith in Visual Representation', *European Journal of Marketing*, 36(5/6), 570–94.

Bowen, S.A. (2004). 'Expansion of Ethics as the Tenth Generic Principle of Public Relations Excellence: A Kantian Theory and Model for Managing Ethical Issues', *Journal of Public Relations Research*, 16(1), 65–92.

Butchart, G.C. (2006). 'On Ethics and Documentary: A Real and Actual Truth', *Communication Theory*, 16(4), 427–52.

Carter Center (2009). www.cartercenter.org, date accessed 1 December 2010.

El-Astal, M.A.S. (2005). 'Culture Influence on Educational Public Relations Officers' Ethical Judgments: A Cross-national Study', *Public Relations Review*, 31(3), 362–75.

Ferrari, M.A. (2009). 'Overview of Public Relations in South America', in K. Sriramesh and D. Vercic (eds), *The Global Public Relations Handbook: Theory, Research, and Practice*, 2nd edn. New York: Routledge, pp. 704–26.

Fitzpatrick, K. and Gauthier, C. (2001). 'Toward a Professional Responsibility of Public Relations Ethics', *Journal of Mass Media Ethics*, 16(2–3), 193–212.

Freedominfo.org. (2009). www.freedominfo.org, date accessed 1 December 2010.

Freeman, M. (2002). 'Vis-Sat Names as Supplier to e-Mexico Plan', *San Diego Union Tribune*, 24 December, pp. C–1.

Fursich, E. and Robins, M.B. (2002). 'Africa.com: The Self-representation of Sub-Saharan Nations on the World Wide Web', *Critical Studies in Media Communication*, 19(2), 190–211.

Global Alliance for Public Relations and Communication Management. *The Global Protocol on Ethics in Public Relations*, www.globalalliancepr.org, date accessed 1 December 2010.

Grunig, J.E. and White, J. (1992). 'The Effect of Worldviews on Public Relations Theory and Practice', in J.E. Grunig (ed.), *Excellence in Public Relations and Communication Management*. Hillsdale, NJ: Lawrence Erlbaum.

Hawkins, E.T. and Hawkins, K.A. (2003). 'Bridging Latin America's Digital Divide: Government Policies and Internet Access', *Journalism & Mass Communication Quarterly*, 80(3), 646–65.

Hofstede, G. (2010). *Geert Hofstede Cultural Dimensions*, www.geert-hofstede.com, date accessed 1 December 2010.

Hughes, S. and Lawson, C. (2005). 'The Barriers to Media Opening in Latin America', *Political Communication*, 22, 9–25.

International Association of Business Communicators. *IABC Code of Ethics for Professional Communicators*, www.iabc.com, date accessed 1 December 2010.

Kienzler, D.S. (1997). 'Visual Ethics', *Journal of Business Communication*, 34(2), 171–87.

Marsh, C.W. (2001). 'Public Relations Ethics: Contrasting Models from the Rhetorics of Plato, Aristotle, and Isocrates', *Journal of Mass Media Ethics*, 16(2–3), 78–98.

Martell, C.R. (2007). 'Municipal Government Accountability in Brazil', *International Journal of Public Administration*, 30(12), 1591–619.

Molleda, J.C. (2000). 'International Paradigms: The Latin American School of Public Relations', *Journalism Studies*, 2(4), 513–30.

Molleda, J.C, Athaydes, A. and Hirsch, V. (2009). 'Public Relations in Brazil: Practice and Education in a South American Context', in K. Sriramesh and D. Vercic (eds), *The Global Public Relations Handbook: Theory, Research, and Practice*, 2nd edn. New York: Routledge, pp. 727–48.

Molleda, J.C. and Moreno, A. (2008). 'Balancing Public Relations with Socioeconomic and Political Environments in Transition: Comparative, Contextualized Research in Colombia, Mexico, and Venezuela', *Journalism & Communication Monographs*, 10(2), 115–74.

Morgan, N.J. and Pritchard, A. (2005). 'Promoting Niche Tourism Destination Brands: Case Studies of New Zealand and Wales', *Journal of Promotion Management*, 12(1), 17–33.

National Press Photographers Association. www.nppa.org, date accessed 1 December 2010.

Newton, J.H. (2001). *The Burden of Visual Truth: The Role of Photojournalism in Mediating Reality*. Mahwah, NJ: Lawrence Erlbaum.

Pratt, C.B. (1991). 'Public Relations: The Empirical Research on Practitioner Ethics', *Journal of Business Ethics*, 10, 229–36.

Roberts, L. (2006). *Good: An Introduction to Ethics in Graphic Design*. Worthing: Ava Publishing.

Roth, N.L., Hunt, T., Stavropoulos, M. and Babik, K. (1996). 'Can't We All Just Get Along? Cultural Variables in Codes of Ethics', *Public Relations Review*, 22(2), 151–61.

Skinner, C., Mersham, G. and Valin, J. (2003). 'Global Protocol on Ethics in Public Relations', *Journal of Communication Management*, 9(13), 13–28.

Wheeler, T.H. (2002). *Phototruth or Photofiction? Ethics and Media Imagery in the Digital Age*. Mahwah, NJ: Lawrence Erlbaum.

Note

1. This is a reference to citizens of authoritarian regimes who were removed from their homes or workplaces by the authorities and never heard from again.

Part V
Is Education the Answer?

12
The Invisible Dimension of International Communication: Is It Possible to Teach Others 'the Right Ethical Standards'?

Svetlana Sablina and Bella Struminskaya

The process of globalization and, consequently, the increasing cross-border flow of goods, labour forces, information and knowledge, as well as the integration of different countries into the world economy, are accompanied by the development of special communication practices in the international context. Since the collapse of the Iron Curtain, Russia has been actively participating in different international communication processes that have taken place at interpersonal, group, organizational and public levels. Russia's cooperation with European countries within the context of the Bologna Process contributes to the formation of the European Higher Education Area (EHEA). More students of this and upcoming generations will undoubtedly work in multinational corporations, which brings certain challenges along with benefits. Williams raised one of the key questions with regard to preparing students for work in diverse cultural contexts: what intercultural communication skills should be developed in order for the communication to be successful (1992, p. 247)? In addition, one of the important questions, both theoretical and practical, remains: is it possible to teach students 'the right ethical standards' to be used in the process of international communication? Questions of this kind are of great importance not only because of the formation of EHEA but also in relation to the global education arena. International education programmes become more widespread and give rise to the interest in ethics-related teaching and research (Himelboim and Limor, 2008, p. 241).

The concept of communication ethics has a long history, beginning with the Ancient Greek rhetorical tradition. Ethics is studied by the scholars as a communication theory as well as a practice: 'The subject matter of ethics is the justification of human actions, especially as those actions affect others' (Schwandt, 2001, p. 73). In a broader sense, ethics is a form of orientation of a person within a society and it presupposes the reflection of one's own moral norms. As Denzin and Lincoln explained: 'Moral frameworks are fundamental for orienting us in social space' (2005, p. 154).

Our research is based on the concept of discourse ethics developed by J. Habermas (1990). Central to his theory is the concept of *communicative action*, which refers to the kind of interactions in which individuals coordinate their actions by achieving mutual understandings. This concept is particularly meaningful for the educational context that serves as the basis of our study. The educational system of any country is influenced by its culture as it naturally passes on values and cultural patterns. To save its integrity, every culture forms certain means of *social control* – mechanisms that regulate individual actions. Among these means are *social norms*, or expectations of an approved or disapproved behaviour. These norms are formed by perceptions of what is *good* and *bad*, *acceptable* or *unacceptable*; in short, social norms are derived from social values. Social norms are learned to be one's own (*internalized*) as a result of a process called *socialization* for which the educational system serves as one of the main agents. Members of a society perceive these norms as social prescriptions for or bans against doing something in various situations. The norms, along with other elements such as ethical standards, form the system of behavioural standards for each individual. These ethical standards are defined here 'in terms of the norms which direct the participants in the communication activity' (Greenberg, 1991, p. 12).

According to Habermas (1990), as long as an individual is only in contact with people from his or her own culture (in one's own *subjective life-world*), social norms and ethical standards are taken for granted and do not need to be justified. As Hofstede said: 'The norm is absolute, pertaining to what is ethically right' (1991, p. 9). It can be called external control – the regulation of an individual's communicative action by the cultural system.

Being included in the process of international education, a person is no longer bound by his or her own culture; instead, acquaintance with other normative systems regulating the behaviour of individuals takes place. Interaction with foreigners on a regular basis leads to the actor's understanding that other moral systems exist and that one has to interact with people who use other moral principles as guidelines for their actions. Cultural patterns are therefore no longer taken for granted.

In an international context, a very specific 'type of situation in which communication occurs' (Infante, Rancer and Womack, 1993, p. 12), an objective social world is formed, which is different from an individual's 'life-world' (Habermas, 1990, pp. 138-9). Since new cultural patterns differ from those which people are accustomed to and are socialized in, they are far from self-evident and ethical standards can be considered an *invisible* (latent) dimension of international communication (Sisko and Reinhard, 2007, p. 358).

In this chapter, we analyse ethical issues occurring in actual communication activities. 'Moral issues are never raised for their own sake; people raise them seeking a guide for action' (Habermas, 1990, p. 179). Thus, the study of moral and ethical dilemmas in a broader sense is also incorporated into action theory. Understanding ethical problems and proposed ways to solve them should therefore serve as guidelines for actions. According to Boltanski (2007), as one acts according to moral principles, a reference group – absent at the moment of action – becomes co-present. Since the reference group is capable of performing sanctions for unanticipated behaviour, the actor rationally orients himself or herself based on the group's ethical standards. In our study, actors are perceived as rational individuals with certain cultural norms internalized and they are well aware of the costs and benefits of following ethical standards in a different environment.

The focus of our attention lies in the interpersonal level of international communication, the key topic of which can be defined as cultural differences in ethical standards (Williams, 1992, p. 234). A person usually operates on more than one level of communication at any given time. The complexity of each communication situation can be explained by an overlap of the situational contexts and the possible dissonance between the moral patterns of the actors. This complexity manifests itself as ethical dilemmas faced by the participants of the communicative action or as conflicts between participants' expectations of the behavioural patterns of others and the reality of such patterns. Solving moral problems calls for specific efforts on the part of the actors who behave in such a way that would enable the action to be successful. Behavioural strategies that lead to the success of the communicative action represent the topic of this study.

Method

Both data collection and the analysis of empirical materials are based on qualitative methods. The researchers used indepth open-ended interviews of students and professors of the Centre of European Studies at Novosibirsk State University (NSU), Russia. A specific type of communication known as *active* interview was used: 'The speakers are viewed as competent observer-analysts of the interaction they are involved in' (Silverman, 2004, p. 163). This presupposed more symmetrical peer-to-peer-like relationships with the participants.

The data were generated in two steps: during the 2002/3 (N = 18) and 2005/6 (N = 21) academic years. Dozens of Russian students, 15 of whom had had at least some previous academic exchange experience with European universities, were interviewed for the study. Almost all of the professors (a total of 12) had no previous professional experience in Russia, and came from Belgium (1), the Netherlands (2) and Italy (9). Some students and professors also had some academic experience in the US. Having actors, who simultaneously played various roles, participate in the interviews allowed for a more indepth analysis of the ethical problems faced by the actors.

Interviews were carried out either after all the communicative episodes had taken place at NSU (at the end of foreign professors' stay in Novosibirsk) or with Russian students upon their return from different exchange programmes abroad. This method had both its advantages (it was easier to collect the immediate impressions that can fade away as time passes) and disadvantages (little critical thinking over the situation develops because the time for analysing the communicative episodes is too short and an individual cannot immediately include this experience in his or her life-world).

The underlying logic of the interview implied opinion exchange on three major elements of the communicative action – objectives, rules and principles (values) that served as main elements of the framework of moral reasoning. Interviews were aimed at elaborating on the following issues: regulation of the communicative action needed for success of the educational process; the scope of permissible behaviours; and desirable models of interaction. Direct questions about the ethics of the communicative action were not included in the questionnaire. This phenomenon was studied indirectly by discussing rules that guided students' and professors' behaviours. Students and teachers could have generated their own understandings of ethical codes (Somekh and Lewin, 2005, p. 126) in ways we could not entirely foresee. Hence, every communication episode was analysed as a situation that hypothetically could encourage one to think about or become aware of moral issues. Within the logic of the discussion, interviewers purposefully did not draw attention to those questions and did not use such words as 'ethics' and 'moral' or their derivatives. Consequently, the emergence of such indicators in the discourse of actors was of particular importance. According to Habermas, the action situation is not to be separated from the speech situation (1990, p. 135). Therefore, the statements or *speech actions* of respondents – competent representatives of their cultures – were interpreted in line with this idea.

The results of the textual analysis of the interview transcripts were compared with those of participants' observations. The problem of researcher bias, due to the inherent subjectivity of this method, was partly solved by aggregating the results obtained by various investigators. All of the interviewers participated in the same educational programmes as students and therefore were able to understand the context in relation to which the respondents made their statements. Therefore, interviewers were also direct observers of the communication processes. This combination of two methods – interviews and observations – allowed us to minimize misinterpretations of the rules and principles of the communicative action.

Several limitations of the study should be mentioned. Firstly, two groups of participants of the educational process are over-represented in the analysed communicative episodes: students of NSU and professors from European universities with interaction taking place in Russia. Differences in ethical standards that were found should therefore be interpreted with this prevalence of roles in mind. Other groups – such as foreign students and Russian professors – were beyond the focus of our study.

Secondly, cross-cultural differences in Europe were not studied in detail; rather, European practices were compared with Russian customs, traditions and habits. This has to be taken into account because Europe cannot be considered a unified sociocultural arena with a common educational tradition.

Thirdly, certain ethical problems were context-dependent – they were actualized by the participants in the *here-and-now* manner and were derived from each specific situation. Therefore, these dilemmas cannot be considered to be universal. Moreover, possible influences of the degree of differences between cultural patterns and personal characteristics of participants on the perception of ethical problems were not studied either.

Although the limitations mentioned above allow only for limited generalizations of the results, this particular attempt to study the nature of ethical and moral problems in the international educational context may still be quite useful and informative.

Results

In spite of the absence of direct questions about ethics in the interview, certain deliberations of moral codes that set the boundaries of allowed and acceptable behaviours were present in the discourse. Latent ethical standards often took on the form of the *visible* dimensions of international communication as communication partners broke the normative models. Contradictions between expected and real behaviours caused a certain dissonance that took the form of astonishment, antipathy, alienation or shock.

These contradictions (ethical problems) attracted the attention of actors to the competing values of representatives of different cultures and norms in which they were socialized and which they perceived as absolute. Deviations from common behavioural rules often caused actors to reflect on moral principles that varied across different sociocultural environments. Common everyday practices, and therefore *invisible* regulators of the communicative action, then needed to be justified.

Several ethical problems faced by actors and perceived by them as inconsistencies between their expectations of behavioural principals and patterns of their partners and reality were identified. These dilemmas can be classified as either *descriptive* or *explanatory*.

Descriptive dilemmas provide the outline of the problem in the form of a narrative in which the problem is identified but there are no efforts present to explain or to solve it. These dilemmas were often accompanied by emotions of astonishment, anger or guilt. In this case, personal emotional experience played a greater role in moral justifications for the partner's behaviour. For example, students often drew attention to the non-verbal form of communication of Italian professors during lectures and seminars (lively gestures, quick changes in posture, facial expressions), which seemed unusual to Russian students and distracted them from the topics of classes. In the Russian educational sphere, more reserved behaviour is common and showing one's emotions may be rather disapproved of:

> When one of the professors rushed in during the other one's class and started telling what happened to her, interrupting the class and crying that something burned down [*laughs*], this annoyed me a little. When our professors come in the middle of the class of the other, they open the door carefully and ask [the other] to come out saying 'Excuse me, could you come out for a second?' But this one just flew in [*laughs*]. (Respondent 28,[1] student, NSU)

In turn, Italian professors were concerned by the reserved character of the Russian students – the absence of facial expressions, except for constrained politeness, and their distant attitude. It surprised the professors and was seen as a lack of interest in the subject:

> What surprised me the most is that in the beginning the communication climate was very cold. Everybody was quiet and all seemed far away from me. But during the break or at the end of class they were very nice, so that I thought I was mistaken and they were very interesting people, very kind, very nice and friendly. But they did not look [like] that. I don't understand passiveness, absence of reaction. I think when there is passiveness there is a lack of interest. (Respondent 36, university professor, Italy)

Explanatory dilemmas exploited rational methods of thinking for which actors not only used their knowledge and intelligence to make sense out of various situations, but their previous social experiences as well. Participants were trying to justify the behaviour of others by searching for reasons as to why their counterparts' actions differed from what was expected. Explanations were often preceded by descriptions of dilemmas encountered; however, reflections on the ways to solve the problems were mostly absent. For example, students, who did not expect to have to evaluate the course or that the professors would want to decide together with them on the form of the final exam, were surprised that professors encouraged questions and discussions. But the longer the interaction, the more different schemes of action converged:

> When professors from abroad came, our students had problems. It is not common to say whether you liked the course or not. Although every student has his or her own preferences [as to] which course they liked and which they didn't, they don't talk about it. When the professor asks [the student] to evaluate the lecture, give recommendations, problems arise – because they [students] don't know how to put it, what to say, what to write. (Respondent 16, student, NSU)

Some actors not only acknowledged the differences of normative models but, considering their interests, adopted the perspective of all other participants of the action. This illustrates the process described by Habermas (1990, p. 65). The acknowledgement serves as a basis for solving moral problems. The desire to solve such dilemmas calls for special efforts, the absence of which makes communication less successful.

The example of the presence of Russian professors at lectures delivered by their foreign counterparts illustrates this point:

> In my classes [in Novosibirsk] not only students but Russian professors were always present. It's silly but in Italy a professor wouldn't come up with a thought to listen to another professor's lecture together with students. 'I am a professor and I cannot be here with students.' For us it is a rule. Here [in the international education context] it is silly and works against success. You've broken that rule. (Respondent 35, university professor, Italy)

Our analysis of cases confirms that the ethics of norms, rules and ideas is not external to human beings. This revelation becomes evident when participants treat ethical standards differently from the normative patterns of their culture. Expectations for the partner's behaviour are derived from models common to one's own culture and may disagree with the actual actions of the counterpart who acts according to different behavioural standards. The rejection of one's own culturally imposed (and therefore not requiring justification) forms of social control demonstrates the readiness of actors to reach a consensus for the sake of the success of education:

> Suppose, if our professor [*laughs*] sits on the table – that irritates me sometimes. When it is done by [foreign professors] – it does not irritate me. (Respondent 25, student, NSU)

> The fact that students come up to me during the break to ask something is a little unusual. In Italy this is not at all natural. When students came up to me after class to ask questions – that was more interesting than the class itself. That was very important for understanding something greater. (Respondent 35, university professor, Italy)

In the studied network of local interactions, ethical principles of a conventional nature were formed, which partly substituted those that were culturally imposed. These principles can be divided into two groups – *general* and *context-sensitive*, that is, having a situational character. The conventional basis in the international community is less stable and more short-term oriented than in a monoculture context. This situation demands more rationality and more readiness from actors to reach a consensus:

> I had an impression that [the attitude towards] international students was not the same as towards regular students. I felt it here

[in Novosibirsk] and there [in Milan] as well. Professors always think that they may offend us, our national feelings. (Respondent 3, student, NSU)

I think [European] professors acted very carefully, they probably set distinct restrictions on themselves. (Respondent 23, student, NSU)

One of the general moral principles of the communicative action is respect for one's counterpart, which appears in the discourse of most respondents as a universal rule of successful communication. Students and teachers define *general* ethical standards similarly – in international education, mutual respect between students and professors becomes more important, while their cultural origin and differences in values and behavioural models pale in comparison. Ting-Toomey supports this argument: 'Human respect is a prerequisite for any type and form of intercultural communication' (1999, p. 276). The aim of reaching mutual respect was referred to as an essential principle of communicative action. A lack of respect towards one's partner was often evaluated extremely negatively, with no regard as to whether the partner who ignored these maxima was a representative of the first party's culture or a foreigner:

I think a teacher, a foreign teacher has to respect [the] values and orientation of the student which, perhaps, to some extent are not the same [as] his values. (Respondent 20, university professor, Italy)

One should be polite and intelligent, by that [I mean] you show respect toward the professor. From one [side] and from another side there should be mutual respect. (Respondent 34, student, NSU)

Respect took different forms in various communicative episodes: kindness to one another, mutual politeness, tactfulness, friendliness, hospitality and tolerance:

[In France] I was very friendly and people treated me the same. And professors tried to make something clear. In general, I noticed that when the foreigner comes we all try to show him or her that we are very nice, very kind and so on. (Respondent 4, student, NSU)

Well, the most surprising and good fact was that people, students, and other teachers are very warm with me, and I do like this. That's [a] good surprise. (Respondent 20, university professor, Italy)

Respondents more experienced in international communication formulated rather *general* principles of moral action which went beyond the context of the analysed episodes. One of these principles is tolerance towards the counterpart, a refusal to impose one's own ways of doing things on the partner who is used to other regulators of behaviour. As a result, the ethics of international actors has become a mix of the norms common to and imposed by one's own culture and of some *context-specific* behavioural norms:

> When somebody acts against the rules of [one's own] culture it is bad. When somebody from the external environment starts to act that way, everybody tolerates it because they understand that he is just not familiar with the rules. This makes one smile, or not. Foreigners are like children: when children act not according to the rules we say they have to learn the rules, they don't know them yet. We do not conceal the situation, but treat it mellow. If you treat it good from a moral point of view there can be no problems. (Respondent 2, university professor, the Netherlands)

In contrast to *general* ethical standards, *context-sensitive* rules are dependent on the peculiarity of each communicational situation in which the roles of students and professors are imposed by the educational context and overlap with cross-cultural differences. Context-sensitive principles are relevant only to each specific communicative action analysed, and their application to a broader context is limited. However, in this context, regulators of behaviour are formed by the actors (internally and consciously) not out of the *frame* of the action, since cultural patterns can be contrasting, but *during* the action.

In the analysed discourse, several *context-sensitive* principals were consistently present. Firstly, there were procedural rules that regulated the multilevel communicative action. Of particular interest were the scripts of formation of conventions relevant to the international educational context. As a rule, at first certain aspects of the action were perceived as problematic by the actors. For instance, in the interviews, students often drew attention to what they considered to be the unusual work schedule of European professors in which attitude towards time as a parameter of educational communication was different from the students' own attitudes. Continuing class during breaktime was perceived negatively as violating the right of students for a break:

> [A topic] critical for all students ... was maintenance of breaks. It was noticeable that they have a very different work schedule. Every time

to adjust to it for the students is not very good, it contributes to a decrease in attentiveness and activity. [A s]triking example is no hint for a break. I mean, I can't say that the class was too tiresome, it was rather interesting. (Respondent 30, student, NSU)

To reach a consensus, the 'victims' justified the unusual behaviour of their partners, transforming it into morally acceptable behaviour. As a result, a tactful reaction of students to the uncommon behaviour of the professor was formed and a mutual work schedule became gradually conventional, not infringing upon the interests of either party:

A [European] professor who gave a lecture on welfare did not stop, he talked permanently. Then, he thought that it was time to have a break and looked at the audience. And he asked one guy to tell him when it was time for a break. That guy literally interrupted him when it was time. [Professors] talk, [they] are carried away and we have to stop them. It is troublesome, uneasy, but we got out of the situation. (Respondent 27, student, NSU)

This could surprise me and seem rather unacceptable for a professor. At NSU professors usually watch the time. For European professors it may be hard to watch [the] time since the lecture was so intense, one needed to talk constantly, show something. But, on the other hand, maybe it served as a way to establish contacts. When we watched the time, we got an opportunity to tell them, and they responded and thanked us for tracking the time. Maybe it is like an initial bridge which allows for establishing ties later on. (Respondent 29, student, NSU)

Another procedural rule of the communicative action was the usage of the most convenient language. In most analysed cases it was the English language, foreign for all of the participants. Students sometimes violated this rule, communicating in Russian with each other, but, when reflecting on this infringement, they acknowledged this behaviour to be unacceptable. The communicative space should be open and comfortable for all of the participants and not only in terms of the use of language, but also in terms of the control of paralinguistic means. Students realized the need to be particularly careful with the use of laughter:

[Students have to] try to communicate less in their native language with each other. [A professor] comes to another cultural environment and when there is a foreign language heard from all the sides ... [the professor] loses his train of thought. (Respondent 23, student, NSU)

Students should try to support the professor morally. We have some kind of our own humour, we laugh in Russian [*laughs*] and the professor doesn't understand what we are laughing about. Students should explain their behaviour. We must not, as it happened, actively communicate in Russian when the foreign professor is present. (Respondent 31, student, NSU)

In addition to the procedural rules, several substantive rules were formed, in which the boundaries of the action regarded as ethically acceptable from every participant's perspective were outlined. Specifically, the most common objective of professors and students towards the success of the educational process formed the perception that behaviours that hindered the attainment of knowledge (those moving the focus of attention to secondary activities) were unacceptable:

There are certain things that one must not do: drink, eat, and use mobile phones. These are written rules in my university [in Brussels]. You cannot bring a switched-on mobile phone to class, as, for example, it was yesterday [at NSU]. You have to switch it off before coming to class. (Respondent 21, university professor, Belgium)

In most cases, partners were attentive to the reaction of their counterparts and were ready to take their partners' interests into account and to change their own behaviour accordingly, even if it meant not abiding by the standards of their own culture:

In Italy it is compulsory: if a student leaves he usually asks, 'Please, may I go out?' Here, this does not happen, these rules don't work here. But, attention! I don't think that this necessarily needs to happen because we are adults. I saw that students leave and come back without disturbing me. (Respondent 35, university professor, Italy)

In the analysed communication episodes, efforts towards reaching a consensus were also made with regard to one important rule – the rule regulating the presence in class of some professors from NSU during lectures and seminars held by European teachers (an example mentioned earlier). Most of the instructors from Italy were surprised to find somewhat older people in the audience who, along with students, asked questions and participated in discussions:

> The situation I experienced those days was special. The audience, for example, was not ordinary, [and] lecturers were present. (Respondent 38, university professor, Italy)

At the beginning, the presence of other teaching staff members caused discomfort, but later on the importance of their presence for the success of education was acknowledged. Actually, NSU professors played the role of intermediaries, competent in questions discussed and knowledgeable about the terminology. Students felt more comfortable in turning to Russian professors for explanations and their presence contributed to a better understanding of the topic.

It should be pointed out that context-sensitive principles of ethically acceptable behaviours discussed by the respondents vary across cultural contexts. Participants link moral foundations of an action predominantly to the sociocultural environment. This link becomes evident when one considers actors more experienced in international communication – those who are familiar with diverse ethical standards (for instance, in America, eating and drinking in class are considered acceptable behaviours):

> I remember from my experience, PhD students in the US eating, drinking [and] in the same time writing on laptop during classes. I'm a tolerant and liberal person as far as I can, but, of course, maybe [at] one point [it] is better to have some break and not be pushing up being active, working and working any single moment, and also skipping the time for having lunches. (Respondent 19, university professor, Italy)

In most difficult situations, serious context-sensitive obstacles appeared on the path to consensus. Actors were not able to solve these problems and form a conventional substance of rules in such communication episodes. These experiences left some participants with feelings of resentment.

The most difficult point for international actors was reaching a consensus about the *desired* rules of behaviour of students and professors. For example, the relatively passive behaviour of students during lectures and the asymmetrical flow of communication between students and professors had been for decades traditional attributes of the Russian educational system. In spite of recent changes in educational practices towards more active participation, the perceptions of students are rather inert and cannot be modified immediately. Thus, traditional patterns of behaviour were justified in the discourse of Russian students and were perceived as conditions for the success of education. In contrast, professors from Europe (or the Western tradition) viewed this behaviour as an obstacle to attaining knowledge:

> It is not only my opinion – many students say that those courses of our professors are easier which are based on this system: simply lecturing, without questions. And if questions arise, one can come up to the professor after class and discuss it one-to-one. Students from the West are used to something different: [the] professor is in constant dialogue with them, they can constantly interrupt him. (Respondent 16, student, NSU)

> I think that you are just used to [an]other style of teaching, rather different from the European one. Between student and professor there is only one-way direction, meaning you expect that the professor tells all he knows and are not ready to interact with him, answer him, and make partial interactions. You are used to being silent. I would have liked some feedback to improve my class, my lectures. I felt a lack of this, of students' feedback. (Respondent 38, university professor, Italy)

Despite acknowledging differences in educational traditions and the resulting diversity of educational methods, actors failed to form a common conventional basis for actions in order to attain the principal aims. This failure was accompanied by feelings of incomprehension, discomfort and dissatisfaction, because it was impossible to overcome the differences in roles:

> We were not eager to answer questions during the lectures; we wanted to listen [to the European professor] and not to have discussions on the topic. Maybe this surprised him. But we were surprised that he expects us to dispute about the subject [and] to express our points of view, since we were disposed to listening [*laughs*]. (Respondent 29, student, NSU)

> When I tried to make students talk during the class, I understood that it was a little complicated. Interactions between them and me

were very friendly, but without asking. (Respondent 35, university professor, Italy)

Participants thought that the failure to solve the problems of communicative action was mainly caused by the short duration of contact and that the episodes were not connected to each other. The amount of time available to think over the contradictions and find solutions was simply too short. The respondents claimed that they could have overcome many difficulties if the amount of time spent interacting had been longer. These problems included psychological problems (shyness and being reserved because of the new and unfamiliar setting), linguistic problems (insufficient conversational language skills) and thematic problems (for example, those caused by a shortage of information on the problems of the European Union):

> One week is too short to get to know each other and to get to control and check whether you understand each other or not, avoid misinterpretation. (Respondent 1, university professor, the Netherlands)

> A lot of us are being shy; the professor should shake us up, encourage discussion, talk over the most problematic themes. Different people live in our countries. (Respondent 27, student, NSU)

While every party oriented itself towards its own cultural patterns, common moral foundations of actions formed in the context of concrete episodes. The educational character of the situation predetermined the main objective of communication, according to which certain ethical standards were reconsidered. For example, the universal disposition to respect European professors was seen by the professors themselves as dysfunctional in relation to the attainment of the main goals of education. The receiving party over-emphasized the demonstration of politeness, which created obstacles along the way to understanding one another. As a rule, such a dysfunctionality was justified by the participants without regard to the extent of its influence on the success of education:

> Politeness of Russian students: is it not something that hinders good communication? They treated me as one who came from abroad, [which] I actually am, with whom they need[ed] to be very polite. I believe they did not use me as much as they could have, which restricts the forms of control of quality of communication. They

demonstrated [a] friendly attitude. But this attitude, accompanied by politeness, restricted the possibility to determine the degree of possible misunderstandings. (Respondent 1, university professor, the Netherlands)

The fact that actors with different cultural backgrounds realized that forms of social control are situational caused them to no longer perceive ethical standards as external to the action. This illustrates the proposition that: 'A moral dimension must be considered intrinsic to human being, not a system of rules, norms, and ideals external to society' (Denzin and Lincoln, 2005, p. 154). Efficient communication in the context of international education, when individuals coming from different countries and representing different cultures can orient themselves to diverse and even conflicting patterns of behaviour and ethical standards, should therefore be based on conventions that imply and articulate the norms and values of *joint action*.

Discussion

Our results show that ethical standards, as latent components of actions, cannot be ignored when dealing with the success of international communication. In an educational context, these standards serve as one of the key parameters of success. The impulse for reflecting on moral principles was often given by situations in which the schemes of actions and normative models, to which one was accustomed and which did not have to be justified, did not work once used as guidelines for actions in a different cultural context. Since cultures form dispositions and patterns of behaviours, and attempt to maintain them by the means of social control and because such behavioural patterns are deeply internalized, it may be suggested that perceptions of consensus on regulators of the communicative action form over time with an increasing number of interactions.

The complex nature of international communication is reflected in the ethical dilemmas faced by individuals operating in a cross-cultural educational context. These problems are largely derived from the recognition of the main contradiction between the aims of actions (efficiency of education) and the means of achieving these ends – orientation on ethical standards formed by one's own culturally imposed normative models. Because 'the contemporary challenge of cultural diversity ... made easy solutions impossible' (Denzin and Lincoln, 2005, p. 152), more creative solutions have to be found. The complex context of communicative action calls for a conventional basis of its moral orientations.

The success of international education is influenced by many factors, not only by the degree of diversity of culturally *given* behavioural patterns, but also by the sociopsychological characteristics of individuals who find themselves at different stages of learning about the world and who have diverse abilities of reflecting on social reality. In spite of the differences in the interpretation of ethical codes, the universal disposition of partners to respect one another is viewed as an important outcome of communicative action. Human respect is considered to be a fundamental starting point for effective international communication. Therefore, the highest stage of moral development implies the recognition of the premise of respect for others 'as ends, not means' by every rational actor (Habermas, 1990, p. 129).

The obtained results are the evidence of the actors' context-sensitivity and willingness to form new conventional rules and principles of behaviour. The participants need to coordinate their actions in order to accomplish the purposes of training. Students and teachers – representatives of different cultures – did not consider ethical principles as criteria external to their actions and just *given* by the culture. These ethical principles arose out of communicational practice and returned to it for verification of their effectiveness.

These results are of interest in the light of current debates that emphasize a 'radical break' from the canonical ethics of individual autonomy and responsibility (Denzin and Lincoln, 2005, pp. 148–9). The challenges of globalization make the mutual responsibility of participants of each interaction more important for the results of their actions. Actors may have contrasting values but they are ready to justify the norms that were not internalized by them and were derived from the situation and were agreed upon.

Communication is successful under the condition that every participant is involved in the formation of its conventional moral basis. Only regular contacts can make the initially problematic aspects of a form of behaviour of the counterparts ethically acceptable. As Habermas said: 'Moral justification will tend to illuminate a problematic action by excusing, criticizing, or justifying it' (1990, p. 51). Therefore, the readiness of actors to criticize moral beliefs formed within their own sociocultural environment has two consequences: a gradual change in one's own actions and/or a modification of how one perceives moral beliefs in general.

This fact is of particular interest to international communication. Changes that take place in international relations also impact on education and create a need to revise and reform educational practices in order to accommodate new cultural dynamics. This important, necessary and timely pedagogical aim can be accomplished by *integrating* the teaching of communication skills and ethical considerations. The main idea is to foster 'ethical sensibilities in students and facilitate their moral development by highlighting the centrality of ethics' (Conn, 2008, p. 140) in international communication practices. As a result, a duality of pedagogical goals becomes apparent: professional skills have to be developed along with some ethics training.

Considering the importance of cultural diversity, we should no longer teach *the right ethical standards*. The normative basis of communicative action is formed during the communication process and is a result of a consensus of its participants. According to the concepts of Piaget, Kohlberg and Habermas, the process of learning is regulated by the insights of its participants (as cited in Habermas, 1990, p. 34). Thus, forms of external control (control of the cultural systems experienced by actors) become less significant than those of internal control (a new situational set of norms and rules that is internalized by every participant and that serves as a set of regulators of communicative action).

Success in international communication can be achieved as participants aim at forming more transparent ethical principles and adjust their actions accordingly. The focus of attention during all training in international communication should therefore be the development of certain necessary skills – such as tolerance to cultural differences, mutual responsibility for decisions and actions, motivation towards critical self-reflection and flexibility – rather than teaching students *the right ethical standards*. An important pedagogical guideline is the concept of moral development that emphasizes a gradual convergence between the moral beliefs and moral actions of individuals.

Authors' note

The authors gratefully acknowledge the help of E. Dunenkova, J. Kotarskaya, I. Lenko, M. Molokeeva and A. Svintitckaya of NSU, Russia, in conducting interviews, as well as the assistance of all the participants of the surveys. Additionally, the authors would like to thank Ryan DeLaney for his thoughtful insights.

References

Boltanski, L. (2007). *La souffrance à distance. Morale humanitaire, médias et politique; suivi de La présence des absents*, 2nd edn. Paris: Gallimard.

Conn, C.E. (2008). 'Communication Pedagogy: A Resumé Case Study Exemplar Integrating Writing Skills and Ethics Training in Business', *Business Communication Quarterly*, 71(2), 138–51.
Denzin, N.K. and Lincoln, Y.S. (eds) (2005). *The SAGE Handbook of Qualitative Research*, 3rd edn. Thousand Oaks: Sage.
Greenberg, K.J. (ed.) (1991). *Conversations on Communication Ethics*. Norwood: Ablex.
Habermas, J. (1990). *Moral Consciousness and Communicative Action*, C. Lenhardt and S.W. Nicholsen (trans.). Cambridge: MIT Press.
Himelboim, I. and Limor, Y. (2008). 'Media Perception of Freedom of the Press: A Comparative International Analysis of 242 Codes of Ethics', *Journalism*, 9(3), 235–65.
Hofstede, G. (1991). *Cultures and Organizations: Software of the Mind*. Glasgow: HarperCollins.
Infante, D.A., Rancer, A.S. and Womack, D.F. (1993). *Building Communication Theory*, 2nd edn. Prospect Heights, IL: Waveland Press.
Schwandt, T.A. (2001). *Dictionary of Qualitative Inquiry*, 2nd edn. Thousand Oaks: Sage.
Silverman, D. (ed.) (2004). *Qualitative Research: Theory, Method and Practice*, 2nd edn. London: Sage.
Sisko, L.A. and Reinhard, K. (2007). 'Learning to See What's Invisible: The Value of International Faculty Exchange', *Business Communication Quarterly*, 70(3), 356–63.
Somekh, B. and Lewin, C. (eds) (2005). *Research Methods in the Social Sciences*. London: Sage.
Ting-Toomey, S. (1999). *Communicating across Cultures*. New York: Guilford Press.
Williams, F. (1992). *The New Communications*, 3rd edn. Belmont: Wadsworth.

Note

1. To preserve the interviewees' anonymity, they are referred to by number only.

13
Instead of a Conclusion: Is Education the Answer? Or What May All This Mean?

Alexander G. Nikolaev

This volume makes an attempt to analyse a whole host of ethical problems in the area of international communication. What is interesting is the unusual variety of issues and fields covered in this book. Sometimes it may seem that they are so far apart that may have little to do with each other. For example, what do problems that college professors encounter when teaching in a foreign country have in common with religious rhetoric, with health communication campaigns or with news coverage of Egyptian traditional rights and ceremonies? But amazingly all of them deal with the same issue – how we make ethical decisions while communicating in an international context.

In other words, the very scope of the problem of international ethics makes it extremely complex. It was a challenge even to just begin working on this issue. But it seems like we have made a good start. Certainly, we only scratched the surface but still managed to address and cover quite a few important areas of international human activities and corresponding ethical problems. In this chapter we will try to briefly summarize the most interesting and important arguments and points raised in the volume, understand what all this may mean and find at least some (even though very tentative) answers to the main ethical questions.

It seems like international ethical problems can be roughly divided into three categories. Philosophical issues deal with deep psychological, cognitive and social dilemmas that occur when people communicate at an international level. Area-specific issues deal with particular fields of international human activities – such as journalism, public relations, education, and political and interpersonal communication. Finally, purely technical dilemmas (such as photo-image manipulation) may also present ethical challenges when one deals with international issues.

The problem is that these categories are not mutually exclusive – they permeate each other. This classification may be better depicted as a pyramid where ethical issues are at the foundation of the entire structure, area-specific problems are the main building blocks of the body and technical dilemmas are just the small tip of the formation.

It will be difficult to analyse this volume category by category because, for example, while discussing problems of political rhetoric we will inevitably stumble into larger philosophical issues, and while discussing technical problems we will actually be addressing area-specific issues. But from the very beginning we tried to structure this book conceptually as an inverted pyramid. We started with general philosophical ideas and then moved towards area-specific and technical dilemmas. So, in this chapter we will go over the entire volume and see what kind of deeper theoretical meaning we can find behind described facts and stories. However, the main problem will be to find a way out of this huge labyrinth of issues. Maybe it is unfeasible, but at least it is worth a try and we may have a lot of fun on our way to this arguably impossible goal. OK, let's start.

Philosophical issues

In Chapter 1, Clifford G. Christians addresses the same issue that was covered in the Introduction to this volume – the philosophical debate between universalists and relativists. And he is also making an attempt at finding a solution to this dilemma. In order to do so, he suggests first divorcing cultural relativism from moral relativism and then finding common (or universal) ethical foundations by using such concepts as *protonorms* and *ethical realism*.

However, first he addresses the issue of the *narrative*. He notices a 'preoccupation with narrative in communication studies', which is not surprising given that narrative *is* communication. Then, he writes in his chapter:

> moral values unfold dialectically in human interaction. Ethical understanding is a cultural product. Moral commitments are embedded in the practices of particular social groups and they are communicated through a community's stories. Moral values are situated in the cultural context rather than being anchored by philosophical abstractions. Contextual values replace ethical absolutes. The domain of ethics shifts from principle to story, from formal logic to community formation.

However, he also believes that:

> *narrative ethics* is conflicted in its own terms about which value-driven stories ought to be valued ... How does one determine the status of context-dependent, everyday discourse within context dependency? What in narrative itself distinguishes good stories from destructive ones? On what grounds precisely does narrative require fundamental changes in existing cultural and political practices? ... [w]hich valuing to value[?]

Christians then discusses two foundation pillars for the new international ethics – *protonorms* and *ethical realism*. Protonorms are primordial and almost biological characteristics of the human nature, as he claims: 'Neuropsychology documents that through evolutionary naturalism, the human species has a sense of right and wrong. This biological inheritance is the ground for universalizing moral development and an ethics of care throughout the species.' In terms of *ethical realism*, Christians says that there is *real ethics* out there (ethics that can be objectively discovered) as opposed to *socially constructed* ethics, which he identified with relativism. He writes: 'From a realist perspective, we discover truths about the universe that exist within it. Discovering values is incommensurable with constructionism.'

In conclusion, Christians summarizes his arguments. He states that: 'Moral relativism justified by cultural diversity yields arbitrary definitions of goodness.' He believes that we cannot accept the ethics of some communities because 'the communities we describe ethnographically are not necessarily good'.

Finally, Christians makes an excellent point:

> In order to make philosophical work on ethical relativism fruitful, media ethics needs to nurture the philosophical imagination across the board. All the ethical issues we face should be rooted in philosophical beliefs about the character of human beings and the meaning of life. Debates over issues such as ethical relativism are not only an intellectual exercise but a venue for learning how to live.

This is a great statement. Let's indeed try to be creative and think about all this more. Probably, in this case we will be able to find a way to solve this complex theoretical dilemma.

Both chapters in Part II of this book are also philosophical in nature, although formally they belong to the category of political rhetoric. But we know that rhetoric and philosophy are inseparable. Therefore, most of the issues raised and discussed in these chapters are deeply philosophical.

For example, Gerard Elfstrom in Chapter 3 explores the use of the idea of democracy in international political rhetoric. He shows tolerance by saying that nobody is right or wrong when choosing one form of government or another. Such different forms are based on the strength of emphasis that different cultures and nations place on *the collective* versus *the individual*. It has been argued for a long time that the idea of Western democracy tramples over the collective element in favour of the individual. Consequently, it is not appropriate for the rest of the world. This argument has traditionally raised quite a large amount of controversy among politicians, international communicators and scholars. One of the attempts at solving this dilemma is covered in Elfstrom's chapter – the one suggested in the 1970s by John Rawls and Robert Nozick. Elfstrom writes that they 'distinguished between the requirements of a political order and the values individuals should be allowed to pursue in their personal lives'. He then continues:

> They argued that defensible governing structures must place ultimate value on individual human lives. Nonetheless, within this overarching concern, individuals, while leading their private lives, should be allowed to pursue such values as they see fit. Of course, this view has the unsettling implication that some people may gain greatest value for their lives by devoting them to some other cause or movement. However, if that is what gives their lives greatest fulfilment, the jarring note disappears since their devotion to a cause is what gives their lives value ... The only governmental order that will allow each of these diverse individuals with distinctive values and personalities to achieve maximal gratification is for government to remain aloof from these private matters and allow each individual to pursue them as he or she desires.

In the philosophical part of the chapter, Elfstrom reminds us of a common point argued by Kant that only the notion of individual autonomy could serve as a moral ground for ethics. This argument is something of a favourite with many Western philosophers. It is an interesting point that we will discuss later on in this chapter.

As in any morality-related discussion, religion is front and centre in the international ethics debate. And this is not surprising. First of all, religion serves as the foundation of morals for many people in the world.

Secondly, it shapes the culture to a large extent. And certainly, with the considerable variety of cultures, state systems and religions, this factor could not be missed in our book. As such, we asked a professional theologian to explore the use of religious appeals (specifically the language of 'good' and 'evil') in international *political* rhetoric. We needed a deep religious exploration that would uncover the spiritual roots of the political rhetoric of 'good' and 'evil' and would provide us with the evaluation as to the use of this language by secular people for political purposes. Do they use it correctly from the theological point of view? Anna Kasafi Perkins did this very well in Chapter 4.

The main thesis of Kasafi Perkins's chapter is that 'evil' is a deeply theological concept, which raises questions concerning the nature of divine omnipotence and the meaning of innocent suffering. It is also deeply moral as it calls into question the roles of individuals and nations in the *fight* against evil. Kasafi Perkins believes that in dividing the world into 'us' versus 'them', 'good' versus 'evil', the term harks 'back to a Manichean notion of the world that ignores the ambiguity of the motives, actions and justice of the self-proclaimed "good side"'. What is called 'evil' is also automatically beyond redemption, beyond discourse, beyond comprehension and understanding. Yet there is no need to locate this stark dualism in the Manichean realm only; Christianity has a dualism embedded in its doctrine which gives expression to the presence of evil in the world. In Chapter 4 we read that by some: 'The earthly struggle against evil is viewed as a reflection of the battle between God and Satan which, having been lost by Satan in heaven, has continued on earth (Rev. 1:7–9). It is a futile battle, however, as God has already won.' Therefore, it is possible to argue that the usage of the term 'evil' in international political rhetoric has deep soteriological roots, that is, salvation will be brought about, in this case in the form of civilization and democracy. But a political system cannot serve to destroy evil for good. Viewed theologically, such attempts are futile because in Christian theology it is not nations that rid the world of evil, but rather God and the people of God when they exercise moral conscience.

This is a fascinating idea. Indeed, civilization and democracy is not the heaven on earth and, from the theological point of view, all earthly battles are in vain because the way to salvation is through the righteousness of the people of God. It is not up to separate nations to win the victory for God. And righteousness simply cannot be expressed in violence. In terms of the West, we could easily find a connection between the contemporary American religious right political rhetoric and the rhetorical traditions of the Puritans. In terms of the East, the similarities between the speeches by contemporary Jihadists and the language of Saladin in the twelfth century are quite striking. And the main conclusion from all this is quite interesting. It seems as though people on both sides (radical Christians or fanatical Muslims) who use the rhetoric of 'good' and 'evil' in religious terms are (to put it mildly and politely) not very smart individuals because they clearly do not even understand the basic principles of their own religions and badly misinterpret and misrepresent them.

For Christians, non-violence, peace, love, understanding and moral integrity are the pillars of their religion. For Muslims, 'jihad' is a fight against one's own imperfections, an eternal striving for personal development and a quest for moral enlightenment. From a theological point of view, it has nothing to do with violence and cutting human heads off. It seems like people who declare crusades against Muslims or violent jihad against Christians are precisely those who know nothing about these two great religions and understand precisely nothing of the concept of spirituality. All that these blind people see is this earthly world and its political struggles, which has nothing to do with religion. There is another explanation: they shamelessly use religion to stir up hatred and, by so doing, to augment their personal wealth and power. But in either case – whether due to stupidity or propaganda – the use of the religious appeal of eternal 'good' and 'evil' in *political* rhetoric is utterly inappropriate and consequently unethical.

It is interesting that the chapter just discussed (Chapter 4) closely intersects with another chapter – Chapter 2, written by Stephen M. Croucher. Croucher's chapter is quite fascinating because he did something quite unusual in terms of international ethics research. He did not just ask a bunch of superficial questions and convert them into a host of almost meaningless numbers. He went out and actually talked to people. And he was really listening to them. He did not lead them with crafty questions to the conclusions he wanted to receive (as many researchers unfortunately do – intentionally or unintentionally). He let them talk openly. He let them express their honest opinions and deep-seated feelings, which is quite refreshing. That is why his material is extremely interesting.

Croucher was exploring the opinion of people on the ethical aspect of international communication at the interpersonal level. Specifically, he examined opinions of Muslims and Christians who live in Europe on the matter of interpersonal conflict. And his findings are at the same time encouraging and discouraging (unfortunately, rather the latter than the former). This is so because, although we see some pan-human reactions and emotions, it is still clearly visible that the differences are quite substantial. First of all, it seems like so-called Christians ('so-called' because many of them do not practise their religion but merely associate themselves with a certain type of culture) are more prone to conflict in everyday life than Muslims. Quite a few of them expressed a higher tolerance for conflict ('let's just get it done with' or 'it will clear things up') than Muslims. Secondly, Muslims seem to be slightly more likely to use religious and, consequently, moral considerations in interpersonal conflict situations than so-called Christians. In general, Muslims employ mostly religious considerations and Christians employ mostly societal (secular) considerations in such situations. Finally, it looks like so-called Christians are much worse educated about their own religion (with which they allegedly associate themselves) than their Muslim counterparts. This can clearly be seen from their own statements. They say that they 'were taught' or 'got used to' being aggressive and dominating in a conflict situation. They are striving for a win. For anybody who has ever read the New Testament and understands the character and the teaching of Jesus Christ, it is clear that being aggressive, dominating and winning in an open conflict are actually counter-Christian qualities. All this is directly correlated with quite disappointing conclusions that can be drawn from Kasafi Perkins's chapter: people, especially in the West, do not actually know and understand their own religion. It seems that a purely secular type of Western education renders a great disservice to the character of some people who think that dominating others is consistent with being a Christian.

Generally speaking, the conclusions from Croucher's chapter are not particularly promising. It seems like no matter what we do or say, both sides still consider the other side's actions and positions unethical and their own actions deeply moral. And all this happens in places where people live and work side-by-side and even have friends in the other community. And the eternal question of 'what can be done here?' still goes unanswered, although we will suggest *an* answer in the part of this chapter dealing with education.

Area-specific issues

Journalism and media behaviours

Part III of this book covers ethical problems in the area of journalism, but it also touches upon other types of media behaviours such as advertising and cinema. The first chapter in the part (Chapter 5) is the most diverse and demonstrative in terms of cultural insight into international ethical issues. Its author – Iman Roushdy-Hammady – is a native of Egypt, but she is a Harvard graduate and her field of expertise is medical anthropology. She is more qualified than anyone to expose and analyse deep cultural problems that occur during the process of international communication and also to provide her opinion on such cultural practices as female circumcision.

The first part of her chapter is devoted to this practice or, to be more precise, to an accident that occurred when a Western media outlet (namely CNN) aired a report, which was filmed in Egypt, on this subject. It is interesting that Roushdy-Hammady, as a medical anthropologist, neither openly defends nor condemns this practice. What she is saying in her chapter is that it is a complex cultural matter that has to be examined very carefully and dealt with by Egyptian society itself, but without foreign interference. She highlights the efforts that the government undertakes in order to outlaw this ritual and to conduct educational programmes in the strata of Egyptian society that practise it. Certainly, these efforts have varying degrees of success, but the main point is that Egyptian officials do not sit idly by – they try to deal with it in a culturally sensitive and evolutionary (rather than revolutionary) manner.

At a very delicate political moment (during an important international conference), a CNN crew finds its way into the home of a very simple and not very highly educated man, who definitely could not understand all the problems associated with his actions, and makes a report that manages to insult the entire country of Egypt (its government and its culture). It clearly shows how dangerous it is when representatives of one culture barge in with their own ethos into another culture, and what kind of consequences it may have. In this case, CNN clearly violated journalistic ethics when they, chasing after the profits that a sensational report would generate and even allegedly having some hidden political agenda, decided to air the footage without any regard for the safety of people involved and the issue they supposedly cared about so deeply.

Some philosophers would say that considering the consequences of human actions is rather a teleological than a deontological idea and therefore has little to do with the concept of ethics. The CNN people did what they had to do in their opinion. This is a very formalistic and hypocritical argument. Isn't the concern for people the foundation for human ethics? Can it actually be separated from ethics? And if it can, do we need such ethics if concern for people is not included in the code? Also, 'their opinion' was formed by their culture and clearly was not compatible with the local culture. Are the journalists supposed to consider the local ethical standards while working in other countries and cultures? These are questions for all foreign correspondents to ponder over.

The other two parts of Roushdy-Hammady's chapter deal with advertising. One of them – in *Vogue* magazine – is quite clear-cut. The stereotypical, outdated and insulting use of an image of a Muslim (or Arab) woman provoked a series of protests even in the US. It can only be compared to the Blackface minstrel routine of the nineteenth century that became synonymous with racism in the US. It is amazing how sensitive we are when we talk about certain ethical standards *inside* our own country and how insensitive we can be when applying them to *other* cultures. Using double standards in terms of morals is definitely unethical.

The other advertising case is rather more complex. There are no clear-cut answers in that situation and this may be a good thing, because not everything is easy in this world. It just seems that the CIA, while conducting their media recruiting campaign on American Arab-language TV channels, somehow missed the mark and aired adverts that, instead of recruiting people, created a sense of cognitive dissonance in the hearts and minds of Arab Americans. Instead of feeling patriotic, they felt torn between their two identities – their Muslim-Arab identity and their American identity. It seems like something went wrong. What exactly? Only professionals in the fields of psychology and anthropology could probably answer this question. But one possible answer is quite obvious. It seems that there was a lack of cultural analysis during the process of designing the adverts. We can only hope that next time they will do better.

Finally, Roushdy-Hammady's chapter ends with a case of when an interesting piece of art – a film – fell victim to a whole host of political and cultural contradictions in the Middle East. It demonstrates the simple fact that, although we are supposed to judge art on its merits, we still use culture-specific judgments. And this is where the entire situation gets really discouraging. If we cannot make an objective judgment call even about a simple and good film, can we actually be at least slightly objective about anything foreign? If not, the hope for a working international ethics system is very slim.

Chapter 6 of this volume talks about one of the most respected quality newspapers in the world – the French daily *Le Monde*. This is an interesting case because this particular paper prides itself on being as close to objective as possible and on having very high ethical standards for its journalists. Indeed, its reputation is very high in the media world.

Secondly, the chapter covers probably the most pressing and important issue in international journalism ethics – using so-called universal ethical appeals to promote personal or national interests.

The chapter's author, Élisabeth Le, conducted a thorough research of the newspaper's editorials devoted to international issues. She found that in those types of materials, *Le Monde* could assume three rhetorical identities – *Le-Monde-ness*, *French-republic-ness* and *universal-ness*. In other words, it can position itself as a carrier of ethical values of this specific publication, of the French nation or of the entire civilized world. Le shows how the newspaper plays with these identities depending on specific topics and situations. And what she finds is quite interesting:

> In *Le Monde*'s case, it would seem that the greater [ethical] danger would lie in calling upon universal principles under the identity of universal-ness to promote *Le-Monde-ness*. In other words, it would be like saying 'do as I say not because *I* say it but because *my* point of view reflects *universal* principles that must be followed by everyone' while one is *really meaning* 'do as I say because my own specific point of view must prevail'. The specific danger for *Le Monde* in this respect is the ease with which it can go from the latter to the former type of reasoning because of how its identities overlap.

It seems that even *Le Monde* quite often uses this trick – calling upon so-called universal ethical standards to justify its own or the French government's points of view and actions. It seems like this is one of the most widespread violations of media ethics but, at the same time, is probably the most difficult to combat (if it is possible to fight it at all). When national interests and personal feelings come into play, ethical considerations somehow fade away.

However, regardless of the problem discussed above, Le concludes that:

> [a]lthough French national values (liberty, equality, fraternity) have been called upon as universal values for national aims, the five editorials given as examples in this chapter *do not appear to display any unethical strategy* according to *Le Monde*'s French understanding of the top-down application of natural law (as stated in the Preamble of the Declaration of the Rights of Man and Citizen). (Emphasis added)

It seems like an appropriate conclusion. But it may still require some reservations and limitations to be attached to it because some people may look at the facts a little differently. For example, in the article entitled 'L'Europe politique existe', *Le Monde* practically demands that the democratically elected right-wing government of Austria be boycotted by other European governments and hinted that it would be nice if the Austrians somehow changed it. It seems like in that article *Le Monde* uses a universal principle (democracy) in trying to deny people of Austria their democratic right – the right to choose the government they want. Whatever attitude we may have towards right-wing parties and politicians, if they are democratically elected, they represent the will of the nation. And it may seem like *Le Monde* in this case uses so-called universal values to attempt to deny the people of Austria their liberty of political choice. The newspaper may also have violated the value of equality by trying to impose on the Austrians how they are supposed to act. This may be considered as a violation of communication ethics, even 'according to *Le Monde's* French understanding of the top-down application of natural law'.

In the last chapter in Part III (Chapter 7), Richard Lance Keeble very interestingly demonstrates quite a few specific cases when the national media, reporting on issues of international importance, relinquished their ethical responsibilities in the face of pressure from the national government and, instead of providing the public with reliable information, either hid the truth or served almost as a propaganda arm of the government. Keeble also suggests an alternative and deeply ethical way of covering international topics called *peace journalism,* and appeals to people not to be passive consumers of news products and merely complain about the media, but to be the media. He believes that such a phenomenon as *citizen journalism*, made possible by the proliferation of the Internet and contemporary advances in communication technologies, can be a model of morality-oriented media work and a counterweight to unethical journalistic practices of the corporate- and government-controlled media.

International PR and public communication

Part IV of this volume begins with Chapter 8 written by Terry L. Rentner and Lara Lengel. Rentner and Legel examine ethical issues that emerge during international social marketing health campaigns. Some people will be amazed by this chapter. The authors provide an almost completely comprehensive overview of the ethical problems associated with such campaigns, which is very important because many would think that nothing can be wrong with programmes that have such good intentions as fighting underage drinking, smoking or drug addiction. But it seems that at the international level, the problems are plentiful and almost all of them are associated with ethnocentrism and disrespect of *the other*, as well as cultural arrogance and ignorance. In this respect, the authors highlight the importance of understanding and knowledge of culture in the success of international social marketing health campaigns.

One of the main questions in any international campaign of this sort is definitely who makes decisions for whom? If one country finances or conducts such a campaign in another country, the question of culturally acceptable social standards becomes crucial. The authors write: 'Exchange theory, the foundation of social marketing, presents additional ethical issues. Targeted groups are asked to exchange an unhealthy behaviour for a healthier one deemed more socially acceptable. The question becomes *who* decides what is socially acceptable?' In other words, the key ethical issue in such campaigns is social and cultural sensitivity.

The authors also outline their point of view on how international public communication ethical issues should be viewed. This excerpt summarizes their position very well:

> Evanoff suggests that ethics must be fluid, addressing 'particular problems faced by particular people in particular situations. As new problems emerge, new ethical solutions must be found; we cannot simply fall back on past ethical traditions for guidance' (2005, p. 2). He argues that 'ethical systems can be both abandoned and created ... we are constantly in the process of creating new ethical norms to deal with emergent problems, such as advances in medical technology and increased contact across cultures. Rather than seeing ethics as fixed and unchanging, a communicative approach sees ethics as dynamic and creative' (p. 2). Ethics, within the scope of intercultural and international communication, 'can be associated with an ecological model of cultural development which recognizes that cultures may proceed along different lines of development but nonetheless co-evolve through communicative relations with other cultures' (p. 2).

Chapter 9 of this volume, by Cornelius B. Pratt and Wole Adamolekun, is devoted to a more traditional issue – the problem of public relations and public communication programmes conducted by major global corporations in so-called Third World countries, in this particular case Nigeria. The authors show that such big companies conduct substantial PR campaigns in Nigeria and spend considerable amounts of money trying to establish themselves as responsible business residents on the local market. But still, serious problems and incidents do occur – such as the Trovan drug trial case.

In order to improve the communication efforts of global corporations all over the world, the authors suggest four 'prescriptions' as to how to enhance the ethical practices of those companies within foreign locales. One of the most interesting of them is to delineate between participation *in* the communication process and participation *through* the communication process – an issue that very few PR people may even be thinking about. Finally, the authors express their support for such documents as Nigeria's 'Bill for an Act to Provide for the Establishment of the Corporate Social Responsibility Commission'. They believe that documents like this can be helpful in creating international ethical standards for the behaviour of multinational enterprises in relation to foreign locales.

In Chapter 10, Katerina Tsetsura explores the ethical aspect of the phenomenon of media transparency. Undue influence of commercial interests on journalists is an important topic. However, Tsetsura writes mostly about PR practices in Russia. In doing so, she introduces several interesting and specifically Russian terms, such as 'black PR', 'white PR' and *zakazukha*. According to her research, on the one hand, almost all Russian practitioners recognize that paying journalists for media favours is wrong but, on the other hand, it happens quite often in Russia. As to the question of why such a discrepancy exists, Tsetsura answers that: 'Although codes of ethics exist worldwide, specialists point out numerous problems with their enforcement.' From her chapter, it is indeed quite clear that, whether in Russia or in the US, the issue of enforcement of such codes is slowly coming to the fore in the international PR ethics debate.

Technical issues

The last chapter in Part IV of this volume (Chapter 11) focuses on what may be considered technical issues. Some people may ask the following question: ethically speaking, what difference does it make if a website has a survey feature or whether photos appearing on a webpage are digitally manipulated? But the chapter's authors – Melissa A. Johnson and Eileen M. Searson – correctly believe that such things do matter, because they show how honest and socially oriented the website owner is.

For example, they are right to say that the presence on official websites of such features as mailing addresses, contact telephone numbers, search bars and FAQ sections, as well as the availability of page formatting

Instead of a Conclusion: Is Education the Answer? 233

for printing and site maps, actually establish the two-way flow of communication between the site's owner and the users. Consequently, it quite demonstratively shows how *responsive to target publics* the site's owner is.

Another important issue is photo manipulation. Certainly, some people would ask: 'What's the difference if the sea looks a bit brighter and the palm trees a bit greener than in reality?' But the authors are correct in thinking that the issue is much deeper than this. Actually, the problem of visual image manipulation in international PR and journalism is very important and there is a serious body of literature on this topic (see, for example, Nikolaev, 2009). The technical manipulation of images represents an ethical problem and that is why the concept of *visual honesty* suggested by Johnson and Searson in Chapter 11 can be extremely important. They even suggest including visual honestly clauses in international PR codes. According to them, such clauses may sound like this: 'Be accurate and comprehensive in the [visual] representation of subjects' or 'Be accurate and comprehensive in the visual representation of the organization and organizational stakeholders'. Another item for the ethics code could sound like this: 'Be complete and provide context when photographing or recording subjects. Avoid stereotyping individuals and groups. Recognize and work to avoid presenting one's own biases in the work.' This sounds like an excellent idea that warrants serious consideration.

Finally, it is interesting that the authors of Chapter 11 showed what was called the Latin American *model* of or *approach* to public relations, which emphasized such values as family, respect and collectivism. This model looks different from but is by no means inferior to the so-called Western model.

Is education the answer?

Chapter 12 of this volume explores the area of international education and, by so doing, breaks new ground for research as well as for theory formation in the field of international communication ethics. Svetlana Sablina and Bella Struminskaya explore ethical problems encountered by European professors while teaching in Russia. Taking into account cultural differences, the situation was supposed to become a nightmare of ethical entanglements, but in practice everything turned out to be just fine. Moreover, when the researchers tried to answer the question as to why this was the case, their results represented 'a "radical break" from the canonical ethics of individual autonomy and responsibility', as the authors put it. It turned out that the ethical codes that participants used to regulate their communication procedures were not *given* by any culture but were *created* by communicators in the process. This takes the life out of the claim that there is some kind of *given universal* ethical standard that must be followed, because communication ethics turns out to be not *given* but *created* by communicators depending on the cultures and contexts involved. This seems to be the most efficient way to communicate internationally. The authors of Chapter 12 state that:

> Actors may have contrasting values but they are ready to justify the norms that were not internalized by them and were derived from the situation and were agreed upon.
> Communication is successful under the condition that every participant of action is involved in the formation of its conventional moral basis ... The normative basis of the communicative action is formed during the communication process and is a result of a consensus of its participants ... Success in international communication can be achieved as participants aim at forming more transparent ethical principles and adjust their actions accordingly.

Therefore, the authors believe that there is an urgent and absolutely vital change that has to be made in the area of teaching international communication ethics. They emphasize:

> a need to revise and reform educational practices in order to accommodate new cultural dynamics. This important, necessary and timely pedagogical aim can be accomplished by *integrating* the teaching of communication skills and ethical considerations ... The focus of attention during all training in international communication should therefore be the development of certain necessary skills – such as tolerance to cultural differences, mutual responsibility for decisions and actions, motivation towards critical self-reflection and flexibility – rather than teaching students *the right ethical standards*. An important pedagogical guideline is the concept of moral development that emphasizes a gradual convergence between the moral beliefs and moral actions of individuals.

Chapter 12 results in two major conclusions. The first of them is that real communication ethics is not *given* but *created* in the process itself. This means that it can be created only under certain conditions. One of these conditions is that elements of ethical standards of all the cultures involved are usually combined in the final code. Consequently, unconditional respect for other moral codes is the main element of any international communication codes of ethics. This newly created code must have such qualities as fairness, equality, respect and flexibility built into it. Therefore, statements like 'Our moral beliefs present themselves as basic truths about how human beings should act, but we are now supposed to respect incompatible moral beliefs ... By the standards of rationality available in our tribe ... being forced to accept that alternative incompatible moral outlooks ... cannot help but undermine the confidence of reflective moral agents' (Lear, 1984, p. 147) are unacceptable and harmful. But this is the main thesis of the universalist tribe.

The second conclusion may give us all some hope in quite a hopeless situation. In a world permeated with communication but also full of arrogance, ignorance and almost zoological phobias (Islamophobia, anti-Semitism, anti-Americanism, Russophobia, Sinophobia, Iranophobia, etc.) and ruled by political and economic interests, many people see any discussion of international communication ethics as childish. They say that people of different nations will keep hating each other and spreading lies and rumours about each other intentionally or unintentionally, through malice or ignorance. Unfortunately, they are partly correct. There is nothing we can do about malicious propaganda. Arguments like 'shame on you' are not going to work on people who spread lies because of hatred towards others or because of their economic and political interests.

However, there is a lot that we *can* do for people who violate international ethics because of ignorance or a mere lack of knowledge about others. Often these people are simply deceived by malicious propaganda, and what we can do is to dispel these harmful myths and falsehoods. The years of teaching experience of the editor of this book have shown that a short ten-week course is enough to dramatically change students' outlook on this world and to build into them such values as fairness, equality, respect and flexibility. All this is done as a part of a course called 'International Communication'. But the simple presence of a course like this is not going to solve the problem of ignorance. Unfortunately, many professors and textbook writers cannot overcome their own biases and hatreds. Such courses can be useful only if professors teach them honestly – explaining the way things actually are but not the way some want them to be. The material covered in such courses is supposed to be based on actual knowledge, not on stereotypes and misconceptions about other nations. Only in this case can we obtain from education extraordinarily interesting insights into the mindsets of other nations and use these insights while forming our communicational strategies, tactics, methods and approaches.[1]

It seems like education is our only answer to the problem of international communication ethics. But it can be the answer only if we reject universalism. Any alien ethical code, if installed, will ultimately be rejected as a foreign object by the moral body of another culture. But the internationalist approach, as it was described above, can be useful. People can learn how to understand each other and how to form a mutually acceptable code of ethics in the process of communication.

What may all this mean?

It is a very difficult task to make sense out of everything covered above. All the ideas, points and positions covered in this volume are valid, interesting and important. However, the incredible constellation of factors interacting with each other – culture, ethics, politics, philosophy, etc. – makes the entire debate extremely complex. Very often, a seemingly simple idea, when considered thoroughly, turns out to be not so trouble-free.

For example, there is an argument that in order to solve the international communication ethics conundrum, we merely have to separate two types of diversity – cultural diversity is good but moral diversity is bad. But there are at least two problems with this position. Firstly, is it possible to separate culture and morality? Is there a culture without morality and morality without culture? Considering culture without morality is like considering a car without its engine. It seems like it is suggested that cultures are devoid of morality, but morality is something separate from culture, hanging out there in thin air as a huge universal dome over all cultures. And different cultures, which by themselves have no moralities of their own, have to look up to that huge dome over their heads for guidance. This idea – that cultures do not contain morality but that morality is something unrelated and external to them – may seem strange to some people. What is culture in this case? After all, it is not just a bunch of funny outfits that people wear. Isn't it supposed to be deeper than that?

The second and closely related problem is about the origins of morality. If morals are culturally derived, then these two concepts can be theoretically equated. If not, then what is the source of morals? One obvious answer is a supreme being (some call it God), but this answer would be appropriate only for those who believe in God. However, does it mean that those who do not have no moral ground to claim at all? What would the other answer be, except for God?

Then there is the problem of narrative. In international communication, ethics are usually expressed in the form of moral stories or media stories with some moral element built into them. And how can we say who is right, who is wrong, what is good, what is bad, what is indeed moral, what is immoral, and what fundamental political and cultural changes are required to make human practices ethical? For example, when one country requires fundamental changes in the existing cultural and political practices of another country, does it present an ethical problem? These are all excellent questions. These are real and central international communication ethics questions. These are at the root of the issue. But, amazingly, most scholars simply sweep them aside as unanswerable and dead-end forms of inquiry, and by so doing, they practically proclaim the entire area of international communication ethics to be unsolvable. If these are the root questions and we perceive them as merely rhetorical, what's the use?

On a related note, it could also be said that if Zygmunt Bauman uses Nietzsche's perspective that ethics in postmodern times has been replaced by aesthetics (1993, pp. 178–9), he may be right. It seems to be so when an aesthetically appealing myth of liberation and struggle for freedom completely replaces the truth (which is how it was in the case of Kosovo). In other words, saying what actually happens takes a back seat to creating a beautiful narrative, basically, a fairy tale. And it is the universalists who use this aesthetic effect to their advantage because universalism is very appealing and is on the surface aesthetically attractive; that is, universalists are actually the followers of Nietzsche because they replace ethics with aesthetically appealing mythical narratives.

In order to solve the problem of international communication ethics, many scholars suggested the idea of the existence of some universal human values or norms. The value of human life is usually the main value they highlight, but a critical thinker could suggest the following point of view. The problem is that each culture treats human life differently and assigns a different value to it. This is the issue of the meaning of life and the purpose of life.[2] Cultures create their own approaches to this and definitely order their political institutions and social structures *differently* in this respect (abortion, capital punishment, kamikaze or suicide bombers, etc.). It is not that nobody wants to die, it is how we define and conceptualize death for ourselves and others (communication across the cultures). In other words, even if we assume that there are universals out there, we are talking not about their very existence but about communicating them to others. This is where the problem occurs.

It seems like the idea of some overarching norms does not resolve the issue of the differences in cultural interpretations and intercultural transmissions. It is not even clear in the first place whether these universal norms are primordial or culturally derived and defined, or what they have to do with communication ethics in general.

The whole idea of universal norms is based on the presupposition that there is real ethics out there (ethics that can be objectively discovered) as opposed to socially constructed ethics that are usually equated with relativism. This seems like a slightly misguided point of view because relativist ethics can be considered as built by the objective, independent and very real forces of history, environment and culture. How is this different from the real ethics that are constructed by objective and independent forces of nature (environment) and evolution (history)? Both of these can be discovered and both of them are, to some extent, contracted by external forces.

In general, there are some problems with counterposing the process of discovering moral values to constructionism. Firstly, even if we discover the biological basics for ethics, we then have to interpret, define and communicate them. This is where *communication* problems start. Secondly, there are different types of values – *first-order* values (primordial, biological) and *second-order* values (purely socially constructed). In addition, it depends on which type of values we are dealing with. We can also *discover* second-order values that have been previously constructed anyway. And it seems that exactly this type of value is of the greatest interest for communication scholars – values like freedom, democracy, etc.

Some scholars say that it will not be that difficult to translate, so to speak, these values into other ethical languages (metaphorically speaking) of other peoples. However, this is not exactly so. Many meanings and emotions are lost in translation. And this *translation error*, this deviation is precisely our area of inquiry – the area where communication fails in translating from the ethical language of one nation to another. The question is why does this happen if we are so similar and it is so easy? Even if we assume that there are no translation problems with so-called *natural* (discovered) norms (which is by itself a very problematic assumption), what are we going to do with *constructed* values? This is where communication problems are inevitable. And the question of 'what do we do with them?' is still unanswered. In other words, the idea of universal natural norms does not solve the communication problem. Cultures first make norms out of protonorms (the first-order effect) and the deviations are already quite significant. Then, they have to communicate these norms (not protonorms) to the members of their own and other societies (the second-order – communicational – effect). And this is where communication ethics problems arise. Moreover, the idea of protonorms is something so primordial that it borders on to the biological sphere. Thus, it cannot deal properly with morality. There is no biological morality. Sex is not immoral in itself. The predators in the animal kingdom are not immoral creatures, but human predators are. In other words, morality is a social phenomenon and exists only in the social contexts of different societies. There is a huge gap between something nature-given, almost instinct-like, and complex human moral deliberations and emotions. It is quite unclear how this huge gap may be bridged. There is a big missing link here that philosophers still have to discover. Therefore, the idea of the very existence of some universal *real* ethical norms is quite debatable. Even if we assume that they do exist and have something to do with social morality, by themselves (as practically physiology-based) they cannot be philosophically good or bad. However, their social interpretations can, and this is what we are concerned with.

Another interesting point that some philosophers make is that actual moral rules, which exist out in the real world, cannot make the basis for normative guidelines because the mere fact of their existence does not make them necessarily correct. But if we discard what we can actually observe and identify in the real world, in this case, how are we going to discover these universal real norms? Or are they completely detached from reality? In this case, the problem of the source arises once again.

But even more troubling is the logical continuation of the argument above. It follows that if we see some moral norms in action in some communities, they can be discarded as meaningless because they are merely situated in this particular space and time, and cannot serve as a source or even a reflection of the ideal and real universal norms. As some put it, communities we observe 'are not necessarily good'. First of all, dividing world communities into good and bad is a scary idea by itself. What are the criteria? Besides, we *always* apply ethical standards to specific situations. Therefore, we must take context – place and time – into account. Is it precisely the failure to take into account local specifics that leads to the worst ethical violations? Secondly, the local context and moral issues may be meaningless to the rest of the world but not to the people who live in this context and by these moral issues. For them it is very meaningful – it is their entire world, their life and death. Also, for universalists, it is usually meaningless if it is located in Africa, China or Eastern Europe. But if that immediate space is New York City or

Washington DC, somehow it immediately becomes a timeless truth and a universal reality. Finally, isn't it a requirement of universalism to find common ethical features in specific situations from all over the world in order to find universal features? If we reject each of them out of hand, how are we going to find those *real* features? Isn't it supposed to be a presupposition of universalists that at least some of them are *genuine*? And from this follows the important question – who is to decide what is genuine and what is not? It seems like those who are going to assume this role are supposed to possess some kind of supreme knowledge that the rest of the world is somehow missing. And who are these awesome and omnipotent judges?

There was an interesting theoretical suggestion made in this volume to confine cultural relativism to the area of epistemology and then to try to sort out all the communication ethics issues somehow separately. But communication is an epistemological phenomenon. We may not even call it an *epistemological* dimension but a *communicational* dimension, which is basically the same thing. We do not communicate values themselves – we communicate ideas about them, their definitions and explanations, as well as their descriptions. Values by themselves are not even communicable. It is when we *communicate* values to each other that errors occur. Everybody knows that killing people for fun or profit is wrong. We are not talking about that. But when we communicate this very idea, this is where problems start. Now we have to communicate or define what 'killing', 'fun' or 'profit' mean. Then we say: 'We did not kill them – it was collateral damage.' Stealing a loaf of bread is stealing for profit, but stealing a country from its residents because of its huge oil reserves is called liberation. This is what we are interested in – the *epistemological* aspect, the issue of definitions and knowledge-base formation.

In other words, Clifford G. Christians is right when he writes in Chapter 1 of this book that 'Cultural relativism ought to remain in the epistemological realm. In so doing, it serves as a deterrent to ethnocentrism and promotes cultural diversity, that is, a comprehensive and inclusive understanding of our humanness'. It is a correct statement if we take into account that *epistemological* means *communicational*. That is, relativism seems to be the only fail-safe perspective in international communication.

Another point that some scholars sometimes make is that in their opinion, relativism somehow facilitates tyranny, but universalism is conducive to democratic processes. In other words, relativism produces conformity and totalitarianism as well as constraining moral reform, while universalism creates a more free-thinking environment, which can help people find some ways towards moral improvement somewhere out there in the universal moral domain. Everything here seems to be turned upside down. Isn't it the universalist position that everyone must obey the norms of one society (the definitions of good and evil being proclaimed as universal) and to diverge from these norms is to act immorally? That is, the same norms are established for everybody and one must conform. Isn't this the definition of totalitarianism? And again, it is universalism that insists on the prerogatives of a particular nation, caste, religion or tribe only because they managed to monopolize the definitions of good and evil for political purposes and to proclaim them as universal. This position also completely ignores the fact that cultures naturally evolve on their own. So, the moral reform will eventually result as a product of natural cultural evolution. And who says that the source of moral improvement must necessarily lie outside of one's own society, in some set of external moral standards? And if this is the case, where should one look for it?

There is another interesting argument as to why, according to some, ethical relativism gives rise to totalitarianism and therefore is dangerous – because it is rational (as opposed, one can only assume, to idealistic and safe universalism). This seems like a rather arbitrary assumption. It is not exactly clear how the people who make this assumption come up with this more than debatable equation. But even if we assume that they are correct (just for the sake of argument), isn't it in fact completely the other way round? Ethical idealism creates totalitarianism because people push for ideals regardless of the real-life consequences, while any type of rationalist rejects any philosophical ideas that prove to be harmful and dangerous in real life. Whether it is the reckless spreading of democracy or communism, regardless of the cost and consequences, it is ideological idealism and not rationalism that is quite perilous. Die-hard believers (idealists) seem to be the most dangerous people – fanatics.

However, the ultimate and widely used argument against ethical relativism is that it produces arbitrary definitions of good and bad. This seems to be quite a superficial argument. If one looks deeper into the internationalists' point of view, one will see that the definitions of good and bad are rooted in cultural, sociological, anthropological, historical and other elements of each society. Moreover, the definitions have to be accepted by all (or almost all) of the members of that culture. That is why they cannot be completely arbitrary. In addition, any definition is to some extent arbitrary because we are not talking about values themselves but about their interpretations by human beings. So, in every communicative action we have to separate values themselves from their interpretations and definitions.

All the above shows how complex and difficult the international communication ethics debate has been. So, is there any way in which we could to find a solution to this complex theoretical dilemma?

Actually, there have been quite interesting, creative and successful attempts at solving the universalists vs. relativists debate. One of them is the concept of *robust relativism* suggested by Joseph Margolis. He suggests that simplistic, primitive (and rather childish) ways of looking at things as black and white are inappropriate for our complex social world. Indeed, we realize that the absolute majority of social phenomena cannot simply be considered as good or bad. There may be other judgment values assigned to them:

> Grant only that a putatively relativistic set of judgments lacks truth-values (true and false) but takes values of other sorts or takes 'truth-values' other than true and false. For example, if judgments are said to be probable (on the evidence) rather than true, then it is quite possible that judgments otherwise incompatible – as true or false – are equiprobable (on the evidence). (Margolis, 1987, p. 484)

This approach removes the main philosophical problem of relativism – that relativists in their theories still have to claim some absolutes that may be in some way universal. In other words, rephrasing Margolis (1987), we can say that in the context of ethics or of international communication, 'there are *at least* three distinct ranges of judgment that may be strongly defended as tolerating or even *requiring* a relativistic construction' (1987, p. 485, emphasis added).

According to Margolis, *robust* relativism is:

> a relativism that admits some range of *competing* claims, claims for which there are at least minimal grounds justifying the joint application of competing principles – hence, that admits not only incompatible judgments relative to any particular principle but also what may be called 'incongruent' judgments, judgments that construed in terms of truth and falsity would be incompatible *and* that involve the use of predicates jointly accessible to competing principles. (1987, p. 485)

As a result, there are certain consequences that robust relativism would entail:

> (1) the rejection of skepticism and universalism for a given set of judgments; (2) the provision that such a set of judgments takes values other than truth and falsity and includes incongruent judgments; (3) the rejection of cognitivism (entailed by [(2)] ...); (4) the admission of the joint relevance of competing principles in validating the ascriptions or appraisals in question (entailed by [(2)] ...). (Margolis, 1987, p. 485)

This means that some judgment calls may merely be '*apt* rather than *true*' (Sibley, 1968, cited in Margolis, 1987, p. 487, emphasis in original). Margolis believes that such 'a relativistic account is actually required' for 'culturally emergent entities' (1987, p. 495). He writes that:

> culturally freighted phenomena are notoriously open to intensional quarrels, that is, to identification under alternative descriptions; and there is no obvious way in which to show that plural, non-converging, and otherwise incompatible characterizations of cultural items can be sorted as correct or incorrect in such a way that a relativistic account would be precluded ... One has only to think of ideologies, ideals, schools of thought, traditions as well as the deep informality of the so called rules of language and of artistic creation. (1987, p. 495)

He thinks that 'What is initially defective or incomplete, of course, is our understanding' of social phenomena and that 'we cannot be certain that what is supplied by way of interpretation is really in principle descriptively available' in life itself (1987, p. 495).

Robust relativism helps to defeat *ethical cognitivism*: 'the possibility of defending *any* form of cognitivism (moral, aesthetic, or any other) with respect to the values appropriate to persons or to their characteristic work is radically undermined. Consequently, the prospects of avoiding a relativistic account of values (and of value judgments) ... is nearly nil' (Margolis, 1987, p. 496).

This more moderate theory is different from both *scepticism* (the absence of any standards) and *cognitivism* (simple black-and-white judgments), and may help to navigate the labyrinth of international ethical communication problems more assertively.

Certainly, it is 'culturally freighted phenomena' or second-order value definitions that cause the main problems in the area of international communication. Such ideas as democracy and freedom are, probably, the most discussed concepts at the international level. In particular, the debate about the idea of democracy is the main international dispute of our time. What is democracy anyway? Is the West right in its everlasting quest for complete individual freedom or is the East correct in its undying commitment to the communal well-being? Scholars have made many philosophical suggestions of how to untangle the knot of controversy around this idea.

For example, to solve the contradiction between the requirements of the communal social order and individual freedoms, scholars suggest divorcing the concepts of political order and personal values. It is an interesting position if we completely forget that these two concepts are inseparable – political orders are created to support certain values. Then there is a suggestion to keep individual freedoms subject to some loose overarching state order that would still give people an opportunity to achieve the greatest fulfilment. In other words, governments still have to stay out of the way of people in their quest towards maximum gratification in their lives. This is an intriguing idea, but it still contains some inbuilt problems. First of all, the state by itself is a community, that is, the contradiction between the requirements of the communal order and individual freedoms cannot be removed that easily. But even if we forget about it, this suggestion still does not solve the contradiction between the role of the government as a guardian of everybody's interests and the interests of some individuals *who disagree with* the communal values.

For example, the economic crisis of 2009 showed that some individuals, in pursuing their own values, destroyed the lives of millions of people and then argued that the government had to stay aloof and let them pursue their greatest fulfilment. They entirely devoted themselves to the cause of personal material enrichment, a cause that gave their lives the greatest fulfilment. They said that it was unethical and immoral for anyone to interfere in their individual lives, which were supposed to be protected. If the government is supposed to stay away in situations like this (where *the collective* is in conflict with *the individual*), we (the free individuals who also pursue our own values) will have to sort it out for ourselves somehow. Pitchfork justice is the only available option here, which is hardly a civilized and philosophically tenable option. It seems that strictly regulating the Goldman Sachs of this world is a rather more ethical, moral and civilized option than burning them to the ground.

That is, it is something of a fantasy that states and governments can actually remain aloof from involvement in individual values.

Therefore, the problem of traditionally *collectivistic* cultures versus traditionally *individualistic* cultures is at the forefront of international political debates. The West always criticizes the East for its concern over social order at the expense of some individual freedoms. And even when the most prominent representatives of the Eastern cultures mount some defence of their traditional values and explain that their cultures have their own forms of democracy, some Western universalists simply cannot allow those cute little orientals to make their own choices. They still have to tell them what is good for them. So, they cherry-pick people who for some reason (some of the reasons are covered in the Introduction to this volume) at least on the surface seem to agree with them – these people are called dissidents. They would argue on behalf of their Western sponsors that cultures change and that Eastern cultures will soon change as well by abandoning their traditional ways and becoming exactly like their Western counterparts.

This is an interesting argument, but it still leaves some unanswered questions. Is this cultural change good for the Chinese and Koreans or it will play the same role that some cultural changes played in the lives of Native Americans and Australian Aborigines? Do the Chinese and Koreans have to accept them automatically and, if so, why? Yes, cultures change and evolve, but only internally induced change is good. And how do we know that the changes we observe are not just due to foreign influences and are actually damaging to Chinese and Korean societies? Only people from the countries subject to these processes have the right to answer these questions.

Finally, we always have to remember that being a *dissident* by definition means that a person represents a minority view for his or her culture. Using dissidents as representatives for an entire nation is an old propaganda trick. Thus, it seems unwise to place too much weight on the claims of dissidents.

Next, the counterpositioning of *democracy* and *order* is played out as usual, as if democracy cannot be quite orderly and order always means tyranny. The problem is that *order* is an ill-defined concept, but generally it can be said that in ultimate terms, order is the threshold of disorder beyond which a total collapse destroys a society. This threshold is different for every nation, and every culture is free to establish this for itself. If, for example, the Chinese say they need a certain level of order, we have to trust them; to do otherwise would be arrogant and condescending.

The works of the German philosopher Immanuel Kant are frequently used in support of the Western ideas of morality and democracy. In such instances, it is argued that only the individual can serve as a moral ground for ethics, that is, somehow only individualism can serve as a foundation for a societal ethics and anything collective is somehow secondary and cannot be ethically justified. Actually, this is by itself a philosophical controversy because ethics is a social phenomenon and all this is actually based on the badly misconstrued notion of Kantian *autonomy*.

First of all, we have to understand that Kant's point of view is extremely controversial and is far from being universally accepted. People who are familiar with the Hegelian critique of Kant know this very well. But the main problem is that the Kantian point of view here is somewhat oversimplified. For example, *autonomous* does not mean *laws unto themselves*. It relates in this particular philosophical argument to the *concept of autonomy*. To be *autonomous* does not simply mean being *free*. In philosophical terms, it means *self-prescribed* and it is not congruent with the notions of *individual freedom* and *political liberty*. It means to be guided by *communal* moral laws that are *organically* derived from the *rational will* of the members of this community. Moreover, these laws have decisive authority over individuals. The source of morality and freedom here is that the norms come from the *rational wills* of *separate* individuals and are *freely* agreed upon by the members of the community.

So, *autonomy* is the *moral liberty* to *create laws* that are *self-prescribed*; that is, the laws come from common points in the moral judgments of separate individuals. But these common points must be *freely* accepted and approved by the members of the community. In this sense, moral life is self-determination, but *autonomy* is realized in being guided by the general will of a particular community. Therefore, *autonomy* only means the *autonomous* (by each individual *separately* and *voluntarily*) *self-imposition* of *communal* moral laws. In other words, the *self-imposition* of the *communal organic* laws is *autonomy* (again, because people *autonomously* – *independently* and *voluntarily* – impose such norms on themselves). *Autonomous* moral norms simply mean *self-prescribed* – but still *communal* – laws. Isn't that what the Chinese are arguing for – their freedom to *autonomously* and *voluntarily self-impose* on themselves the *communal organic self-prescribed laws* of their society that they *agreed upon* as a nation over the last several thousand years of their history? By no means does Kant argue for individualism. He is actually arguing for a community of responsible citizens – a sort of socialism. As such, the idea that the Western form of democracy alone is consistent with the requirements of human autonomy is rather misguided.³

Then, when all the philosophical arguments fail, there is always the empirical argument. There is a whole plethora of 'research' that is supposed to show that Western democracy is the best way of living. Certainly, there is no need to say that such research is almost always produced or financed by certain Western institutions or governments. For example, some researchers found that famine has never occurred in countries with Western-style democracies and a relatively free press. But how can we account for cases of severe hunger in some countries of Africa, South-East Asia and the Americas where people elect their governments, have presidents, parliaments and 'a relatively free press'? The explanation is very simple: this type of research is usually performed in the form of a self-fulfilling prophesy – if there is a case of famine, the country is not a democracy (and vice versa). And such concepts as 'democracy' and 'freedom of the press' are usually defined arbitrarily or politically. This is an unfalsifiable theory and is thus not scientific. Many Arab countries are not 'democratic' (so to speak) and may even be authoritarian, but may also be highly developed, very concerned with the welfare of their citizens and have no famine – something that some researchers prefer not to explore.

There is also research that finds a strong correlation between the Western form of democracy and the respect for human rights. Please, mention this to the detainees of the Abu Graib prison, the Guantanamo Bay concentration camp, the black CIA prisons in Eastern Europe, the victims of the practice of extraordinary renditions or of the bombings of civilian cities (Belgrade or Baghdad), or the victims of the French colonial adventures in Africa – they may disagree.

Finally, it is always the corruption argument – non-Western governments are almost always portrayed in some 'research' as the most corrupt. But the question is what is corruption and how do we define it? Lobbying, as it exists in the US, is the *ultimate* form of corruption, but it is not called as such by Western researchers because they cannot violate the principle of the self-fulfilling prophesy – if it is a system in the West, it cannot be called corruption. It is another unfalsifiable theory. And certainly it is not even necessary to talk about so-called democratic peace research, one of the most outrageous propagandistic ideas created by some representative of the Western social sciences; this myth has been dispelled profoundly enough. Again, the main question is: who does and who finances this type of so-called research and for what reason?

To finish the examination of the rhetorical argument of *democracy*, it is interesting to point out that we can hardly ever find a definition of the term itself. The differences in the ideas of democracy all over the world were discussed quite thoroughly in the Introduction to this volume. Nevertheless, it is usually automatically assumed that democracy is the Western form of government. Indeed, it is a very misleading term. It literally means the 'rule (law) of people'. But with only the private media on the scene and the unprecedented role of money in the political system, it can be said that, for example, the American government represents big corporations and the wealthy minority rather than the general population of the US. So, it can be called 'moneyocracy'. Therefore, the most that can be said about the *democratic* nature of this particular form of government is that it is seriously unproven. Even if people are allowed to vote, it does not mean that the government is actually working in the interests of the people and carries out their social orders. The representative system does not mean the actual *rule of people* that *is* democracy. The representatives usually rule in their own interests and the interests of their sponsors. What does this have to do with *demos* – the people? And, in general, is there any form of government in the world that actually allows people to rule or make laws?

It seems like democracy is nothing more than a theoretical philosophical concept that has little to do with reality. It cannot actually exist beyond a small group of people. Aristotle believed that only city states were sufficiently small to enable the type of governing arrangements he advocated (Aristotle, 1984, pp. 2104–5), but even cities are probably too big. Only small tribes would be appropriate for this system because unless we know somebody very personally, we cannot vote for him or her clearly appreciating *what* we are going to get as a result of that vote and also firmly recognizing that we would be able to remove that person from power if he or she deceives us. All the rest is just media and political manipulation.

In other words, for one system of government to appropriate the idea of democracy is unethical enough, but to use it for propaganda purposes is doubly unethical. It seems like Churchill said it best: 'Democracy is the worst form of government, except for all those other forms that have been tried from time to time' (House of Commons speech, 11 November 1947). And let's leave it right there.

Certainly, everything above is a set of quite philosophical and general considerations. But international ethics are realized and actualized in practice in specific human actions in certain areas of human activities. So, let's try to look at some of them and see what specific problems are most widespread in these fields, and what kind of problems scholars encounter trying to analyse and solve them.

Definitely, the area of international PR and public communication is one of the most challenging fields. Everybody knows how many ethical problems PR people encounter working simply at the domestic level. When the entire field is elevated up to the international heights, everything becomes even more complex.

For example, the problem of media transparency has already been considered in this volume. The undue influence of commercial interests on journalists is an important topic. The predominant attitude of PR practitioners towards such a practice – especially if it involves direct cash payments to members of the media – is generally negative, and it is quite clear why. But still there remains a great deal of variance in PR–media relationship practices all over the world. For example, such practices may be different in Finland and in Arab and South-East Asian countries (probably because in the latter regions such payments are not actually an example of corruption but a culturally mandated token of appreciation for help). In the US, the traditional (or, at least, self-proclaimed) role of the media as the *watchdog of democracy* has its own effect on the perception of the role of journalists and consequently on what are considered to be socially acceptable media and PR practices.

But when we are talking about such places as, for example, Russia – a country which is stuck in-between the East and the West – we have to be especially thorough with our cultural considerations and research conclusions. As was discussed earlier in this volume, almost all Russian PR practitioners recognize that paying journalists for media favours is wrong but, on the other hand, almost all of them do it. The question is does it mean that they do not care about ethics? Unfortunately, there is no answer in the Western research to this question. The reason for this is very simple – the disregard of traditional universalists for cultural and historical differences. As one author nicely put it, they think that everybody in the world is just a proto-American. However, in the Russian case, such a cultural exploration may be especially instructive.

We have to realize that throughout the entire history of Russia, the media have always been under the strong control of the state. The first national newspaper in Russia was organized by the state (Tsar Peter the Great), while later the media was controlled and censored by the 3rd Department of the Gendarmerie, then by the communists, and even now the newly democratic Russian government controls quite a few forms of media. Thus, because of that history of government control, Russians traditionally have a very low level of trust but a high level of scepticism towards the media. Journalists have always been considered simply as the servants of the government or of private interests. Consequently, in this cultural environment (where nobody trusts the media anyway), credibility is not even an issue. Therefore, journalists and PR people feel free to do anything – nobody trusts them in any case. (Certainly, these are not supposed to be justifications but cultural and historical explanations for some Russian PR practices, or at least some reasons for contemporary attitudes towards the PR profession in Russia.)

The problem here is that Western-financed or Western-conducted research frequently misses the mark in terms of subtle differences between countries. When Western researchers find similarities (which usually support their point of view), they stop right there with a great deal of satisfaction. Probably, it simply does not occur to them that there may be some deeper, more subtle differences lying beneath the surface. For example, in the case of Russia, the researchers were right when they said that most Russian PR people would probably say that it would be wrong to pay for publishing PR materials. But what do they mean by that? There are two issues here.

First of all, contemporary Russians, as a nation, are much more sensitive in relation to commercial influence on the news. This may be a heritage of the 70 years of socialism. They believe that *any* commercial influence is supposed to be disclosed. For example, in the US, if a story is based on a press release or if a company helped a journalist to research a story, it is considered to be OK. In exactly the same situation, the Russians would consider this to be a heavy influence and consequently a commercial material. Secondly, the Russian PR practitioners consider it absolutely fine to pay for any commercial (publicity) material. Their low-paid journalist friends are supposed to be compensated for their work and materially supported by their highly paid PR brethren. It is just fair – the Russian sense of fairness. And again, *any* – even the smallest – commercial influence makes a material *payable* (so to speak). But that payment is supposed to be made in a *fair* way. Therefore, when Russians say that it is wrong to pay for publishing a press release, they very often simply mean that it is wrong to pay a journalist directly in cash, in an envelope, which looks like a bribe. But if a rich commercial enterprise pays for that service officially, in line with some contracts (from bank account to bank account) according to some official tariffs, it is perfectly alright. After all, it is just a commercial transaction and people have to be compensated for their work and help. Therefore, when they say 'it is wrong', many of them mean the way in which it is done, not the fact itself. But again, for obvious reasons, research financed and conduced by the West is very unlikely to uncover such subtle variations. However, it is exactly these distinctions that demonstrate the essence of local ethics and produce differences in professional practices all over the world.

Finally, it is necessary to clarify another point. Often, ethics-oriented PR practices are referred to as the Western model. But we have to understand that such concepts as the Grunigs' *PR Excellence* are just theoretical ideas. Western PR practices can be and often are absolutely outrageous, and some cases are covered in this very book. Certainly, the readers of *Toxic Sludge is Good for You* can add quite a few other cases on top of that. Therefore, regarding the Western PR model as the ethical standard while rejecting cultural deviations in itself raises some serious ethical issues.

PR has traditionally been considered a 'problem child' in the communication family. Yet what about journalists – those self-proclaimed watchdogs of the public well-being: do they do better? It is interesting that at the international level, it is probably journalists (not PR people) who are the perpetrators of the most egregious violations of international communication ethics. PR practitioners at least try to represent their organization or client in the best possible light. But journalists, in their chase for sensationalism and their tendency to gratify their audience at any cost, are more likely to insult somebody at an international level just to make sure that their readers or viewers perceive them as patriotic. Humiliating somebody who is foreign is a usual way of achieving this aim, although it is not exactly clear how insulting others makes one a patriot. Especially demonstrative is the level of Russophobia and Sinophobia in the Western media. And here we are not talking about such channels as Fox – even the self-proclaimed liberal media do it as a matter of normal everyday practice. For example, one well-known MSNBC commentator and nightly TV news-show host called the Chinese national holiday a 'freaky holiday' and was childishly giggling while one of the guests on her show called the Prime Minister of Russia, Vladimir Putin, a part of the species heading towards extinction.

After horrific terrorist acts on the Moscow subway on 29 March 2010, when dozens of people died, CNN devoted exactly one minute to the event, while terrorist acts in London and Madrid warranted almost two weeks of 24-hour non-stop coverage. This means that for them a Russian life is about 20,000 times less valuable than the life of a Western European. And the Russians are lucky. Anything of this sort happening in China does not usually produce any media coverage at all. It seems that for the Western media, Chinese lives are simply worthless. And yet, after all that, they talk about such values as *equality* and *fairness* in their professional codes of ethics.

The editor of this book had a hard time trying to remember when he saw any piece of good news from China or Russia covered by the US media. It seems like practically 100 per cent of news coming from there is bad (to this list we can certainly add Africa, Latin America and South-East Asia). This, of course, distorts the truth and produces a false impression about the way of life in these countries to the American audience. Incidentally, the Russian and Chinese media are doing a much better job covering the West. Terrorist acts that happen in America or Europe receive almost the same amount of coverage as internal events in these countries. In addition, many positive foreign news stories are covered. A big research programme showed that the Chinese media produced probably the most even-handed, deep and objective coverage in the world of the run-up to the 2003 invasion of Iraq (Nikolaev and Hakanen, 2006). To a large extent, all this can be explained by the predominance in the West of privately owned forms of media that are forced to protect the interests of individuals and special interest groups, and make money. Some people even call newspapers, magazines and TV conglomerates owned by private individuals, families and companies 'slave media' (named after people owned by private individuals and families). This might be going too far, but it seems as if, due to being owned by those with private interests, such media are simply not capable of *being free* from manipulation. However, people are forced by centuries of propaganda to equate *private* channels of information with *free* media, which is conceptually incorrect. It appears that the public and state media actually often produce a better journalistic result, at least in terms of foreign news (this is why millions of Americans migrated to the BBC during the 2003 Iraq War coverage).

Often, the violation of basic ethical standards of international communication is justified by the notion of freedom of speech. But most people in the world, for example, cannot understand how publishing humiliating and blasphemous caricatures of the Prophet Muhammad constitutes freedom of speech. For most people on the planet, it is incomprehensible. Even the US Supreme Court ruled that shouting 'fire!' in a crowded theatre does not fall under the protection of freedom of speech. In this respect, the US can be complimented. Their strong hate speech laws make such incidents somewhat unlikely, although the recent *South Park* cartoon controversy raises some doubts in this respect. People cannot be free to insult and humiliate each other. Many countries have laws against hate speech for a good reason – to preserve domestic and international peace and to save human dignity (the value that universalists are arguably so worried about).

Certainly, on the other side of the debate of civilizations, anti-Americanism and the Great Satan rhetoric also make their way onto the pages of many publications all over the world, but at least these journalists do not try to establish themselves as the norm for the rest of the universe. Therefore, the members of the Western media need to take a hard look at themselves first before claiming ownership of the international journalism ethical standard.

Even such respected Western media outlets as *Le Monde* do and say things that can be considered unethical from the point of view of many people in the world. The Chechnya crisis can serve as an example: *Le Monde*'s coverage of this particular issue was such that, in its totality, it appeared to demonstrate either the paper's complete ignorance as to what was actually going on in the region or its unwillingness even to discover (or tell) the truth. The paper mostly covered one side of the story, almost entirely ignoring the other side. In other words, it covered its own emotions and opinions instead of all the facts, but it presented them as facts. It was hiding its ignorance (or bias) behind a veil of anti-Russian rhetoric, which is very popular in the West. That is, what it was mostly selling to the French people as reality was just its own interpretation of the events. Trying to sell interpretations as facts is a major ethical violation. And if we also consider the Kosovo crisis of 1999, which almost exactly mirrored the Chechnya coverage situation, we can say that unfortunately *Le Monde* is also guilty of some violations of international communication and foreign reporting ethics.

It seems that all this means one simple thing: the issue of international communication ethics is very important but is also complex and enormous in scope. Therefore, the process of scholarly exploration of this problem must be continued for the purposes of theoretical explanations as well as finding practical solutions for real-life problems. However, this effort must be honest and free of falsehood and manipulation which, unfortunately, happens quite frequently.

For example, in many books and articles, universalists define relativism as the absence of any ethical standards. This is a clear falsification. They are either cunning or clearly unfamiliar with basic philosophical definitions. The absence of standards may be either *scepticism* or *nihilism* but not relativism. Relativism has clear ethical standards – the standards that are rooted in a certain culture.

The issue of the source of morals and ethical standards is one of the main theoretical and philosophical problems that have to be solved.

Universalists have never been able to explain where their universal standards come from. The only thing they say is 'there must be something'. Unfortunately, this is not an argument, or at least not a valid philosophical argument. They could have claimed a supreme being as the source, but regrettably most of them are atheists and supporters of the separation of religious and societal matters. So, they lose this ground too. Next, they go to Kant, but, sadly enough, they misinterpret him too, as was shown above. But let's assume for a moment (although it is not the case) that Kant actually meant what *they* think he did. In this event, it would be wise to examine the historical context of such claims.

Kant lived in a time when Africans, Native Americans, Australian Aborigines, 'Orientals' and the inhabitants of many other nations were not considered as exactly 'human' by many Europeans. Therefore, *universality* meant *only* the opinion of white, predominantly Judeo-Christian men (not women) of European dissent. Other points of view simply did not exist – people from this majority group were not aware of them and, probably, were not exactly interested. This is exactly what the American founding fathers meant when they wrote 'All men are created equal' – white, predominantly Judeo-Christian men (sorry ladies!) of European dissent. However, since that time we reinterpreted that document and gave it a new meaning. Therefore, it is time to reconsider and reinterpret other antiquated philosophical positions too. Who knows what Kant would have said had he been exposed to modern communication and diversity. After losing their last stronghold – Kant – universalists have practically nothing to hang their hat on. Relativists, on the other hand, firmly ground their point of view in culture, history, language, environment and other natural and social phenomena.

Yet the universalists still argue that everybody on the planet *seems* to agree with such Western documents as the Declaration of the Rights of Man and the Citizen (1789), the Universal Declaration of Human Rights (1948) and the European Charter of Fundamental Rights (2000). And the keyword here is *seems* because, as was explained in the Introduction to this volume, people agree with the *labels* contained in these documents but *not* with their interpretations. And here it is important to understand where the European interpretations come from and why the rest of the world is different.

The contemporary notions of human rights from the European point of view have their roots in the eras of the Renaissance and later the Enlightenment. At that time, people of the continent rebelled against God and proclaimed the whim of man to be the ultimate human value. The human being conceptually became God (the unconstrained and all-powerful supreme being) and Jesus Christ just a good man. In other words, the processes of *theofication of anthropos* and *anthropofication of theos* took place. More specifically, the old religious morality was discarded in favour of the new ethical system that would signify complete freedom for humans. Certainly, this shift was absolutely necessary to provide ideological support for the coming of capitalism – to justify the power of money and the sacredness of private property (the famous 'greed is good'). Since that time in the West, limiting human freedom became immoral even if it meant abridging really dangerous behaviours.

However, the problem is that the rest of the world did not go through the Renaissance and Enlightenment in their Western forms and, consequently, through the processes of *theofication of anthropos* and *anthropofication of theos*. They have never rejected God (in whatever shape or form they worship that supreme being). They never proclaimed the whim of man the supreme human value. They kept their own morality connected to the origins of their cultures. Therefore, when they talk about *freedom*, for example, they mean different things from the Europeans – the freedom from exploitation, fear, injustice, inequality, etc. – even if it means reducing some personal liberties. For example, for Russians (as will be explained later) the freedom to become rich and powerful and, by so doing, to increase inequality and injustice is *immoral* freedom. That is, we have a paradoxical situation when Europe (less than seven per cent of the planet's surface and little more than 12 per cent of the world's population) dictates to the remaining 93 per cent of the planet's surface and almost 88 per cent of the world's population how they are supposed to think about morals and ethics.

But this era of moral dictatorship is coming to an end. A historical event occurred in Moscow in April 2006. The Universal Congress of the Russian Nation adopted a document called the 'Declaration of Rights and Dignity of a Human Being'. With this document, they made a clear break with the Western tradition and notion of human rights. For the first time in history, a nation officially proclaimed that it did not subscribe to the Western idea of what basic human values are and instead claimed its own vision. The Russian President and Prime Minister were present at the adoption ceremony, effectively making it an official document of the Russian nation.

In the Declaration, the Russians say that the West separated morality from human rights. Human rights are a set of official political documents and are rooted rather in civil law than in morality. They also say that humans have freedom of choice but that they are also imperfect. In other words, complete freedom means freedom for wickedness and depravity. They also make a difference between the *value of human life* and the *dignity of a human being*: 'The value is given, dignity is acquired'[4] (Declaration of Rights and Dignity, 2006). This differs from the Western notion where dignity is somehow built into all human beings as a birthright. In the Russian sense, dignity must be earned. Below is a direct translation of some parts of that document, which cannot be found anywhere in the Western media:

> We distinguish between two types of freedom: the internal freedom from evil and the freedom of moral choice. The freedom from evil is self-evident. The freedom of moral choice acquires its value ... when a human being chooses good. In reverse, the freedom of choice leads to self-destruction and harms human dignity when he [or she] chooses evil.
>
> Human rights are based on the value of human character and must be directed toward realization of human dignity. Exactly for that reason the content of human rights cannot be separated from morality. Separation of these rights from morality means profanation in terms of such rights because immoral dignity does not exist.
>
> We are for the right to live and against the 'right' to die, for the right to create and against the 'right' to destroy. We recognize rights and freedoms of human beings as they help every individual to ascend toward good, as they guard that individual from internal and external evil, and allow that person to self-realize in the society in a positive manner. In this sense we respect not only civil, political rights and freedoms, but also social, economic and cultural rights.
>
> Rights and freedoms cannot be separated from obligations and responsibilities of the human being. Every person while realizing their own interests is called to coordinate them with the interests of others, the family, local community, the nation and the entire humanity.
>
> There exist values that are ranked no lower than human rights. These are such values as faith, morality, sacred things and Motherland ... It is impossible to allow for situations when [the] realization of human rights would oppress faith and moral tradition, would lead to insulting religious and national feelings and honored sacred symbols ... We see as very dangerous the 'invention' of such 'rights' that make legal behaviours that otherwise are condemned by morality and all historical religions.

We reject politics of double standards in the area of human rights as well as any attempts to use such rights for promotion of political, ideological, military and economic interests and for the imposition of any certain type of state or social order.

We are ready to cooperate with all well-intentioned forces in the cause of safeguarding human rights. The special areas of such cooperation must become the safeguarding of the rights of nations and ethnic groups to keep their religion, language and culture ... The future of people depends on the degree of success of attempts at solving this problem. (Declaration of Rights and Dignity, 2006, translated by the author)

In other words, according to the Russian idea of human rights, there is only the right for good and there is no right for evil. Certainly, they define 'good' and 'evil' according to their own standards, but they also claim their right to do so. That is why many Russians consider the Western notion of human rights as the right to be bad and to do bad things. They think that legalistic human rights are less important than laws of morality and traditional values. They completely reject individualism. They believe that some so-called 'human rights' were 'invented' or were, simply speaking, fabricated in the West to justify certain behaviours. For example, they consider the European prohibition against wearing any religious symbols in public schools to be an outrageous violation of basic human rights. They would always ask: 'And what, the freedom of religion is not a human right?' They would certainly never consider newspaper caricatures and cartoons of religion and religious figures a moral and ethical behaviour. In their opinion, this behaviour cannot be ethical because it is insulting and degrading – that is, bad and consequently immoral. And there is no freedom for bad and immoral behaviours. And this is really a radical break from the official Western ethics.

As was mentioned above, the old God-based pre-Renaissance and pre-Enlightenment moral systems could not sustain the charted path of future economic development. So, a new *civil religion* had to be invented to create a new ethics that would justify the system of capitalism. As such, it was created with its own ethical system (human rights), prayers (pledge of allegiance), icons (national flags), holy scriptures (constitutions) and prophets (a whole host of the Enlightenment philosophers and, of course, Kant, although badly misinterpreted). Therefore, the philosophy of universalism is just a new form of secular religion imposed by one type of civilization on the rest of the planet – on the people who did not go through the same transformations as Europe (*theofication of anthropos* and *anthropofication of theos*) – to provide ideological support for one specific combination of economic and political systems. It is just an ideology imposed on the world in the same way that Christianity was imposed on Native Americans and Australian Aborigines to destroy their culture and their way of life, and, by so doing, to destroy them. And now people who claim freedom and their right to make their own ethical decisions based on their own moral standards are proclaimed heretics and discriminated against by the same universalists who are so forcefully arguing for the freedom of conscience.

The next question is as follows: if universalist ethics is so well established and uncompromising, why is it so flexible when it comes to its application to the real world? In fact, it is quite amusing that universalists call themselves as such, because their ethics is actually *situational*. The so-called universal values are used, depending on a situation, as weapons against dissidents and are always interpreted in favour of the universalists and their situational allies. In the 1980s, Saddam Hussein was good, whereas now he is bad; in the 1980s, bin Laden was good, whereas now he is bad (although these are the same people doing the same things). Where is the consistency and the uncompromising character of the universalist ethics? They did not care when Hussein killed Iranians and bin Laden killed Russians. They started caring only when those two gentlemen started killing Westerners. That is, their values are *relative* to the national affiliation of the people killed – they are the *ultimate relativists*. All the above shows that universalism is not about honouring pan-human values but mainly about imposing certain *interpretations* of those values on the rest of the world.

On the other hand, *internationalism* (as it was explained in the Introduction to this volume) allows for non-totalitarian and non-imperialist interpretations. It avoids the propagandistic black-and-white picture of this world. It professes the humanitarian and humanistic approach of serious morality-oriented contemplation and deep self-analysis.

But all this is theory. In terms of practical applications in the real world, universalists often put on sheep's clothing and argue that everything they do is for the good of the people. They just want to help people to modernize and democratize their life. This is certainly a false argument. Colonization never led to development or democracy.

Certainly, cultures are not static – they develop and evolve. But they can do so *only* at their own pace and on their own terms. Universalists. with their usual racist undertone, try to tie social and economic problems to cultural characteristics of different nations. But what they prefer not to mention is that all cultures went through historical periods when they had in some shape or form slavery, child labour, lack of women's rights, etc. And those countries that are experiencing something like that now are just at a different stage of their historical journey. They do not need cultural or military intervention to develop. They do not need help in this respect. They will be fine. But most so-called development theories, such as modernization or democratic peace, were created by universalists for exactly this purpose – to justify cultural and military interventions. However, what history shows is that any foreign intervention makes things worse, while absence thereof makes everything better.

For example, in the 1970s, almost all the Western economists believed that India and China would never be able to reach the level of economic development of the so-called First World countries because of the cultural characteristics of these two nations. However, they were wrong. Western interference in the Balkans created a mass of ethnic tensions which will eventually explode, but the absence of such intervention in the case of Rwanda (which itself was created by Belgian colonial interference) allowed for an internal domestic healing process that was simultaneously natural, real, strong and durable.

But one of the most desperate areas in the field of international communication ethics is the problem of *knowledge base* – the information that people receive and have when they make ethical decisions. Humans cannot make any type of decisions (and especially ethical decisions) when they have zero information. This means that the decisions we make almost excessively depend on the information we obtain. However, with the prevalence in the contemporary world of private media conglomerates, almost all the information we receive is, to put it mildly, heavily distorted. There were quite a few recent cases when information distributed in the West about non-Western events was almost completely false. Here we are referring to such events as the 1999 Kosovo problem, the 2008 Tibet unrest involving China or the 2008 Russo-Georgian war. The Western propaganda machine made sure that people in the West would not see a grain of truth about those events. In this case, can people be expected to be able to arrive at correct ethical decisions? The answer is an emphatic *no*. In other words, they are deprived of an ability to make *any* type of ethical calls. So, in this case, does it make any sense even to talk about ethical decisions in terms of international communication?

The answer is twofold – yes and no. The answer is an emphatic *no* if we are talking about decisions based on the information provided to us by the contemporary propaganda machinery that some people idealistically call the media. But answer is *yes* (although *non-emphatic*) if the decision is based on a deeper knowledge of the issue. Once again, education is the answer, and this means education in all respects – culture, history, religion, language (especially language – so that people could read the original news). However, this education is supposed to be real, not distorted by propaganda, which is quite rare (that is why the latter *yes* was *non-emphatic*). Yet it is usually universalism that distorts education, and universalists have many resources to do so. For example, such propagandistic theories as modernization or democratic peace are heavily financed, while the writings of internationalists are forcefully discriminated against. Therefore, in the West, only one side of the story is visible. This book aims to remedy this situation, at least to some extent.

We have to be able to teach people how to make ethical decisions at the international level. This is our only hope. But ethics cannot be taught from the point of view of universalism. In this case, the origins of ethical standards are not clear. Besides, in this case everybody proclaims their version of morality to be universal and a war of all-against-all breaks out. On the other hand, the *internationalist* approach is clear and effective. The origins of ethical standards are clear – culture, history, religion and environment. And there is only one simple universal principle built into it – an unconditional *respect* for every nation's way of life, only in this case such values as *diversity, fairness, equality* and the *freedom* to lead life the way people see fit for their society will be completely realized. We hope that this book will help to achieve this goal.

In conclusion, it is very important to clarify that we are not arguing against moral deliberations in the public sphere. Every nation on earth has to engage in such deliberations while making difficult decisions or facing complex ethical dilemmas. It is extremely important because this is what makes (and keeps) us human. But we have to be very careful while carrying such deliberations across borders and civilizations. It may be possible to do so within the limits of separate culture groups – such as the Protestant Anglo-Saxon culture group, the North Mediterranean or Catholic South European culture group, or the Orthodox Christian East European culture group. But even in this case, it is quite clear that ethical considerations may and will be distorted by politics, economics and other national interests.

Therefore, can we not discuss ethical issues at the cross-national and cross-civilizational levels at all? The answer is probably yes *if* we are extremely careful, respectful and sensitive. Another *if* is if we establish at least a moderately decent system of knowledge-base formation – a more or less objective media system – and, finally, if we educate people properly about other cultures, nations and civilizations. Yet even here we will probably be mostly preaching to the converted – discussing *our own* position with *our own* people on something happening elsewhere (hopefully doing all this without lies and propaganda). But this is all we can do – to carefully *discuss* it. We cannot criticize, demand, require or insist on anything. We must respect the ethical systems of other cultures unconditionally, hoping that they will engage in their own moral deliberations within their national and cultural confines. We must understand that other people's ethical systems are equal to ours and are as vital to them as ours are to us. Otherwise, we are getting dangerously close to colonialism, imperialism, racism and chauvinism because, whatever noble motives people may claim, saying that somebody's morals are worse than your own *is* chauvinism.

References

Aristotle (1984). *The Complete Works of Aristotle*, vol. 2, J. Barnes (ed.). Princeton University Press.
Bauman, Z. (1993). *Postmodern Ethics*. Oxford: Blackwell.
'Declaration of Rights and Dignity of a Human Being'. (4–6 April 2006). The final document of the Universal Congress of the Russian Nation. Moscow, Russia, www.vrns.ru/syezd/detail.php?nid=780&binn_rubrik_pl_news=304&binn_rubrik_pl_news=306&PHPSESSID=54aaac4b8d15cf31c629af5123e27783 (in Russian), date accessed 5 December 2010.
Fisher, G. (1997). *Mindsets: The Role of Culture and Perception in International Relations*. Yarmouth, ME: Intercultural Press.
Lear, J. (1984). 'Moral Objectivity', in S.C. Brown (ed.), *Objectivity and Cultural Divergence*. Cambridge University Press, pp. 135–70.
Margolis, J. (1987). 'Robust Relativism', in J. Margolis (ed.), *Philosophy Looks at the Arts*. Philadelphia: Temple University Press, pp. 484–99.
Nikolaev, A.G. (2007). *International Negotiations: Theory, Practice and the Connection with Domestic Politics*. Lanham, MD: Lexington Books.
——. (2009). 'Images of War: Content Analysis of the Photo Coverage of the War in Kosovo', *Critical Sociology*, 35(1), 105–30.
Nikolaev, A.G. and Hakanen, E.A. (eds) (2006). *Leading to the 2003 Iraq War: The Global Media Debate*. New York: Palgrave Macmillan.
Sibley, F. (1968). 'Objectivity and Aesthetics', *Proceedings of the Aristotelian Society*, Supplementary XLII, 31–54.

Notes

1. Some ideas as to how to structure such courses can be found in Nikolaev, 2007, pp. 281–5.

2. Please, see the Introduction to this volume for the human life value discussion.
3. This issue is nicely covered by the works of a group of philosophers from Stanford University and can be found in Robert Johnson, 'Kant's Moral Philosophy', in Edward N. Zalta (ed.), *The Stanford Encyclopedia of Philosophy*, http://plato.stanford.edu/archives/sum2010/entries/kant-moral, date accessed 5 December 2010.
4. It is important to understand here that *dignity* does not mean in this particular case *worthiness* or *value*; rather, it has a social meaning. Who receives the right to a voice in society and whose opinions are supposed to be respected and consequently heeded? Such social respect (or *dignity*) in this case is supposed to be earned or *acquired* through a striving for *good*. It is not inherent in the mere existence of a human being.

Index

Abbott, K.A.   143
abortion   11
action theory   203
active interview   204
Adams, Eddie   129
Adie, Kate   128
Adolino, J.R.   38
advertising   228
　alcohol harm reduction   145
aesthetics   28, 185, 194–5, 237
Afghanistan, US/UK occupation   120
Agence France-Presse   68
Al Arabiya   97
Al-Saati, Samia   90–1
Al-Shaqiqi, Muna   97
Albright D.   37
alcohol harm reduction, young people   144–6
alcohol health promotion, *see* social marketing health campaigns
Algeria   39, 93
Ali, M.M.   37
Allen, N.   184, 185
Allen, Stuart   132
Alloula, M.   94
Alton, Roger   122
altruism, social marketing health campaigns   139–41
anarchism   61
Andreasson, S.   144, 146
Andrew, Prince   125
anthropofication of theos   255, 258
anti-Americanism   253
apocalypse   73
Appiah, K.A.   103
Arab Americans   95, 96
Arab-Israeli film   98–100, 228
Arabic television   95–8, 228
area-specific issues   220, 226–32
Arendt, Hannah   75
Argentine, Internet   186
argumentation   115, 116–17
Aristotelian ethics   160

Aristotle   61–3, 64, 248
Asian culture   56, 58–9
Askehave, I.   106
Athaydes, A.   186
attitudes, changing   4
Austria, *Le Monde*   110–11
authoritarianism   56, 59, 60
authority, religious and secular   58
autonomy   60–1, 246–7
'Axis of Evil'   71, 72

bad news   252
Bakhash, S.   58
Bakri, Saleh   99
banality of evil   75
The Band's Visit (film)   98–100
Bangladesh   66
basic truths, moral beliefs as   5
Battle of Seattle   131
Bauman, Zygmunt   28, 237
Baumann, D.   155
BBC News   145
Beaufort (film)   99
beliefs, culturally based   35
Bell, Martin   127
Bellah, R.N.   76
Berkowitz, A.D.   147
Bhutan   68
bin Laden, Osama   74, 258
The Birth of Tragedy   28
black PR   176–80, 232
Blackwood, E.   160–1, 167
Blair, Tony   77
Blind Spot   131
blogs   132
Blum, W.   6
Boas, Franz   24
bogeyman   122
Bologna Process   201
Boltanski, L.   203
Book of Revelation   79
Borgerson, J.L.   184
Bowen, S.A.   184

Boynton, L.A. 172
branding of nations 187
Brazil, public relations 186
Brent Spar 159
Brew, E.P. 37
bribery 172
Britain 38
British Nationality Act 38
Britt, A.B. 143
B'Tselem 132
Bush, George W. 55, 74, 75, 76
  'Axis of Evil' 71
  shoe throwing 96–7
  West Point speech 77
Butchart, G.C. 184

Cable News Network (CNN), female genital cutting story 88–92
Cai, D. 37
Cairnes, D.R. 37
capital punishment 11
capitalism 257
Carpentier, N. 163
Carroll, J. 80–1
cash for news 172, 175–6, 177–8
Casmir, F.I. 37
Cassara, C. 173
casualties of war 120, 125
categorical imperative 162, 166
cathedralness 13
Catholic Church, authority of 58
Centre for Corporate Responsibility 148
Chamberlain, M.E. 38
Chan, Jackie 59
Chan, Stephen 71, 73, 80
Chaudhri, V. 166
chauvinism 261
Chechnya 114, 253
children, moral development 49
China 14, 55, 59, 114
Ching, C. 142
Choi, H.-L. 142
Chomsky, N. 128
Christian fundamentalism 72
Christianity 37, 224–5
Christianity and Islam, *see* cross-cultural and cross religious study
Christiano, T. 63

Christians 36, 41–4, 225–6
citizen journalism 132, 230
city states 62
civil religion 257–8
clash of civilizations 1
Clinton, Bill 76–7
cognitivism 243
Cohen, A.B. 36
coherence analysis 106
Cole, D. 63
collectivism, and individualism 245
collectivity 223
colonialism 38, 39
Committee to Protect Journalists 125
commodification, image of Middle Eastern women 94
common sense, norms and values as 8
communication
complexity of 203
  cross-cultural 25
  globalization of 24
  international 201–18
  public 18
  and social responsibility 162–3, 166–7
  valuing diversity in theory and practice 23–4
  visual 183–96
  see also ethical standards, teaching study
communication ethics 29, 201–2
Communication Ethics and Universal Values 30
communication research, neglect of Islam 36
communication studies, preoccupation with narrative 26
communication technology 26, 103
communicative action 202
competition 37
complexity 2, 216, 220
concern for people 227
conflict 37–8, 44–8
conflicts and wars 1
Confucianism 59
Conn, C.E. 218
consensus, moral 9–10
constants in human values 3

Constitution of the Fifth
  Republic 107
constructivism 106
context-dependency 205, 210–13
Cooke, Mel 74–5, 78, 80–1
Coombs, W.T. 166
Cooper, Thomas 29
cooperation, economic 1
corporate social responsibility (CSR)
  155, 160–1, 164–5, 231–2
  see also social responsibilities study
corruption, and democracy 68, 247
cost-effectiveness 146
Craig, D.A. 172
creativity, limits of 31
credibility 174–5
criminality 143
Cronn-Mills, D. 38, 39, 44
cross-cultural and cross religious study
  Britain 38–9
  context 38–41
  definition of morality 41–4
  findings and discussion 41–9
  France 39–41
  interviews 41
  method 41
  morality and conflict 44–8
  need for further research 49
  participants 41
  similarities and differences 48–9
cross-cultural communication 25
cultural context and moral values 26
cultural diversity, as enriching 25
cultural homogeneity and
  resistance 26
cultural influences and conflict 37–8
cultural projection 4
cultural relativism 23–7, 32–3,
  185, 240
cultural sensitivity 149
cultural stereotypes 15
cultural tradition, in foreign
  policy 72
cultural uniqueness 9
culture
  as changeable 59
  complexity of 2
  Eastern 245
  in international communication 2

social marketing health
  campaigns 140–1
variability 8
visibility of 10
Curtin, P.A. 141–2

Davenport, C. 68
Davies, M.W. 6–7, 13, 15
Davies, Nick 122
Davis, H. 71, 75
Davis, K. 154
death 25
'Declaration of Rights and Dignity of
  a Human Being' 255–7
Declaration of the Rights of Man and
  the Citizen 107–8
*Deliver Us from Evil: Defeating
  Terrorism, Despotism, and
  Liberalism* 76
democracy 223–4
  arguments for 56
  and Asian culture 56
  as brand 55
  as contested idea 13–15
  and corruption 68, 247
  defining 248
  direct and representative 61
  and economic development 68
  as fundamental right 60, 64
  and human rights 68, 247
  instrumental value 65–8
  Latin America 186
  Le Monde 110–12
  and middle class 62–3, 64–5
  and order 245
  and prosperity 66–7
  requirement for fully human
    life 60–5
  and social order 60
  and wars and conflicts 67
  and welfare 67–8
  see also rhetoric of democracy
Democracy Now! 127–8
democracy, rhetoric of, *see* rhetoric of
  democracy
democratization wars 4
demonization 121
Denzin, N. 202, 216
deontology 160–1, 184, 185, 195–6

Derderian, R.L. 40
development, humanitarian 16
development theories 259
devoir d'ingérence 108
Dewey, John 64
DiClemente, C.C. 147
difference
  in images of women 94–5
  social marketing health campaigns 141
dilemmas 206–7
diplomacy, theological perspective 74
discourse ethics 202
disorder, and individualism 59–60
dissidence 245
diversity
  in communication theory and practice 23–4
  cultural and moral 236
  religious and personal 58
Doh, J.P. 161, 164
Donaldson, T. 3, 6
Donnelly, J. 6, 9
Donovan, John 125
double standards 167
Doyle, M.W. 67
Drèze, J. 63
droit d'ingérence 108, 114–15
Drudge, Matt 126
Drudge Report 126
duty to interfere 108

East Timor, *Le Monde* 113
Eastern cultures 245
economic circumstances and behaviour 16
economic cooperation 1
economic development and democracy 68
economic integration 1
Edelman, Richard 179
Egypt
  female genital cutting, CNN story 88–92
  media bribery 178
El-Astal, M.A.S. 184
elections 64
embedded journalists 123–5

Entman, R.M. 106, 112
envelope journalism 172
environmental charges 159–60
equality 107–8
eschatology 79
ethical codes, creating 18
ethical dialogue 142
ethical egoism 160
ethical issues 2, 4, 220–1
ethical labelism 15
ethical premises, mutually acceptable 18
ethical principles 208–9
ethical rationalism 29
ethical realism 31–2, 222, 238, 239
ethical relativism 23, 27–9, 33, 160, 195–6, 222, 238, 240–2, 253, 258
ethical standards, sources of 253–5
ethical standards, teaching study 201–18, 233–6
  bias 205
  dilemmas 206–7
  discussion 216–18
  ethical principles 208–9
  limitations of study 205
  method 203–5
  overview and context 201–3
  results 206–16
ethical understanding, as cultural product 26
ethics
  and morality 36–7
  visual, *see* visual ethics
ethnic self-consciousness 23–4, 26
ethnocentrism 9
European Charter of Fundamental Rights 109
European Higher Education Area (EHEA) 201
European Union, *Le Monde* editorials 110–12
Evanoff, R. 149, 231
evil 224–5
  association with terrorism 76–7, 80
  banality of 75
  Bush's view of 71
  deliverance from 82
  human role in eradication 79–81

in international discourse 72–3
liberal explanation 76
moral vision of 72
in popular rhetoric 75–6
theological view of defeating 77–9
US foreign policy discourse 71–82
US mission to confront 75–7
see also religion
evolutionary naturalism 30
Eweje, G. 155, 159
exaggeration 145
Excellence Project 176
exchange theory 140
exoticism 100
ExxonMobil 156, 159, 162, 166

fairness 13
family values 14–15
fanaticism 93
Fanon, F. 93, 94
Favell, A. 36
Fawzi, Mufid 90, 91
Feldman, A. 38
female genital cutting, CNN story 88–92, 227
Ferrari, M.A. 186
Fetzer, J.S. 36, 38, 39
Figes, O. 55, 56
Figueriedo, L.R.A. 143
films, Arab-Israeli, *see* Arab-Israeli film
Fink, F. 37
Fisher, G. 8, 9, 10, 11, 14
Fisher, Michael 25
Fisher, W. 26
Fisk, Robert 39, 122, 127–8
Fit Watch 132
Fletcher, Joseph 160
Flora, J.A. 141
fluidity, of ethics 149
Foot, Paul 123
force, one-way flow 11
foreign policy
 cultural and religious tradition 72
 religion in 74–5
Foweraker, J. 59, 67
Fox TV 125
Fox, Vicente 186
fragmentation, political 11
France 38, 39–41

fraternity 107–8, 112
Free Press 178
freedom 12–13, 15, 60–5, 104, 255
freedom of speech 12–13, 252
Freeman, M. 186
French, W. 37
Fuller, R. 36
fully human life 60–5
fundamentalism 93
Fursich, E. 187

Gaither, T.K. 141–2
Galtung, Johan 129
Ganley, E. 40
gatekeepers, media as 172, 175
Gaza, Israeli attack 96–7
Gbadamosi, R. 157–8
Geertz, Clifford 36
Ghazi, J. 98
Gibbs, Sir Phillip 124
Glaser, B. 41
Glasnost 174
Global Alliance 185
global corporations 18
 social responsibilities, *see* social responsibilities study
global economic crisis (2009) 244
global ethics 87
global village 103
globalization 1, 10–11, 24, 201
God 43–4, 78–9
Goodman, Amy 127
Goregin, A.G. 174
Graff, J. 40
Graham-Brown, S. 93
Grant, M. 148
Greater London Authority 39
Green, C. 126
Greenberg, K.J. 202
grounded theory 41
Grynko, A. 172, 175, 176, 177, 180
Guay, T.R. 161, 164
Guivarch, J. 106
Gulf War 123, 128
Guttman, N. 139, 140, 141, 148

Haas, T. 166
Habermas, Jürgen 142, 202, 203, 205, 207, 217

Hadith al-Madinah (The Talk of the City) (TV show) 90
Haider, Jörg 111
Hakanen, E.A. 252
Hall, B.J. 37, 141
Hall, Stuart 143
Hammer, J. 66
Hammond, P. 123, 128
Haneef, S. 37
Hannity, Sean 76
Häring, H. 77, 79–80
Harkins, C. 148
Harro-Loit, H. 174, 175
Harry, Prince, reporting blackout on 125–7
Hartley, R.F. 165
Hasan, Farkhanda 90
hate speech 252–3
Hawkins, E.T. 186
Hawkins, K.A. 186
health communication, personal responsibility model 140
Hecht, M.L. 106
Hegel, Georg 63
hegemony 100
Herman, E.S. 128
hidden advertising 177–8
Hill, P.C. 36
Himmelboim, I. 201
Hirsch, V. 186
Hobbes, Thomas 37
Hocker, J. 37
Hodge, Sh. 9, 10, 12
Hofstede, G. 202
Hoge, W. 38
Holmes, P. 173
homogeneity 10–11, 26
Hudson, Miles 127
Huffman, S. 124
Hughes, S. 186
human life
  meaning 12, 15
  measurement of 11
  relative value 251–2
  requirement for fully human 60–5
  as sacred 30
  value of 11–12
human nature 6, 8, 30

human rights
  assumptions not shared 9
  defining violations 6
  and democracy 247
  in French context 107–9, 112
  invention 257
  Le Monde 115
  ten minimum 6
  universal interpretations 7
humanitarian development 16
humanitarian interventions 1, 4
  Le Monde 112–13, 114–15
humans, role in eradicating evil 79–81
Hunt, M. 73
Hussein, Saddam 65–6, 258

identities
  Arab Americans 95
  ethics and international communication 103–17
  local 24
  media and society 108–9
  sociocultural, and ethics 115–17
identity, integrative approach to 106–7
identity politics 26
ideology 6, 258
images, war and peace, reporting 128–9
immediacy 26
immigration 38, 39–40
implicit social role, of government 14
independence, journalism 104, 174–5
India 60, 63, 166
individual freedom, and social order 244
individual sacrifice 11
individual, value of 56–60
individualism 223
  in Asian culture 59
  and collectivism 245
  denunciation of 56–7
  and disorder 59–60
  libertarian 13
  social marketing health campaigns 140
individuals, in Asian culture 58–9
IndyMedia 131
Infante, D.A. 202

information, as basis of ethical decisions   259–60
information sources   172, 175
'Ingérence en Tchétchénie [Interference in Chechnya]'   114–15
Institute for War and Peace Reporting (IWPR)   129
integration, economic   1
integrative approach to identity   106–7
internal monitoring   165
International Association of Business Communicators (IABC)   185
International Centre for Alcohol Policies   148
international communication   201–18
  and culture   2
  ethical issues   2
  in French context   103–17
  see also Le Monde
  language   211–12
  see also ethical standards, teaching study; international media
international education   217, 233–6
  see also ethical standards, teaching study
international journalism, principles   104
international media   87–101
  Arab-Israeli film   98–100
  CNN female genital cutting story   88–92
  and ethics, reflections on   100–1
  formulation of ethics   87–101
  overview of study   87–8
  Vogue story   92–5
international negotiations   25
international public relations   18, 230–2, 249
  see also public relations (PR)
International Public Relations Association (IPRA)   185
international relations, religion in   74–5
internationalism   3, 258
internationalist-universalist debates   2–16
Internet   103, 186

Iran   55, 58
Iraq, current situation   65–6
Iraq invasion   55, 122–5
Islam   13, 37, 40, 225
  see also Muslims
Islamic republic   58
Ismael, J.S.   122
Ismael, T.Y.   122
Israel, attack on Gaza   96–7

Jaksa, J.A.   4
Japan, view of democracy   14
Jeffery, Renée   72, 76–7
Johanneson, R.L.   37
Johannson, C.   166
journalism   17–18, 226–32
  citizen journalism   132
  embedded journalists, independence   123–5
  ethical violations   251
  influence on PR in Russia   173–4
  principles   104
  self-censorship   127
  Universal Declaration of Human Rights   130–2
  see also war and peace, reporting
journalism of attachment   127
Journalists Against Nuclear Extermination (JANE)   129
journalists, responsibilities   130
judging, ethical situations   4
July 7, 2005 attacks   39

Kandath, K.   36
Kano, drug trials   158–9, 161–2
Kant, Immanuel   60, 67, 162, 166, 184, 223, 246–7, 254, 257
Kapoor, P.   144
Kaufmann, W.   28
Keaton, T.D.   36
Kellner, D.   141
Kershner, I.   99
Ketchum PR agency   178–9
Khomeini, Ayatollah   55, 58, 73
Kidd, W.   40
Kienzler, D.S.   183, 184
Kim, M.   37
Kim Dae Jung   59
Kittredge, C.B.   73

Kluckhohn, Clyde 27
Klyueva, A. 172, 175, 176, 177, 179
Knightley, Phillip 124, 128
knowledge base 259–61
Koltsova, O. 173, 174
Kosovo 113, 128, 253
Kotler, P. 138–9, 148
Kovach, B. 172
Krauss, C. 159
Kristof, N. 55
Kristol, William 78
Kroeber, Alfred 24
Kruckeberg, D. 3, 5, 6, 9, 11, 172, 173, 175, 176, 177
Kupolokun, F. 157–8
Kurz, W. 79

labels 3, 6
Landman, T. 59, 67
language 29, 30–1, 99, 211–12
Larsson, J. 144, 146
Latin America, transparency 186
Latin American School of Public Relations 185–6
Latin American websites study 183–96, 232–3
  conclusions and discussion 192–6
  expertise 192
  focus of sites 188, 190, 192–3
  honesty 188, 189–90, 193–5
  measures 188
  methodology 187–8
  overview 183–96
  research questions 187
  responsiveness to target publics 189, 191–2, 193
  results 189–92
  sampling 187–8
  transparency and communication 185–7
  values 189, 190–1, 192–3
  visual communication and visual ethics 184–5
  visual ethics 195–6
Laurence, J. 36
Lawson, C. 186
lawsuits, Shell 159–60
Le Monde 104–17, 228–30, 253
  argumentative strategies 116–17
  code of ethics 105
  editorial positions 109, 116
  editorials 105–6
  on EU 110–12
  identities 108–9, 112, 115, 116–17
  international issues 112–15
  material studied 107
  political position 104–5
  sociocultural identities and ethics 115–17
  summary and conclusions 115–17
  theoretical framework 106–7
  universalism 115–17
Le style du Monde 105
leaders, choosing 13–14
Lear, J. 3, 5, 235
Ledingham, J.A. 166
Lee Kuan Yew 56, 58–60
Lee, N.R. 138–9, 148
Lee, S.T. 104
Leung, T. 37
L'Europe des maladroits [Clumsy Europe]' 112
L'Europe et la Serbie [Europe and Serbia]' 111
L'Europe politique existe [There is a Political Europe]' 110–11
Leviathan 37, 41
Levidow, Les 128
Lewin, C. 204
libertarian individualism 13
liberty 107–8
life 11–12, 15, 30, 237, 251–2
Lightowlers, C. 148
Limbaugh, Rush 125
Limor, Y. 201
Lincoln, B. 73
Lincoln, Y. 202, 216
Lloyd, Terry 125
local identities 24
losers, as heroes 13
low-intensity conflict 120
loyalty, assumptions of 96
Luoma-aho, V. 176
Lynch, Jake 129, 130

MacArthur, Brian 124
Madison, James 63–4

majority, tyranny of 63–4
Maksimov, A.A. 176, 179
Marcus, George 25
marginalization, social marketing health campaigns 142–4
Margolis, Joseph 242–3
Marsh, C.W. 184
Martell, C.R. 186
Martin, S.C. 142–3
Matusik, M.B. 80
May, L. 37
McDonald, H. 3, 12
McDonald, M. 56
McDonough, S. 179
McGoldrick, Annabel 129, 130
McGraw, Mike 175
McLaughlin, G. 123
McNair, B. 174
McNamara, Robert 9
McReynolds, L. 173
meaning of life 12, 15
media behaviours 226–32
media ethics 23–33, 104
media hyping, military operations 120–1
media non-transparency 18
media opacity 172
media transparency 232, 249
  black and white PR 176–80
  hidden advertising 177–8
  influence of journalism on PR 173–4
  overview 172–3
  Russia 172–80, 249–51
  see also non-transparency
Melhem, H. 97
meningitis 161–2
Merrill, J.C. 160
Mersham, G. 185
Methven, N. 128
Mexico, Internet 186
Meyer, M. 106
Middle Ages, Catholic Church 58
middle class and democratic government 62–5
Middle East International Film Festival 99
Middle Eastern woman, portrayal of 92–5

military operations, media hyping 120–1
military spending 119
military strategy, journalists' understanding of 120–1
military superiority, and universalism 11
Mill, John Stuart 166
Miller, David 124
Milmo, C. 124
Milosevic, Slobodan 111
mindset 8–9
misinformation, alleged, ExxonMobil 159
missed opportunities 146
Mitchell, B. 35
Mitchell, George 97
modernism, failure of 28
Molleda, J.C. 185, 186, 192–3
Moltmann, Jürgen 73
Money vs. Ethics: A Balancing Act 174–5
Moore, K. 87, 92
moral, being 35
moral beliefs, as basic truths 5
moral consensus 9–10
moral justification, for wars and conflicts 1
moral relativism 25, 32
moral superiority, of West 4–5
moral truths 3, 4
moral values, and cultural context 26
moral vision of evil 72
morality
  as branch of philosophy 37
  and conflict 44–8
  cross-cultural and cross-religious analysis 35–49
  definitions 41–4
  and ethics 36–7
  nature and purpose 37
  as social product 23
Moreno, A. 186, 192–3
Morgan, N.J. 187
Morgan, Piers 123
Morleo, M. 148
Mubarak, Hosni 89
Mucchielli, A. 106

Muslims 35, 41–4, 225–6
  see also Islam
mutual respect 101
myth of redemptive violence 81–2

Nakayama, T. 141
narrative 26–7, 221, 237
narrative ethics 26–7, 222
Nathan, A.J. 56
national branding 187
national media 103
nationalism, and myth of redemptive violence 82
Native Americans, alcohol abuse 143–4
negotiations, international 25
neuropsychology 29–30
news, bad 252
newspapers
  Daily Mail 123
  The Guardian 122
  The Independent on Sunday 122
  The Mirror 122–3
  News of the World 122
  The Observer 122
  The Sun 122
  The Times 122
Newton, J.H. 185, 194
Nietzsche, Friedrich 27–8, 33, 237
Nigeria, *see* social responsibilities study
nihilism 28
No Child Left Behind programme 178–9
Nocera, J. 159
non-transparency 18, 172, 174–6, *see also* media transparency
'Nord-Sud: la fracture [North-South: The Split]' 113–14
norm, US as 4–5
normative guidelines 239
normative models 29–30, 33, 207–8
norms 237, 238–9
  as common sense 8
  and conformity 32–3, 142
  as eroded concept 28
  as historically embedded 29
  social 147–8
Nozick, Robert 57, 61, 223

Obama, Barack 96–8, 101
  contested Americanness 95–6
objectivity, journalism 174–5
O'Connor, J. 148
Oetzel, J. 36, 37
Okeke, C.N. 160
Olaniron, B.A. 166
Olbrechts-Tyteca, L. 115
Oluleye, O. 157–8
ontological realism 31
open information 26
order, and democracy 245
orderly society 59
otherness 94, 141–3
Ozouf, M. 107–8

paid news 172
Palazzo, G. 155
participatory communication 162–3
Pashentzev, E.N. 177, 179
Pasti, S. 172, 175
paternalism, Britain 38
pathological democracy 66
Patriot Act, US 63, 81
Patton, M.Q. 41
pay for play PR 173, 179
peace journalism 129–30, 230
  see also war and peace, reporting
Peace Journalism 129
Peace News 131
peace research theories 129
Peak, S. 123
Perelman, C. 115
Perkins, H.W. 147
Permission to Fire 125
personal responsibility model 140
Peukart, H. 30
Pfizer 158–9, 161–2
Philipsen, G. 41
philosophical issues 220, 221–6
philosophy, morality in 37
photo manipulation 233
photography, Middle Eastern women 94
Pierson, R.M. 141
Pilger, John 123
pluralism 116
Pojman, L.P. 35, 36, 37, 40
political fragmentation 11

politics, as career   62
postmodernism   28
Poulet, B.   107
power and structures, social marketing health campaigns   141–7
press freedom   173
Pritchard, A.   187
Pritchard, M.S.   4
Prochaska, J.   147
professional codes of ethics   179–80, 183, 184
Promaco Public Relations   177–8
propaganda   130, 174, 177, 260
prosperity, and democracy   66–7
protonorms   29–31, 33, 222, 238–9
public communication   18
  and international public relations   230–2, 249
public relations (PR)   251
  black and white   176–80
  ethics   142, 183–4
  as information sources   172
  professional ethical standards   177
  visual ethics   183–96
  see also Latin American websites study
  see also international public relations
Purdman, K.   38

Race Relations Act 1976 (UK)   38–9
racism   258–9
Ragozina, I.   173
Rahim, M.A.   37, 45
Ramadan, television   95–8
Rancer, A.S.   202
Rankin, J.G.   142, 146
Rao, S.   104
Rasler, K.   67
rationality as human quality   60
Rawls, John   57, 223
Reagan, Ronald   72–3, 76
realism   31–2, 222
reciprocal respect   5
redemptive violence, myth of   81–2
reflexivity, of language   30–1
Rehnman, C.   144, 146
Reinhard, K.   203

religion   35, 44–8, 74–5, 223–4
  see also evil
religious discrimination, Britain   39
religious groups, legal protection   38–9
religious symbols, wearing   40
religious tradition, in foreign policy   72
repercussions, fear of   11
reporting, war and peace
  see war and peace, reporting
research, moral consensus   9–10
respect   5, 104
responsibilities, social marketing health campaigns   140, 145
responsiveness, to target publics   189, 191–2, 193
Revel, Jean-François   108
reverence, for life   30
rhetoric   17, 75–6
rhetoric of democracy   55–68, 223–4
  instrumental value of democracy   65–8
  requirement for fully human life   60–5
  value of the individual   56–60
  see also democracy
right to interfere   108, 114–15
Roberts, L.   184
Robins, Kevin   128
Robins, M.B.   187
Robinson, P.   123
robust relativism   242–3
role models, societal   16
Rossing, B.   71
Roth, N.L.   3, 141, 184
Royal Society   159
Ruggie, J.G.   160
Russia
  black and white PR   176–80
  democracy   55–6
  hidden advertising   177–8
  influence of journalism on PR   173–4
  international communication   201
  Le Monde   112, 114–15
  media transparency, *see* media transparency
  need for further research   179
  view of democracy   13
Ryn, C.G.   72

Sabanci, Vuslat Dogan 178
sacred violence 81
sacrifice 11
Saks, K. 174, 175
Salmon, C.T. 139, 140, 141, 148
salvation 74, 78
sanitization of war 127–9
Sankt-Peterburgskie Vedomosti (Saint Petersburg Gazette) 173
Sardar, Z. 4–5, 6–7, 13, 15
Saro-Wiwa, Ken 159
scapegoating 166
scepticism 243
Scherer, A.G. 155
Schieffer, Ron 124
Schooler, C. 141
Schroeder, J.E. 184
Schwab, K. 155
Schwandt, T.A. 202
Scranton, P. 77, 80
secessions 11
secularism, France 39
self-censorship 127
self-confidence of universalism 11
self-consciousness, ethnic 23–4, 26
self-evident truth 7
self-regulation 165
Sen, A. 63, 66–7
Serbia, *Le Monde* 111
Sharratt, S.C. 37
Shell 157–8, 159–60, 162, 166
shoe throwing 96–7
Silverman, D. 204
Silverstein, P.A. 39
Simon, B. 106–7
sin 78–9
Sisko, L.A. 203
situational ethics 184, 185, 258
Skinner, C. 185
Smid, M. 155
Smith, W.A. 139
Snow, C. Jr. 155
sobornost 13
social constructionism 31–2, 222, 238
social contract 37, 41
social control 202
social expectations, of business 154
social good, defining 137
social marketing, concept of 137–8

social marketing health campaigns 18, 137–49, 230–1
altruism 139–41
criticisms of 139
cultural factors 140–1
early applications 138
implementation process 138–9
individualism 140
marginalised groups 142–4
nationality, ethnicity and effectiveness 147
omissions 147
overview 137–8
personal responsibility model 140
responsibilities 140, 145
stigmatization 139
structures and power 141–7
summary and conclusions 148–9
sustainability 146–7
tailoring 141
targeting 139, 141
unintended consequences 140
social morality 239
social norms 202
social norms theory 147–8
social order, and individual freedom 244
social responsibilities study 154–67, 231–2
application of CSR 160–1
communication 162–3, 166–7
conclusions 166
corporation studied 156
environmental charges 159–60
ethical theories and corporate behaviour 159–62
ExxonMobil 156, 159, 162, 166
literature review 154–6
Pfizer 158–9, 161–2
research implications 165–7
role of government 164–5
self-regulation 165
Shell 157–8, 159–60, 162, 166
territorialization 163–4
theory building 167
see also corporate social responsibility (CSR)
socialization 202
societies, value systems 8

Index 275

society, orderly 59
soldiers, attitudes to 12
solidarity 63, 113
Somekh, B. 204
Soper, J.C. 36, 38, 39
'sousveillance' 132
Soviet Union, as evil empire 72–3
Spaemann, R. 6, 14
Spellings, Margaret 179
stages of change model 147
Stainer, John 127
Stalin, Joseph 56
state of nature 37
Stephens, J. 158, 161
stereotypes 15, 145
stigmatization, social marketing health campaigns 139
Stockholm International Peace Research Institute, annual report 2008 119
Stockholm, the Beer Campaign 145–6
stories 26
Strauss, A. 41
structures and power, social marketing health campaigns 141–7
subjective life-world 202
Suess, P. 82
Sullivan Principles 155–6, 161, 162, 165–6
Sunday Times 122
Sunstein, C.R. 64
super powers, universalists as representatives 11
supreme deity, authority of 58
sustainability, of changed behaviours 146–7
Sutherland, A. 177
Swales, J.M. 106
Sylvester, J. 124
Szmigin, I. 145

tailoring, social marketing health campaigns 141
taking for granted 10
targeting, social marketing health campaigns 139, 141
Taylor, John 129
technical issues 220–1, 232–3

technologies of communication 103
Teegen, H. 164
teleological ethics 160
television
  Arabic, *see* Arabic television
  CNN female genital cutting story 88–92
temperance 142–3
territorialization, and social responsibility 163–4
terrorism 39, 75–7, 80
theocracy 58
theofication of anthropos 255, 258
theoretical debate 2–16
Thomas, S.M. 74
Thompson, W.R. 67
Tiananmen Square 55
Timmons, H. 159
Ting-Toomey, S. 209
togetherness 13
tolerance 24, 104
Tomasky, M. 56
Tomlin, J. 125
totalitarianism 29, 240–1
Toth, E.L. 166
Traber, M. 30
translation error 238
transnational communication 25
transparency 172–80, 186, 189–90, 232
Transparency International 68
treason 81
Trente Glorieuses 39
tribalism 26
Trovan 158–9, 161–2
trust 166
Tulloch, John 126
Twitter 132
two-way symmetric model of PR 183
tyranny of the majority 63–4

Union of Concerned Scientists 159
uniqueness, cultural 9
United Nations Global Compact 155–6, 161, 162, 165–6
United Nations' International Conference on Population and Development (ICPD) 1994 88

United States
  as divine agent 76, 78
  evil as notion in discourse 71–82
  as Great Satan 73, 253
  media bribery 178–9
  military spending 119
  mission to confront evil 75–7
  as norm 4–5
  Patriot Act 63
  perceived human rights violations 7
  recognition of human rights 6
  as 'saviour nation' 72
  viewed as good or evil 73
  voting 56
universal communication ethics 103–4
Universal Congress of the Russian Nation 255
Universal Declaration of Human Rights 55, 109, 130–2
universal human nature 8
universal human rights, use in debate 6
universal values 11
universalism 185, 195–6, 237, 238, 239–41, 253–4, 257–60
  defining 2
  ideology of 6
  Le Monde 115–17
  non-imperialist 17
  as philosophical impossibility 7–8
  self-confidence of 11
  as Western approach 3
universalist-internationalist debate 2–16
utilitarianism 160, 161, 162, 184, 185, 195–6
utility, principle of 166

Vaisse, J. 36
Valin, J. 185
value, of individual 56–60
value systems 8
values 237
  as common sense 8
  constants 3
  family 14–15

  Latin American websites study 189, 190–1, 192–3
  nature of 3
  orders of 238
  universal 11
van Dijk, T.A. 106
veche 13
Védrine, Hubert 108
veil, use of image 93
Velasquez, M. 33
Venâncio, R.P. 143
Vertovec, S. 38
Vietnam War 9
violations of rights, defining 6
violence 81–2
virtue, moral consensus 9–10
visibility, of culture 10
visual communication and visual ethics 184–5
visual ethics 18
  and communication 184
  major issues 185
  in public relations (PR) 183–96
  see also Latin American websites study
visual honesty 233
Vogue 92–5, 228
voting 61, 67

Wakil, Muhammad 178
Wallis, J. 78
Walsh, D.C. 138, 144
Walzer, M. 80
Wang, J. 166
war and peace, reporting 119–31
  blackout, Prince Harry 125–7
  casualties, journalists 125
  changes over time 129
  embedded journalists, independence 123–5
  fracture of pro-war consensus 121–3
  Iraq invasion, 2003 122
  overview of study 119
  peace journalism as critique 129–30
  responses to invasions 121–3
  sanitization 127–9
  understanding US/UK military strategy 120–1
  Universal Declaration of Human Rights 130–2

use of images   128–9
see also journalism; peace journalism
War on Terror   80
warfare, attitudes to   12
'Warrior Prince' saga   126
wars and conflicts   1, 67
websites   187, 232–3
welfare, and democracy   67–8
Weller, P.   36, 38
Wertheim, M.   9
West, moral superiority of   4–5
Western interference   259
Wheeler, T.H.   184, 185, 194
white PR   176–80, 232
Wiebe, G.D.   138
Wight, Martin   74
Wikileaks   131–2
Wilkins, Lee   29
Will to Power   28
Williams, Armstrong   178–9
Williams, D.E.   166
Williams, F.   201, 203

Wilmot, W.   37
Wines, M.   59
Wink, Walter   81–2
Wiredu, Kwasi   29
Wodak, R.   106
Wolff, Michael   124–5
Wolff, R.P.   61
Womack, D.F.   202
women, images of   92–5
World Health Organization   147
Wuthnow, R.   30

young people, alcohol harm reduction   144–6
YouTube   132

Zakaria, F.   56, 58, 59, 60
zakazukha   173, 177–8, 232
Zaltman, G.   138
Zassoursky, I.   173
Zhirkov, G.V.   174
Zuo, L.   172, 175, 176